Carom Billiards: Half Table Circle Patterns

3-Cushion Billiards Championship Shots

From International Competitions
(Test Yourself against Professional Players)

Allan P. Sand
PBIA Certified Instructor

ISBN 978-1-62505-230-8
PRINT 7x10
ISBN 978-1-62505-420-3
PRINT 8.5x11

First edition

Published by Billiard Gods Productions.

Santa Clara, CA 95051

U.S.A.

For the latest information about books and videos, go to: http://www.billiardgods.com

Acknowledgements

Wei Chao created the software that was used to create these graphics.

Table of Contents

Other books by the author …

    3 Cushion Billiards Championship Shots (a series)

    Carom Billiards: Some Riddles & Puzzles

    Carom Billiards: MORE Riddles & Puzzles

    Why Pool Hustlers Win

    Table Map Library

    Safety Toolbox

    Cue Ball Control Cheat Sheets

    Advanced Cue Ball Control Self-Testing Program

    Drills & Exercises for Pool & Pocket Billiards

    The Art of War versus The Art of Pool

    The Psychology of Losing – Tricks, Traps & Sharks

    The Art of Team Coaching

    The Art of Personal Competition

    The Art of Politics & Campaigning

    The Art of Marketing & Promotion

    Kitchen God's Guide for Single Guys

Introduction

This is one of a series of Carom Billiards books that show how professional players select shots, based on the table layout. All of these shots have been mapped out based on shots played at international competitions.

This book contains a wide variety of examples where the player shoots the pattern within a half table area.

These shots put you inside the head of the player beginning with the ball positions (shown in the first table layout). The second table layout shows the shooting decision and the results of the player's choice.

About the Graphic Layouts

There are two graphics for each shot. The first graphic shows the ball positions on the table. The ball labeled "A" is always the player's CB. The first graphic the ball positions on the table. The second graphic shows how the shot was played.

Each table graphic in this book is a black & white representation of a standard 5 x 10 carom billiards table. Balls are represented with these three symbols.

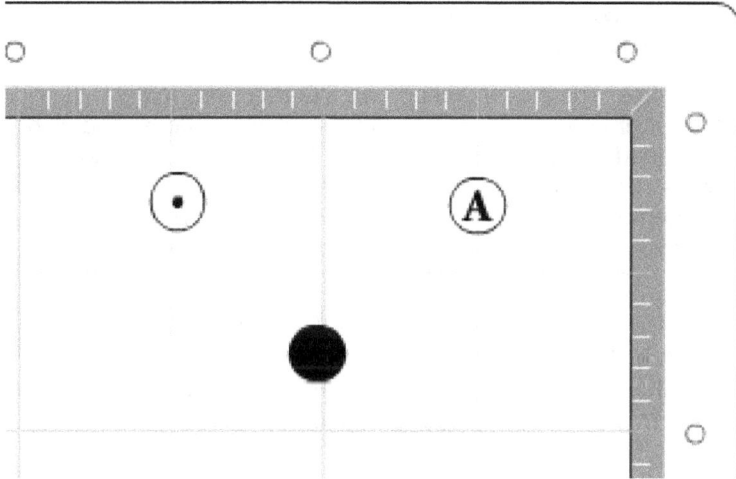

(A) The white "A" ball "A" is ALWAYS the shooter's cue ball.

(•) The white "center dot" ball is always the opponent's cue ball.

● This is the red Object Ball, represented in the layouts as the black ball.

Each shot is represented with two layouts on each page. The first layout shows the ball position setup BEFORE the shot. The second layout shows the ball pathways that the balls travel during the shot.

Table Setup

1. Use donuts (paper reinforcement rings) to mark positions for the carom balls. These are available at any office supply store.

2. Place chalk cubes at the locations where the CB contacts each rail.

When you play the shot, observe where the CB pattern and each rail contact. You may need several attempts as you make adjustments to the CB spin to properly follow the pattern.

Purpose of the Layouts

These are examples of shots that champion 3-cushion players from all over the world had to play. The first graphic provides the layout. The second graphic provides the results of their shooting solution. These layouts are provided for two purposes.

*   Use the first layout as a mental exercise. The player picked one, but there are many possibilities. From the comfort of your armchair, you can consider multiple options, and work out the pattern using the spin and speed you would have applied. These help stretch and extend your skills in tactical analysis. Then consider how the player decided how to shoot the shot. From the patterns you can determine how the CB was played and the type of applied spin. It's helpful to use a pointer (or your finger) to trace the pattern as you work out how the shot was played.

*   The second purpose is to take these layouts to the practice table. Position the paper reinforcement rings in place for each ball. You are going to shoot the layout many times, so these donuts help mark the ball positions for each attempt. BEFORE you experiment with your own "solutions", shoot the pattern until you can easily duplicate the paths. This means you will do a lot of experimentation to find the spin/speed used by the original player. Only AFTER you understand and can execute the pattern should you experiment with your own ideas.

This combination of mental analysis and practical table practice will boost your growth as an intelligent and thinking carom billiards player.

A: Basic Half Table Circles

On these shots, the CB comes off the first OB and into three rails. When the CB comes out of the third rail, it contacts the second OB for the score.

A: Group 1

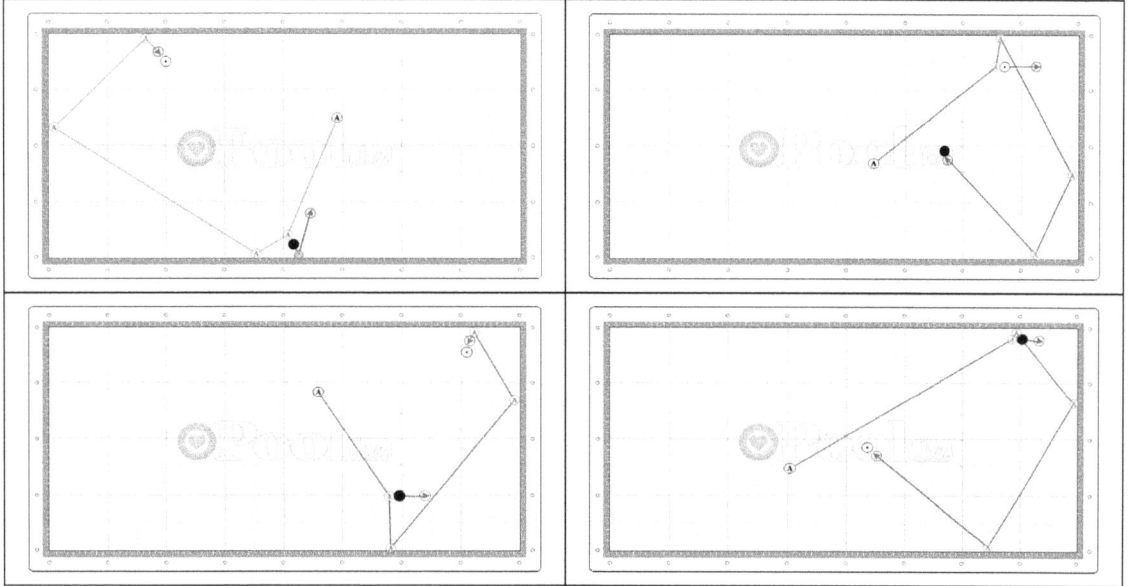

Analysis:

A:1a. _____

A:1b. _____

A:1c. _____

A:1d. _____

A:1a – Setup

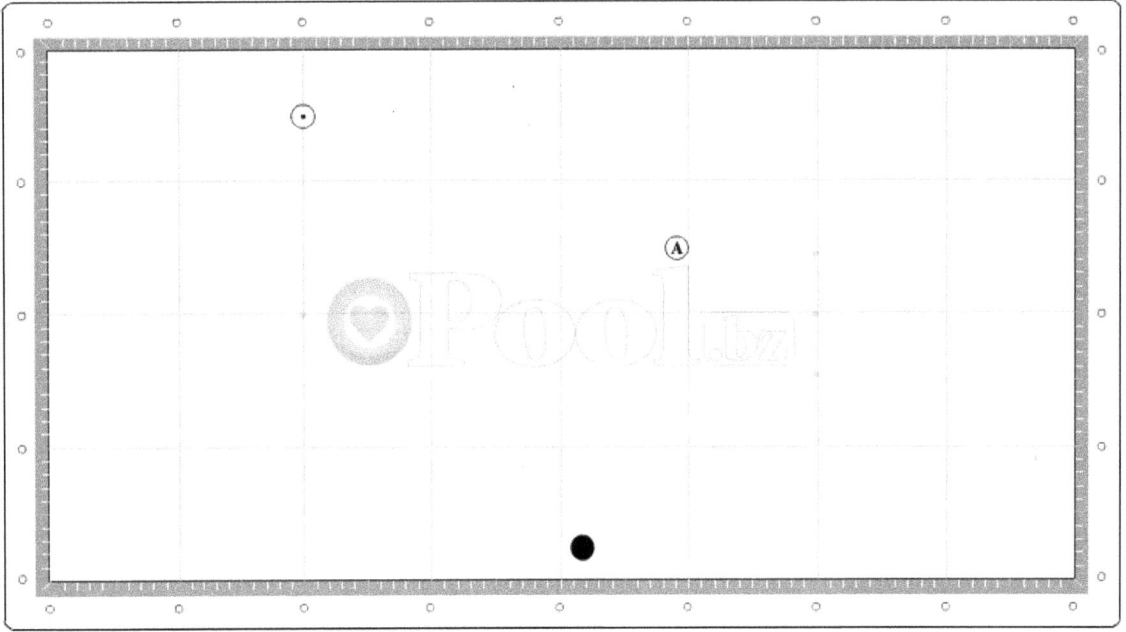

Shot Pattern

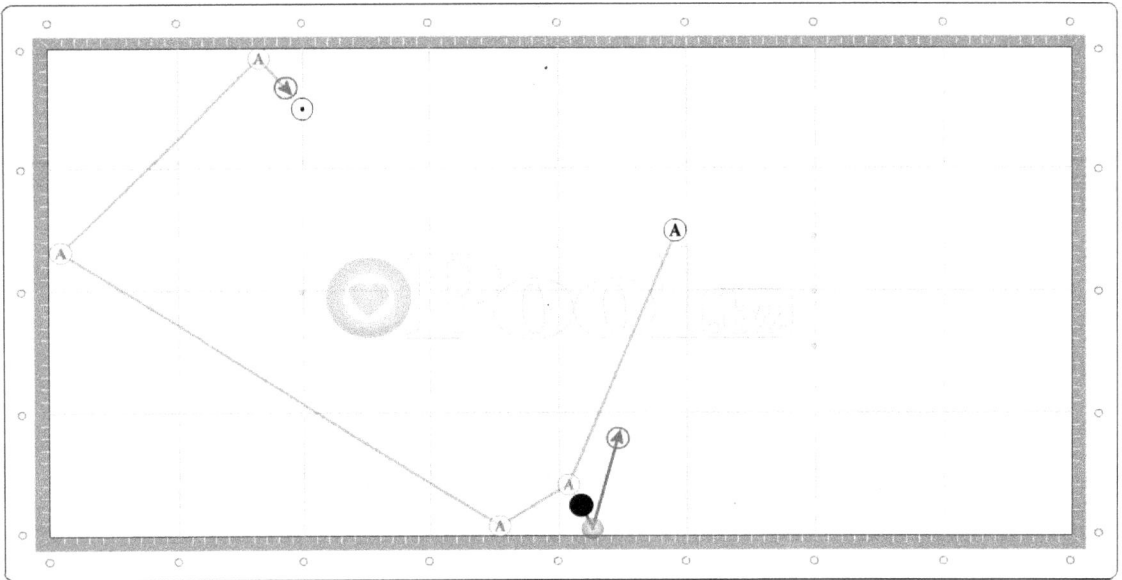

A:1b – Setup

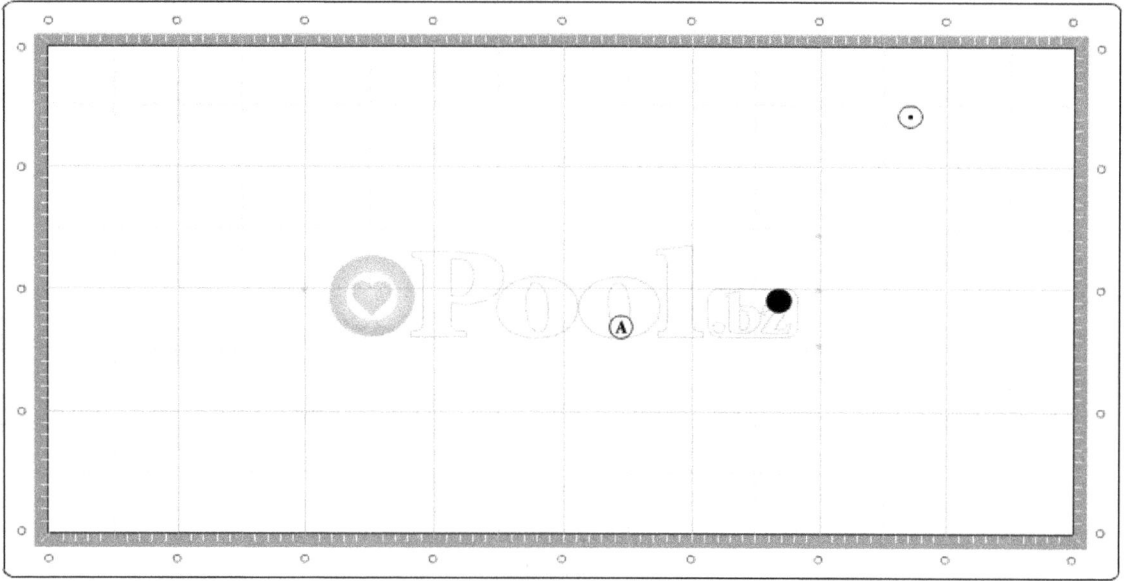

Shot Pattern

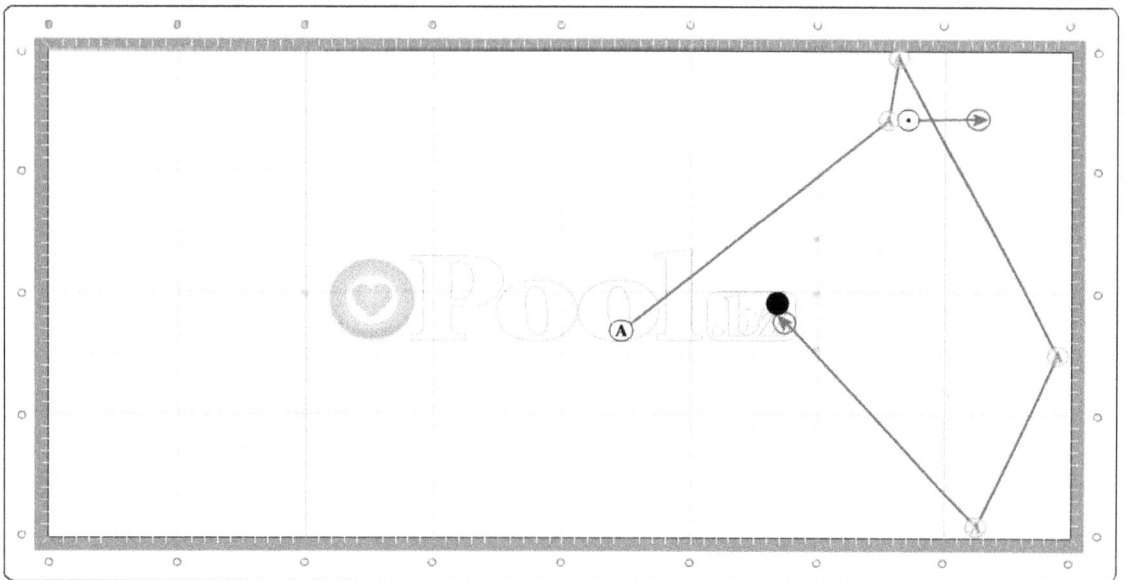

A:1c – Setup

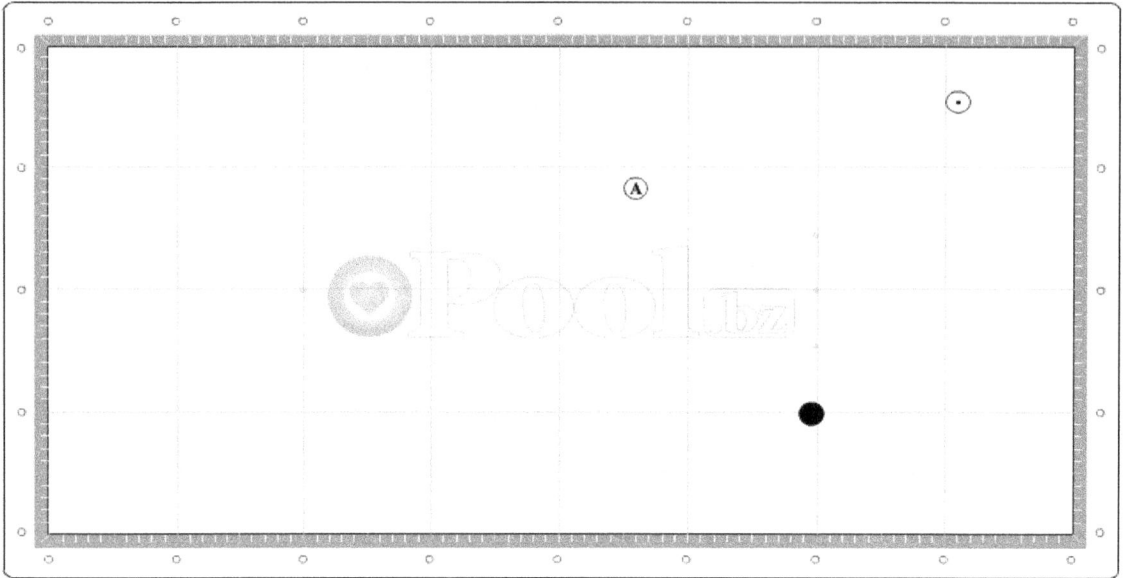

Shot Pattern

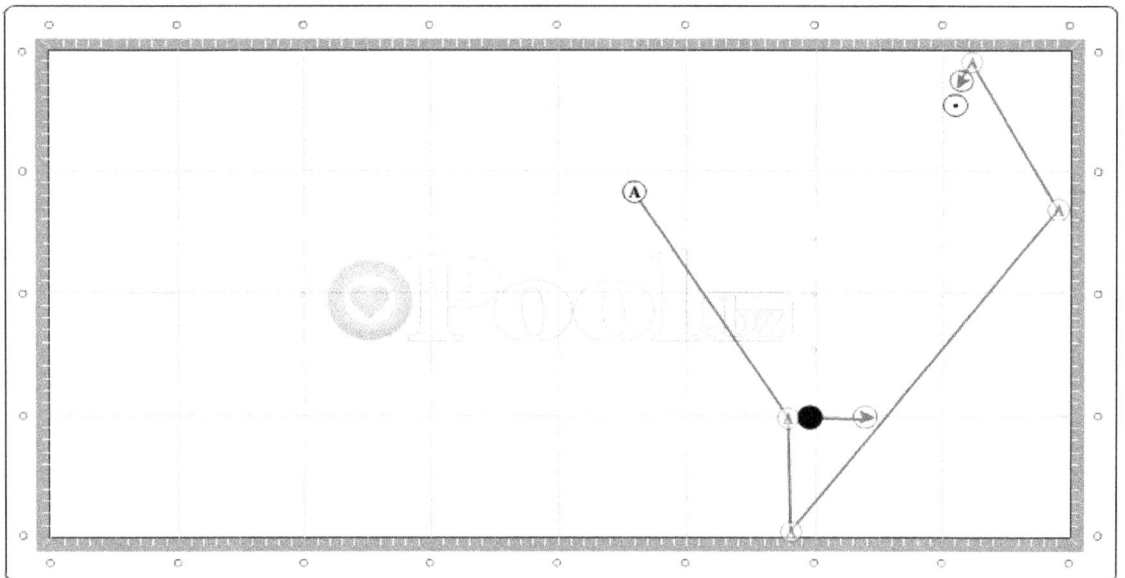

A:1d – Setup

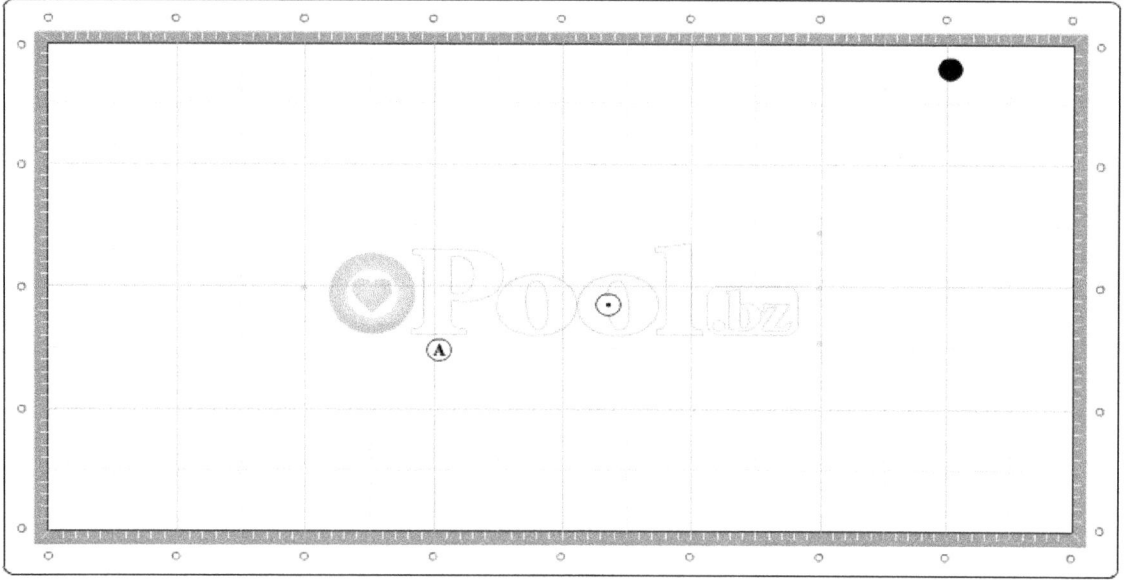

Shot Pattern

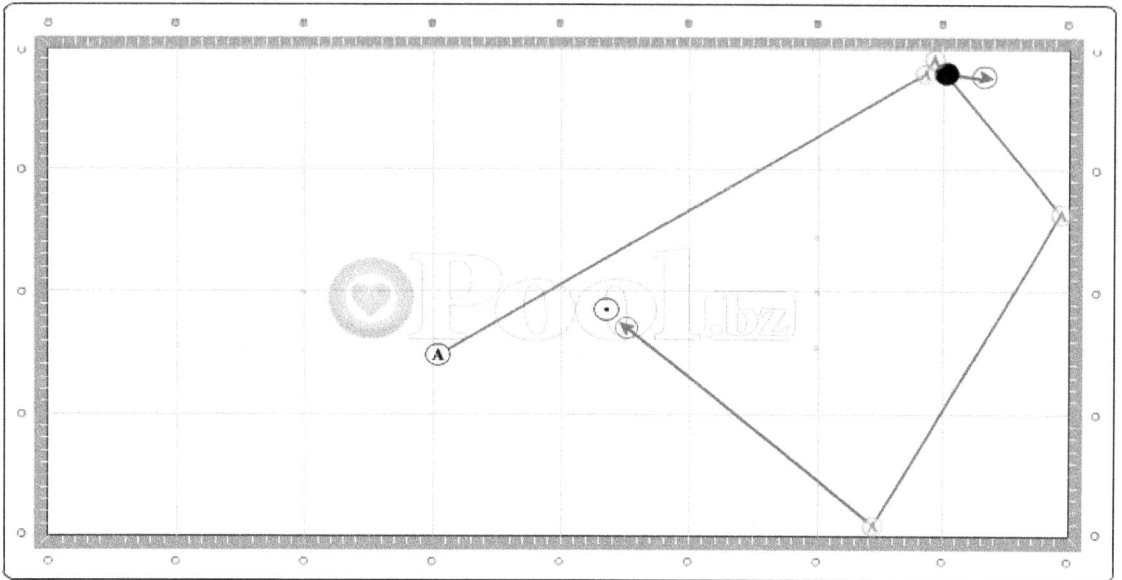

A: Group 2

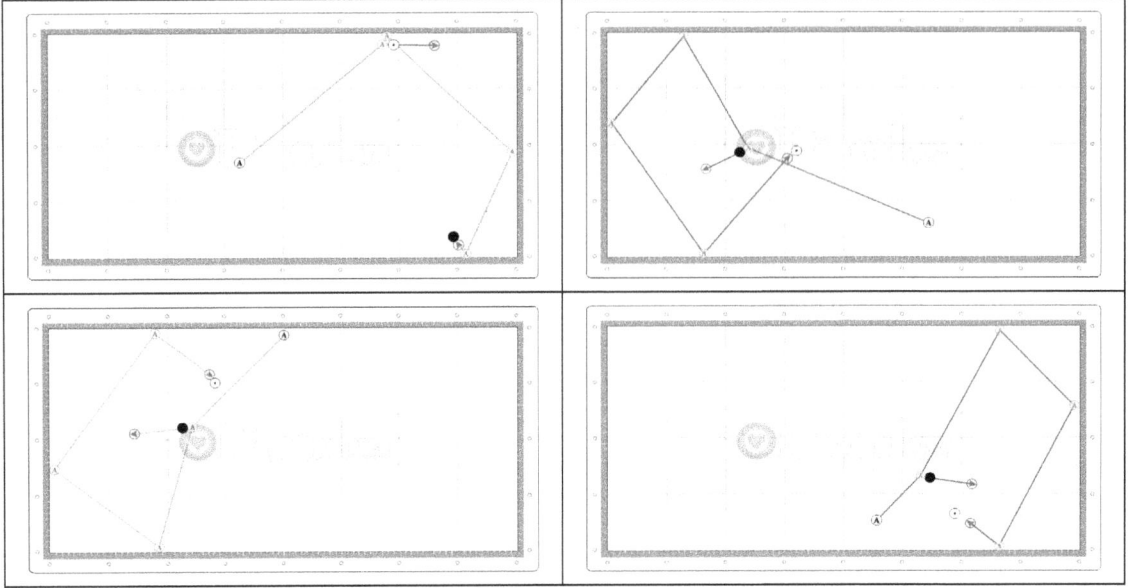

Analysis:

A:2a. _____

A:2b. _____

A:2c. _____

A:2d. _____

A:2a – Setup

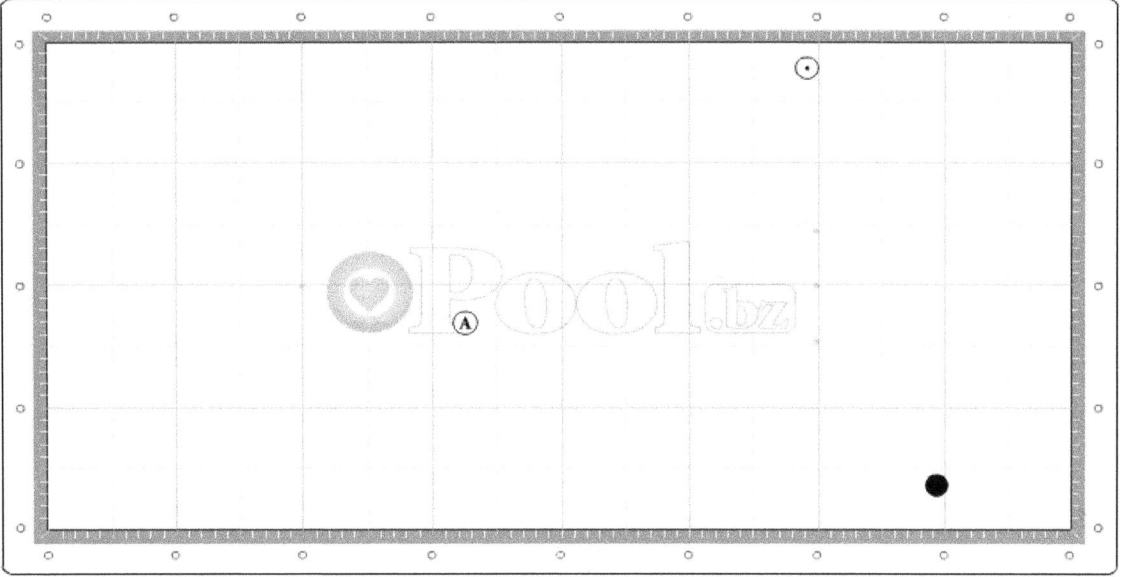

Shot Pattern

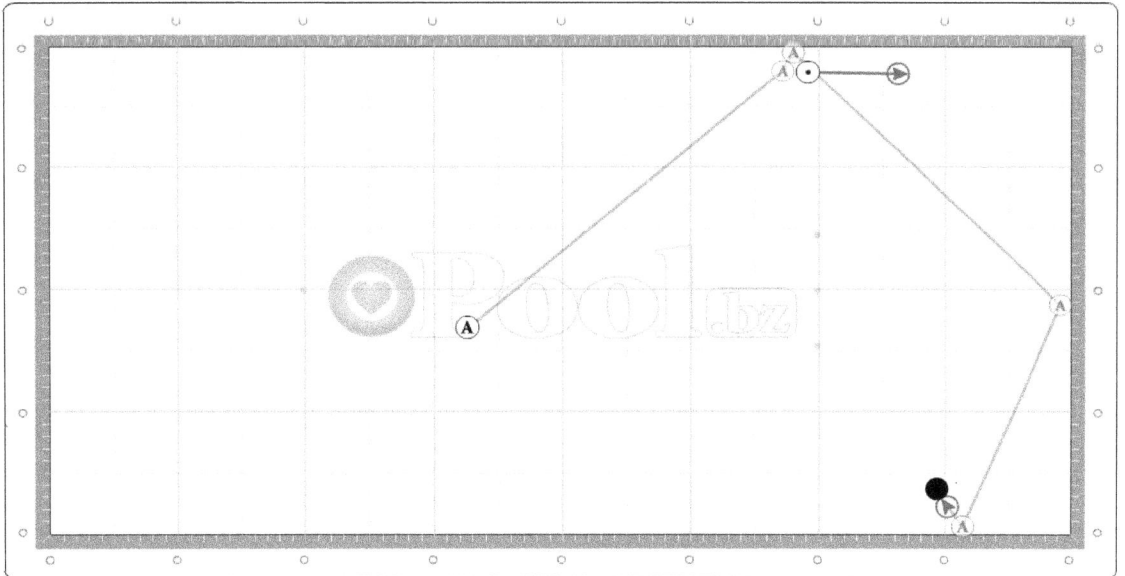

A:2b – Setup

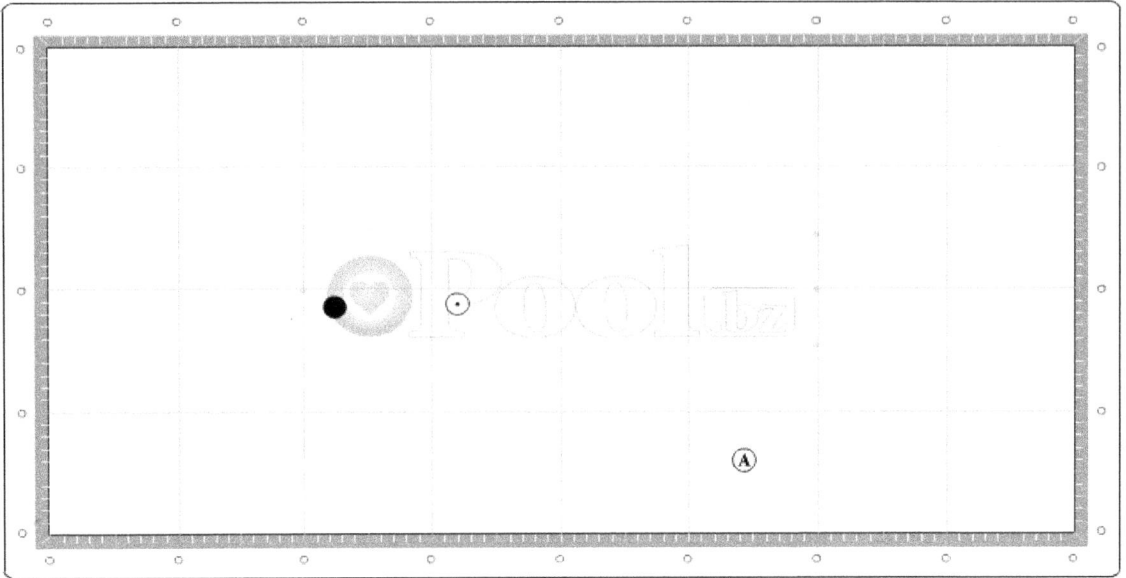

Shot Pattern

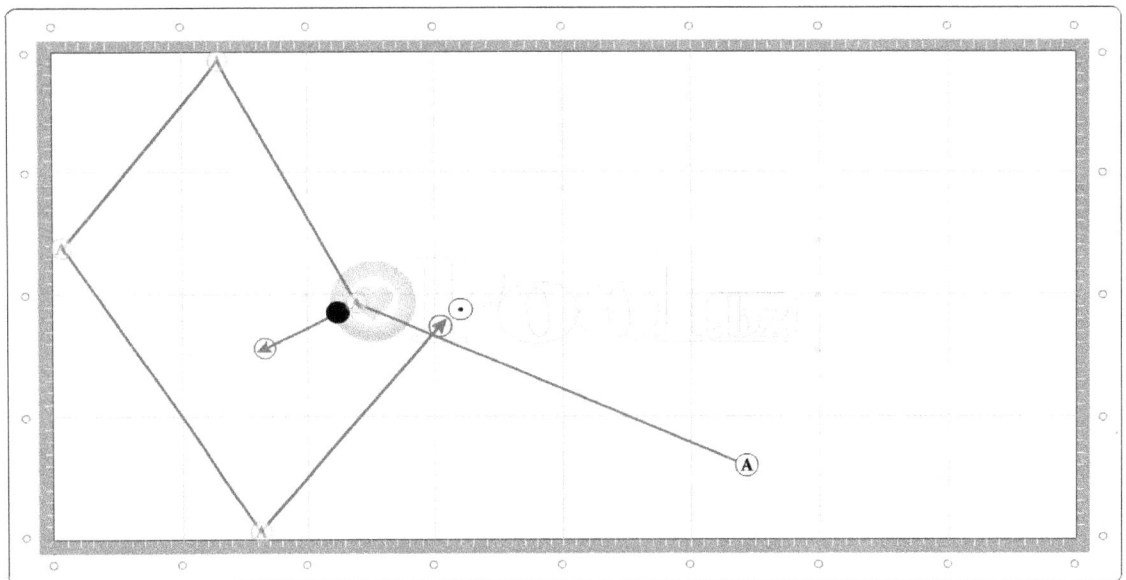

A:2c – Setup

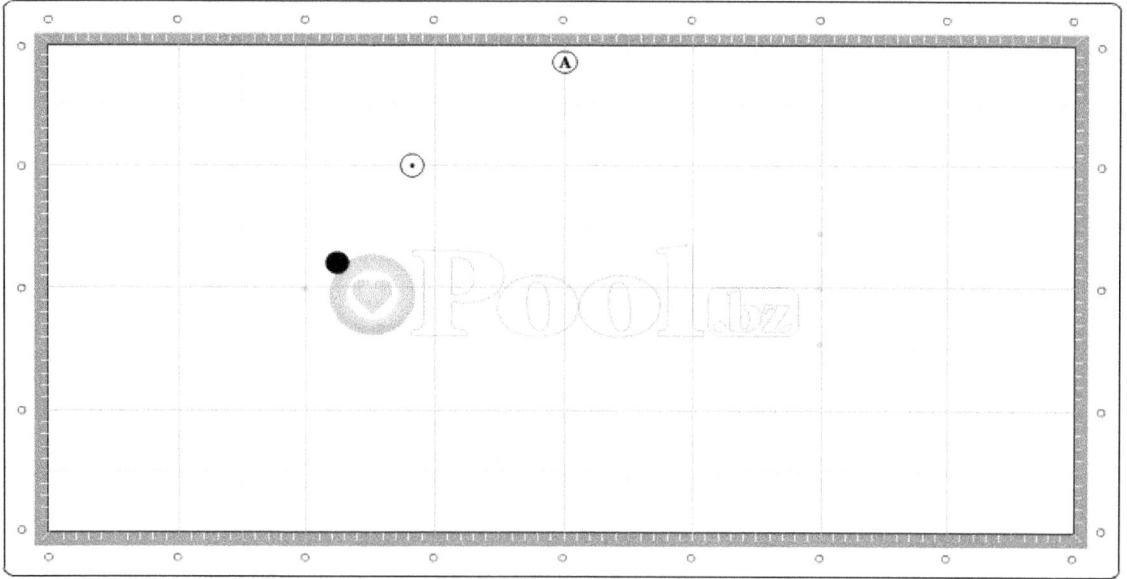

Shot Pattern

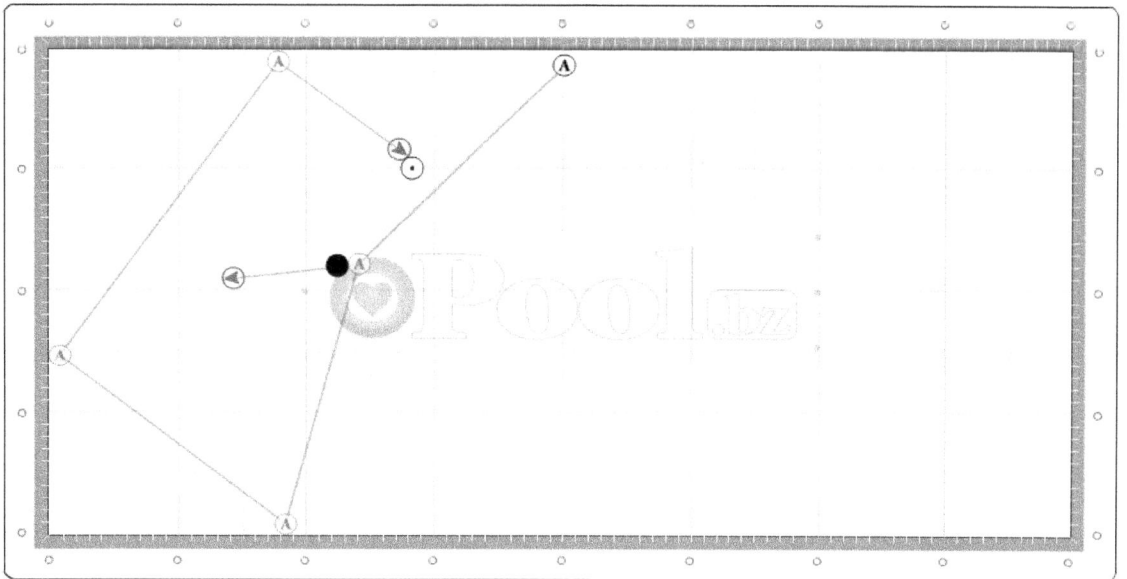

A:2d – Setup

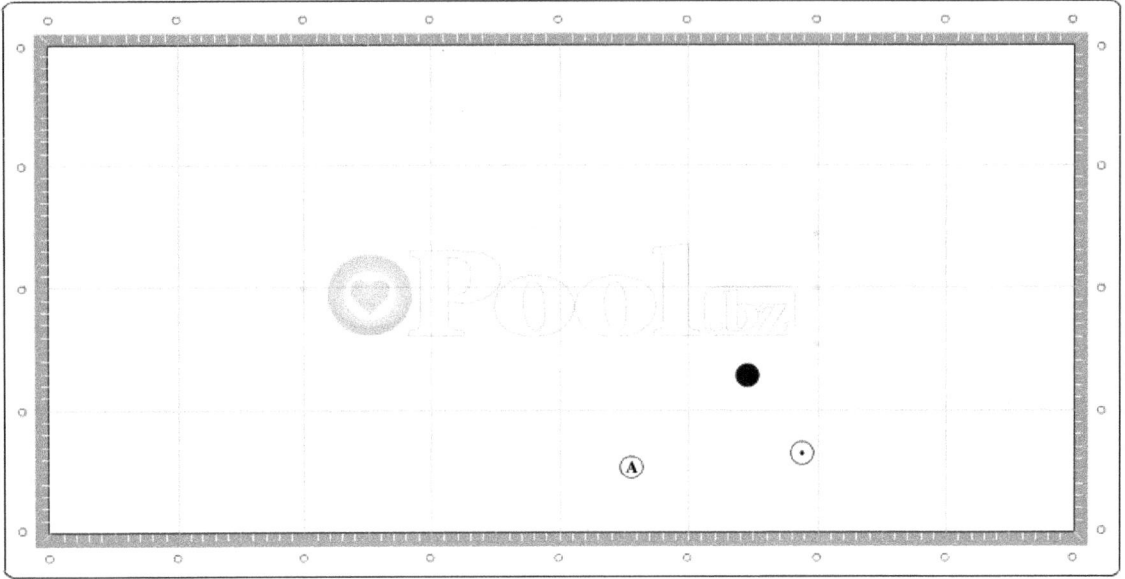

Shot Pattern

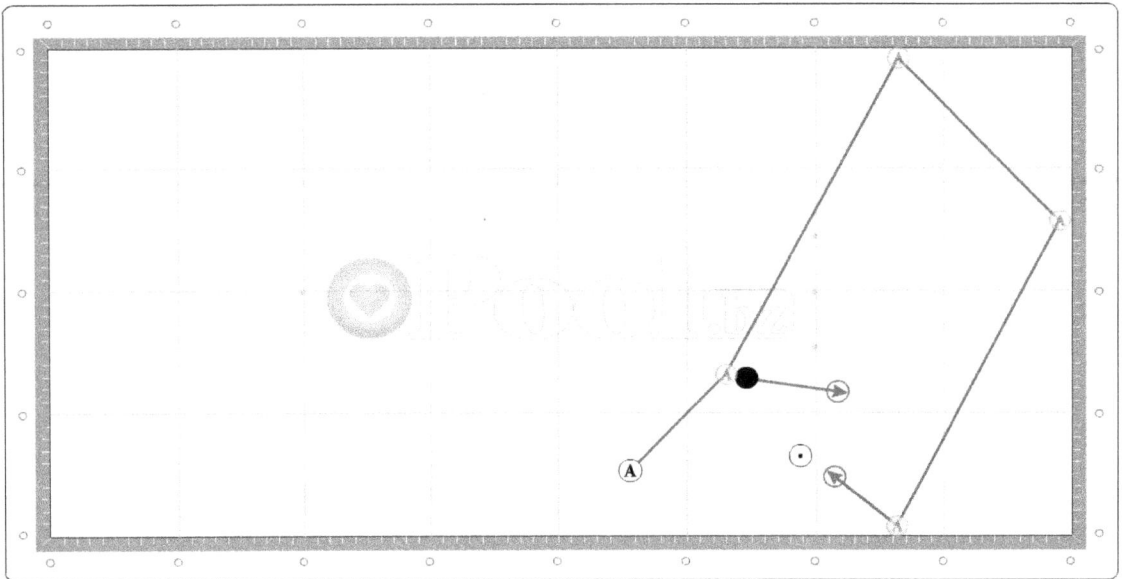

A: Group 3

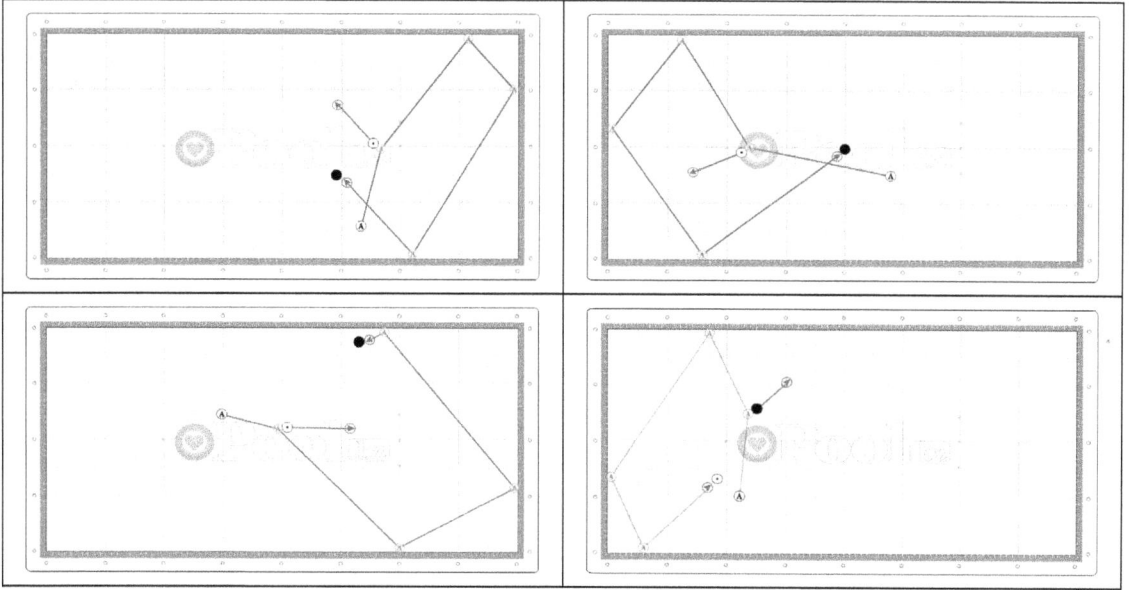

Analysis:

A:3a. _____

A:3b. _____

A:3c. _____

A:3d. _____

A:3a – Setup

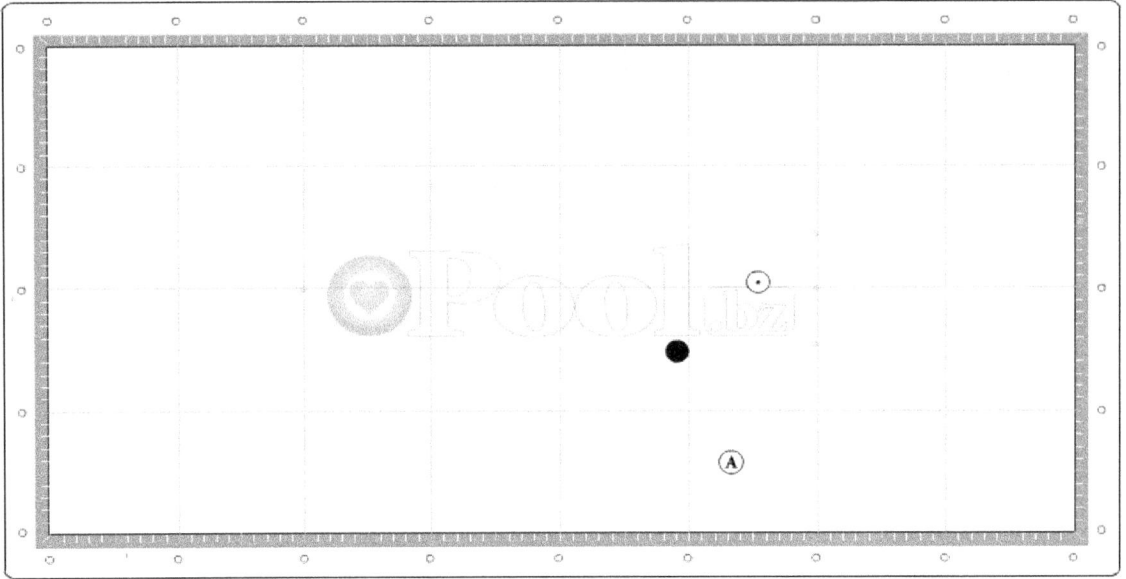

Shot Pattern

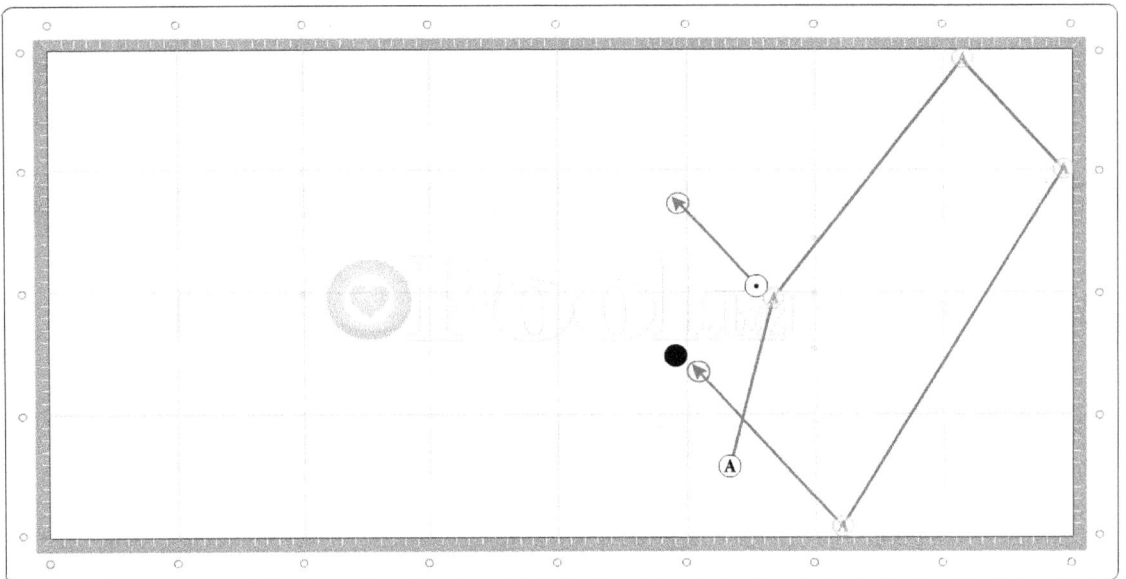

A:3b – Setup

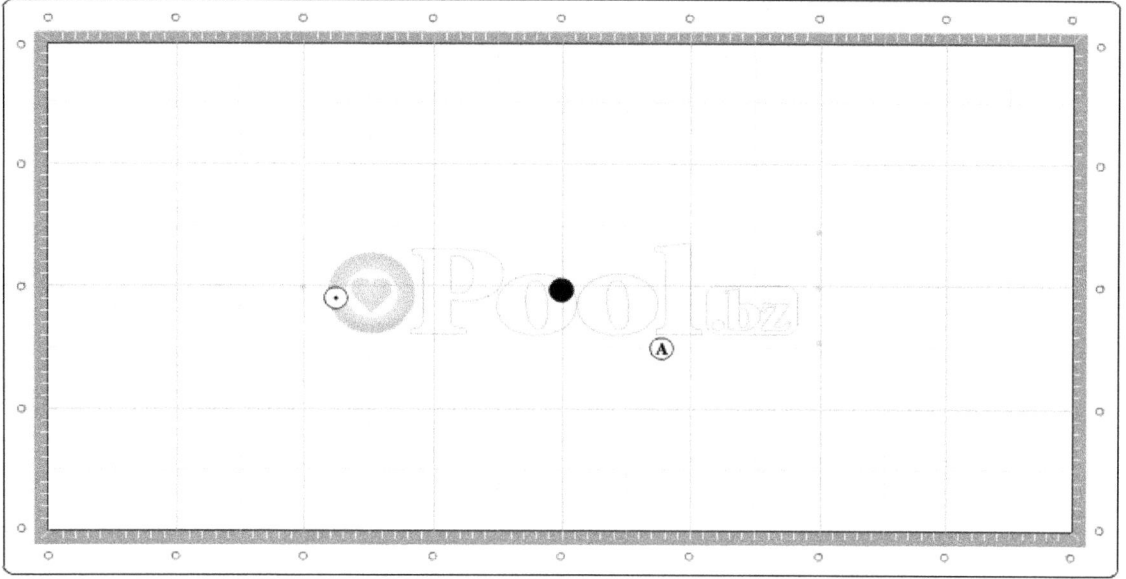

Shot Pattern

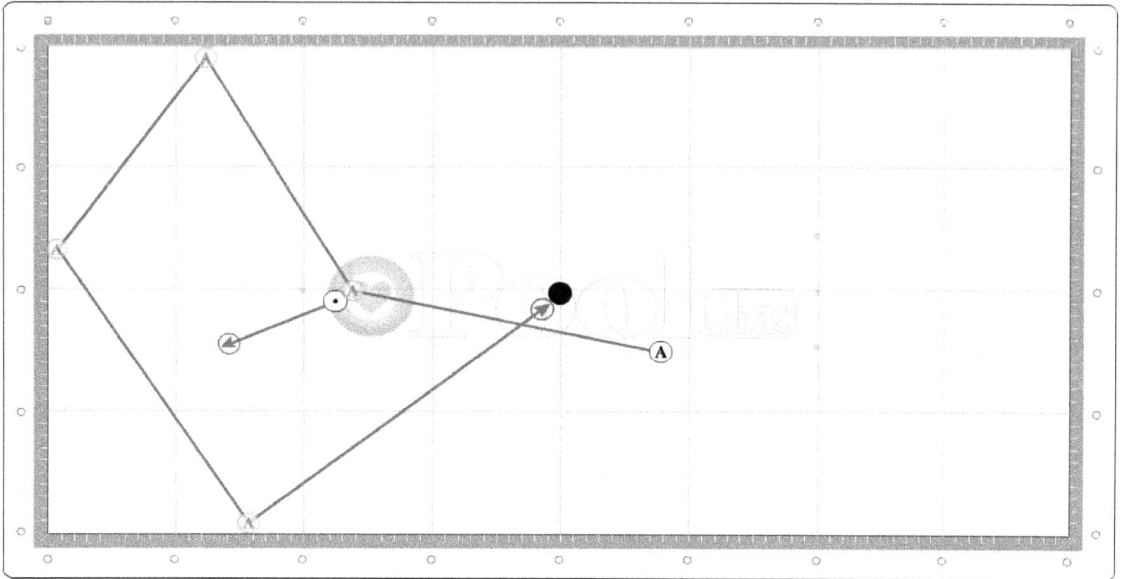

A:3c – Setup

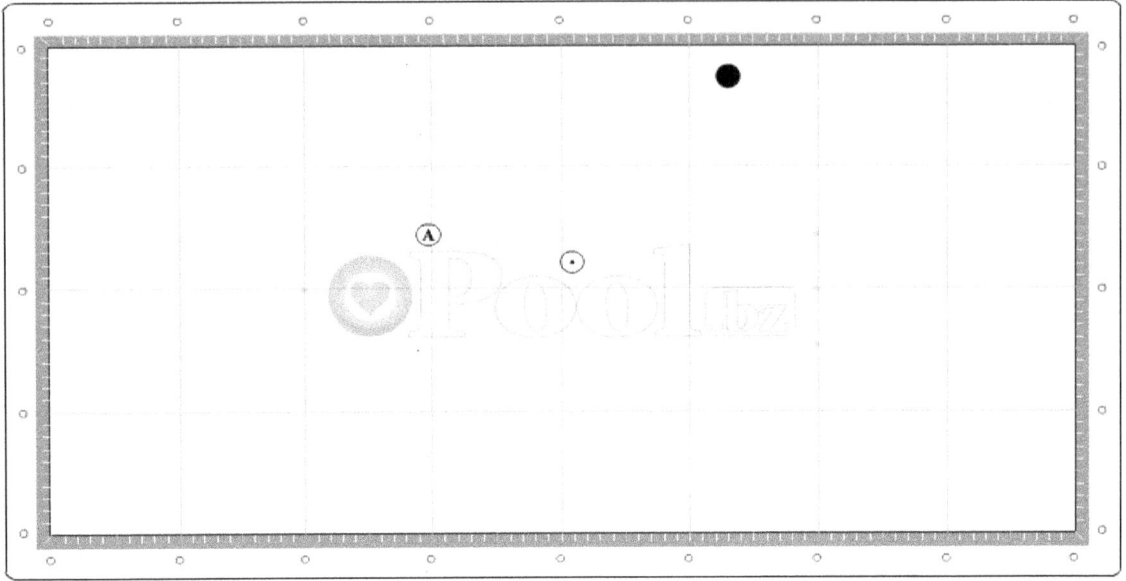

Shot Pattern

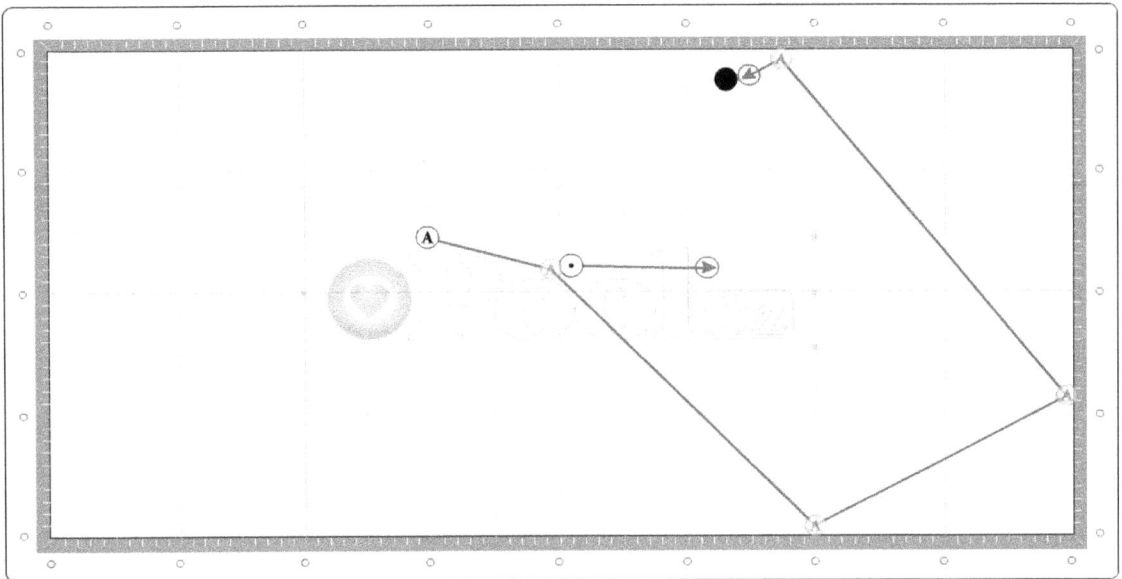

A:3d – Setup

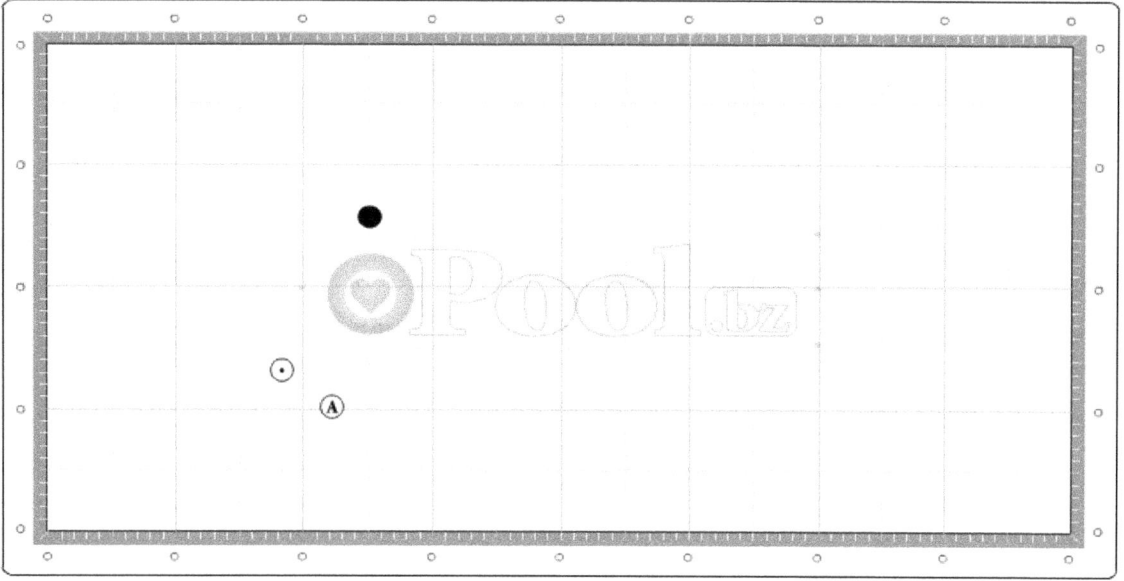

Shot Pattern

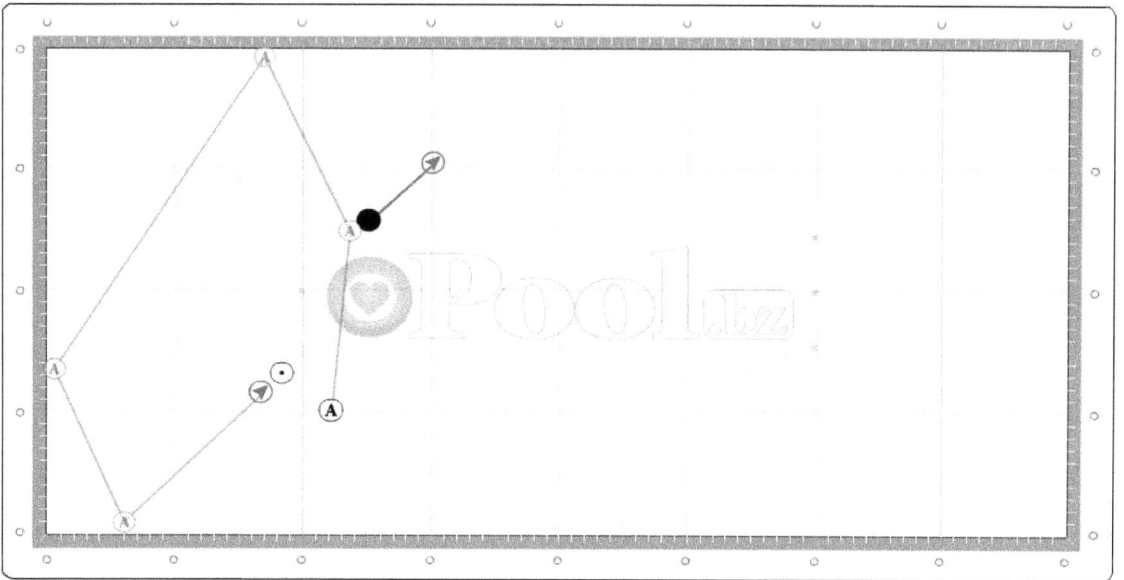

A: Group 4

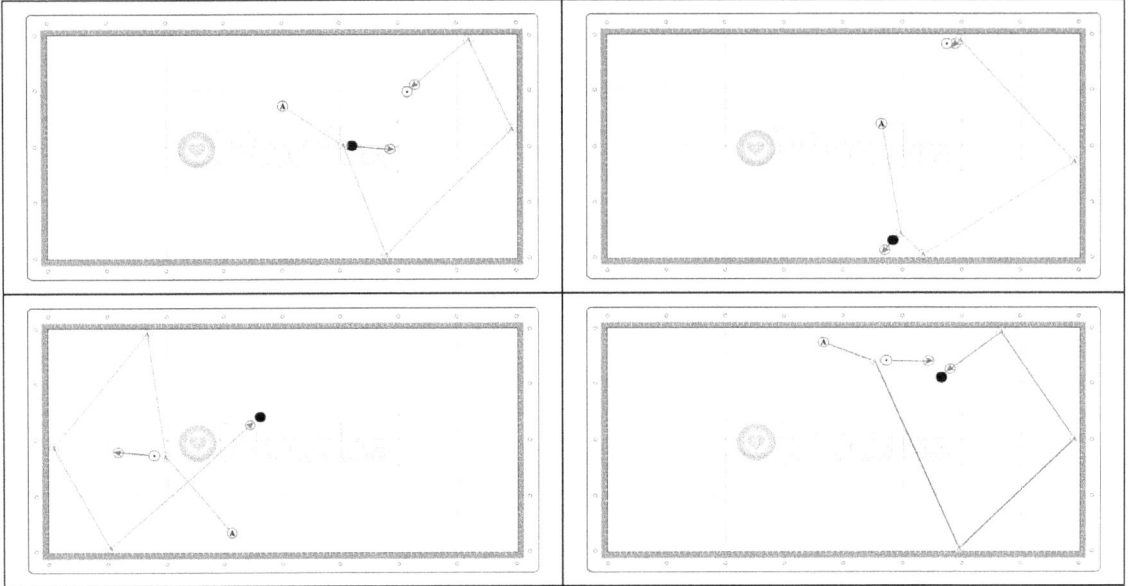

Analysis:

A:4a. _____

A:4b. _____

A:4c. _____

A:4d. _____

A:4a – Setup

Shot Pattern

A:4b – Setup

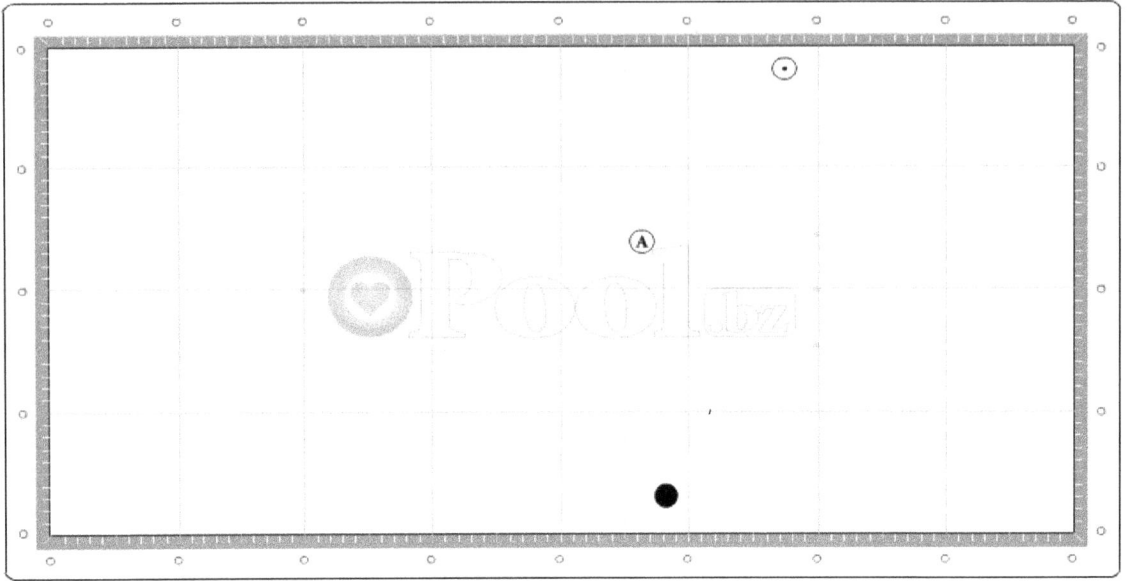

Shot Pattern

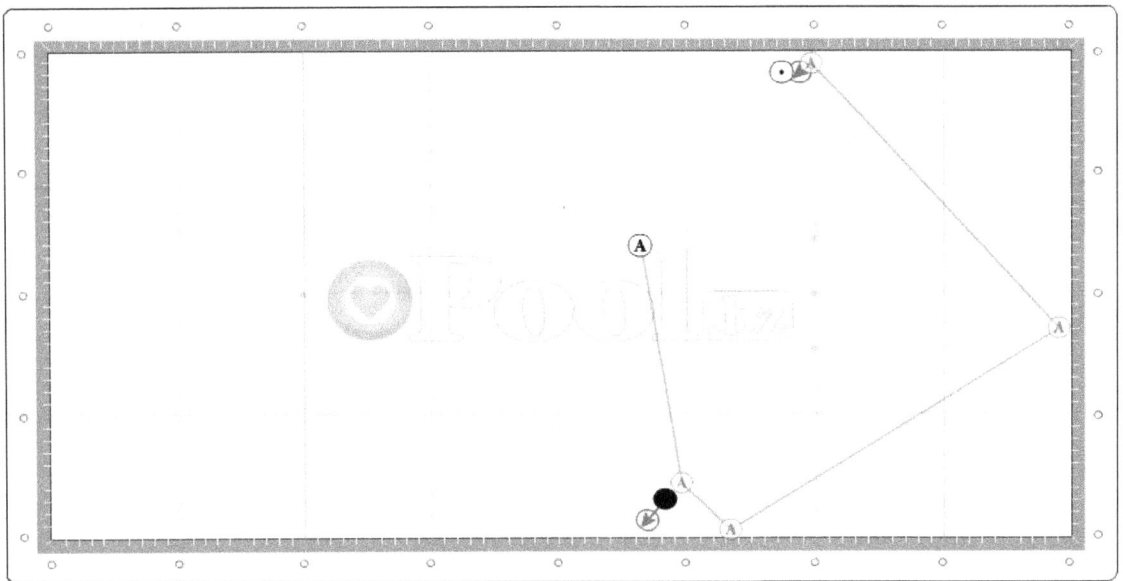

A:4c – Setup

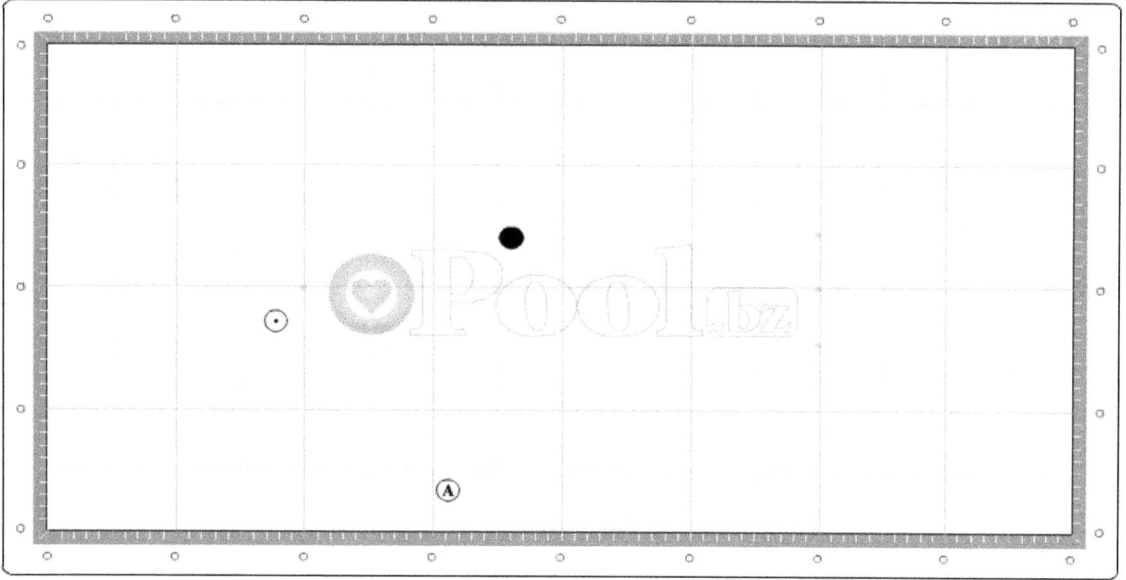

Shot Pattern

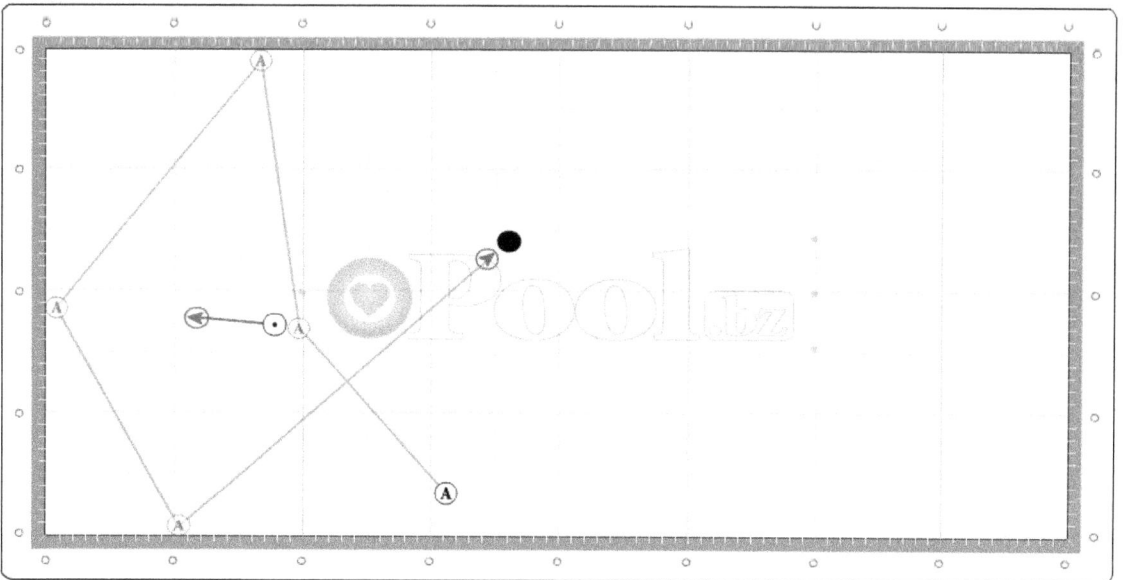

A:4d – Setup

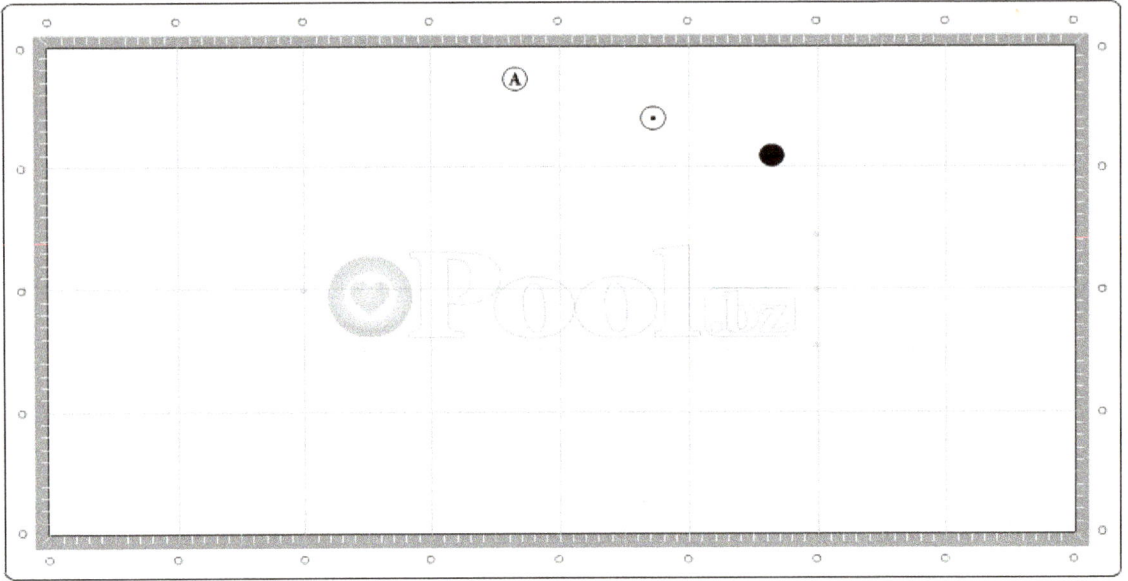

Shot Pattern

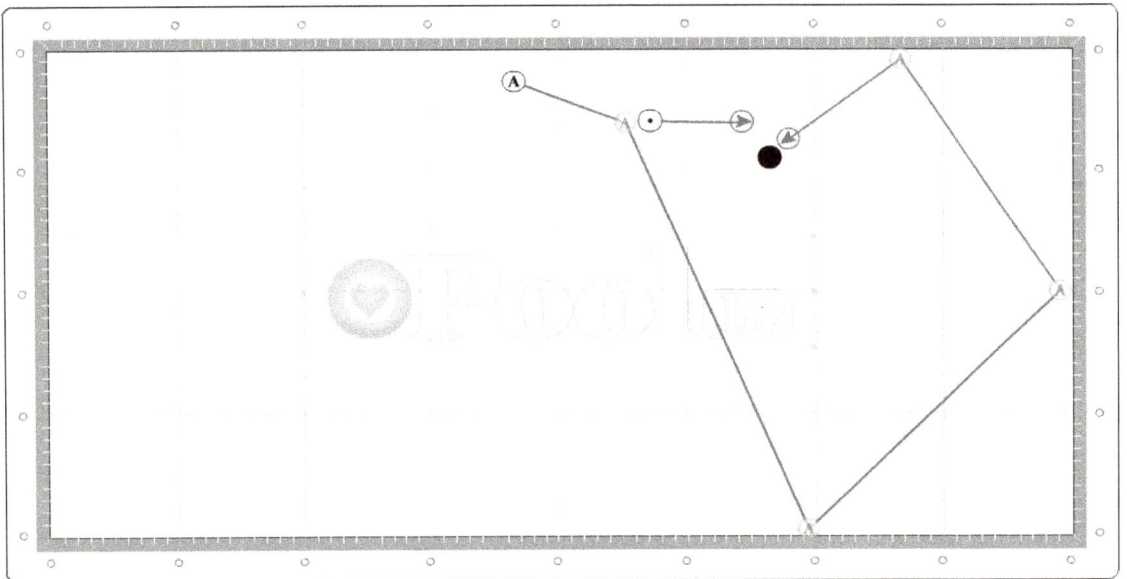

A: Group 5

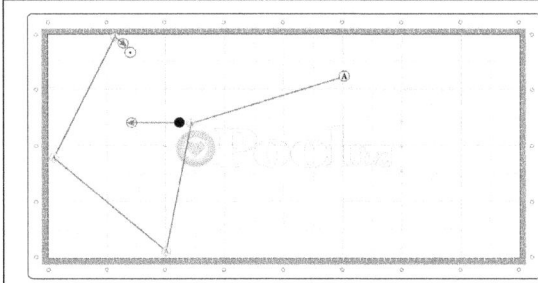 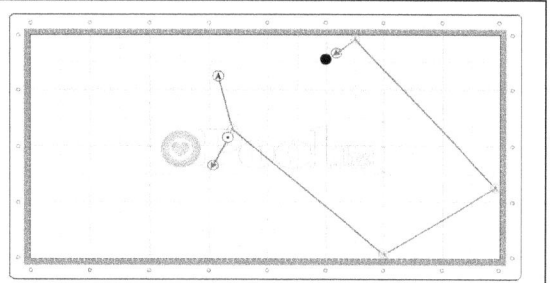

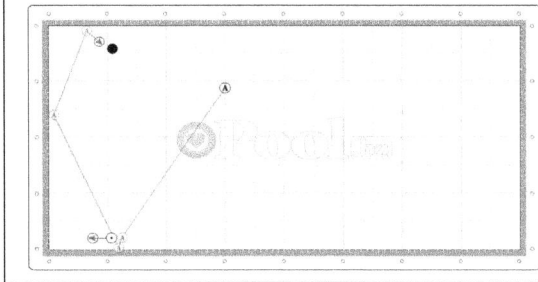 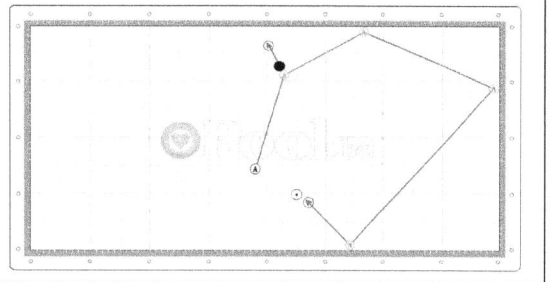

Analysis:

A:5a. _____

A:5b. _____

A:5c. _____

A:5d. _____

A:5a – Setup

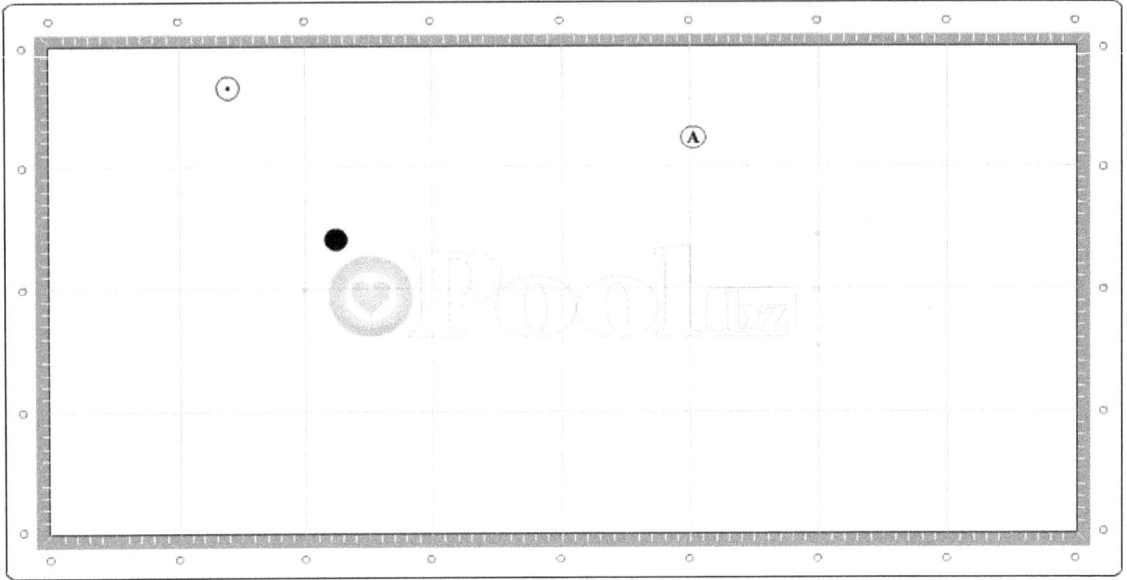

Shot Pattern

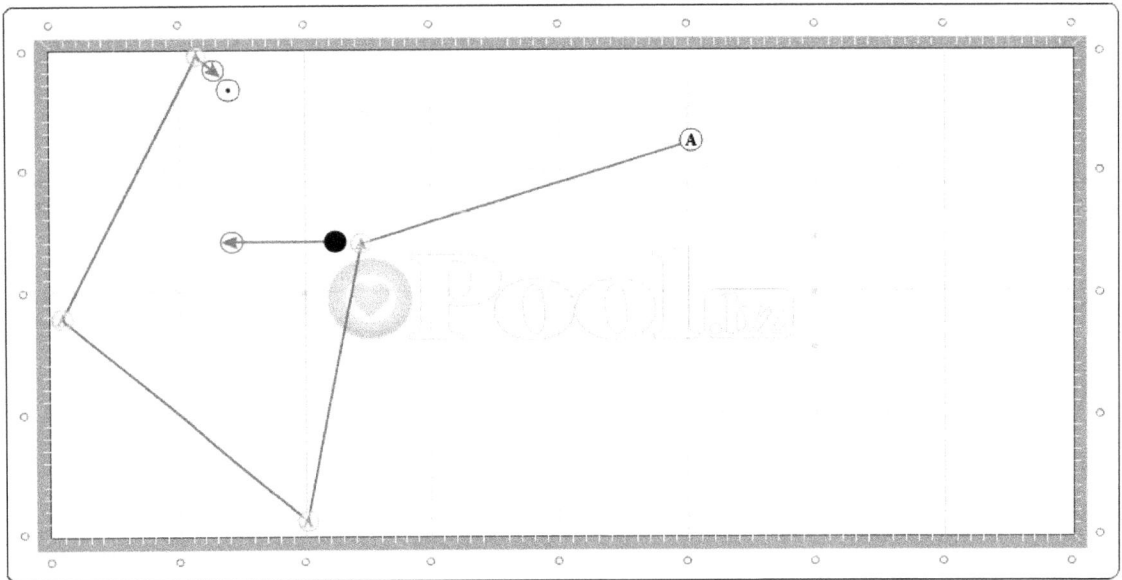

A:5b – Setup

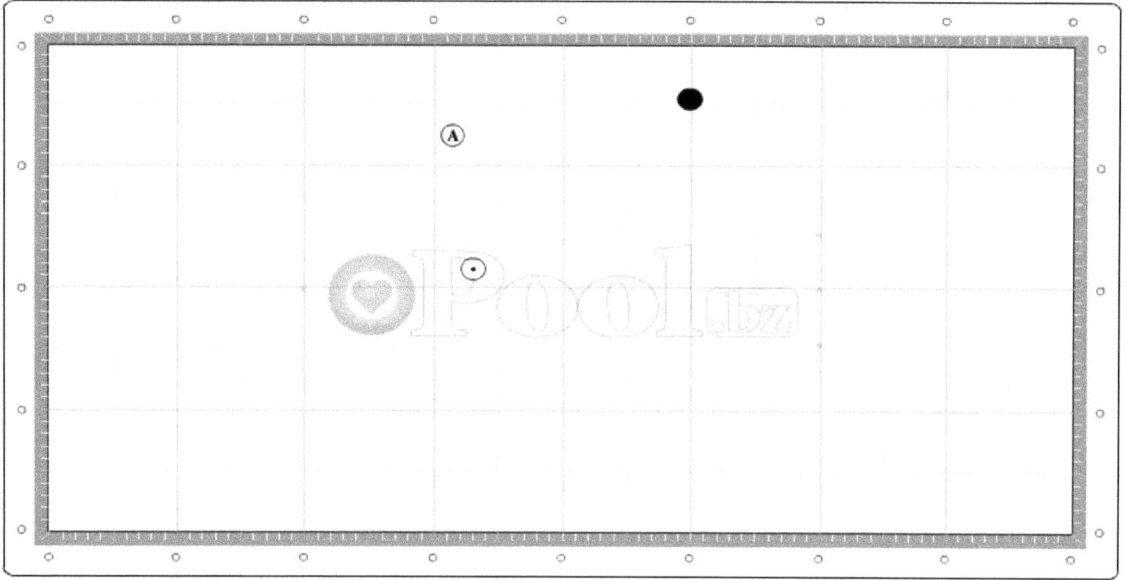

Shot Pattern

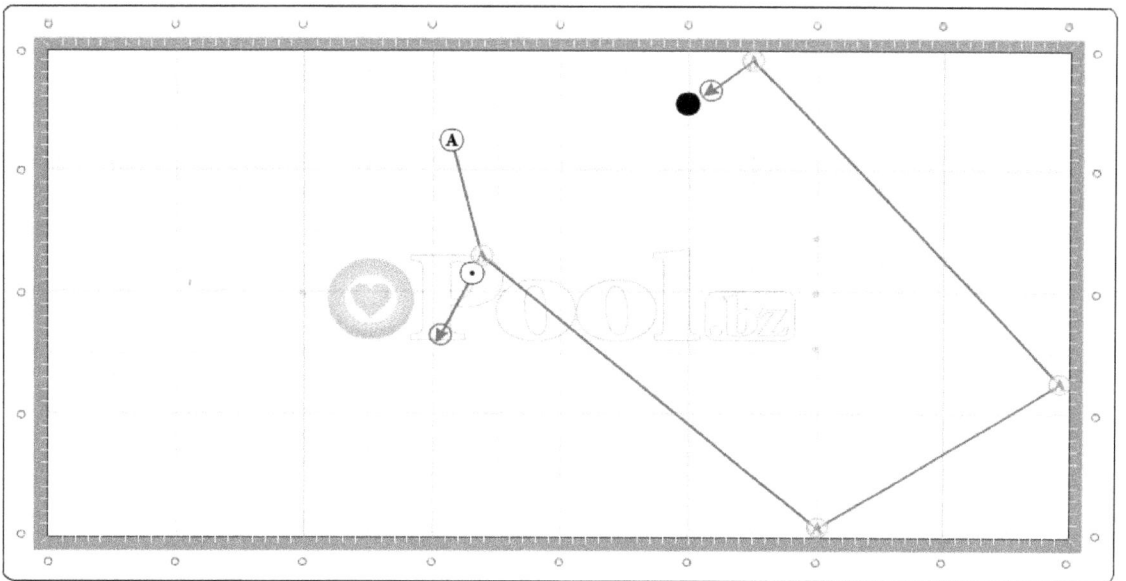

A:5c – Setup

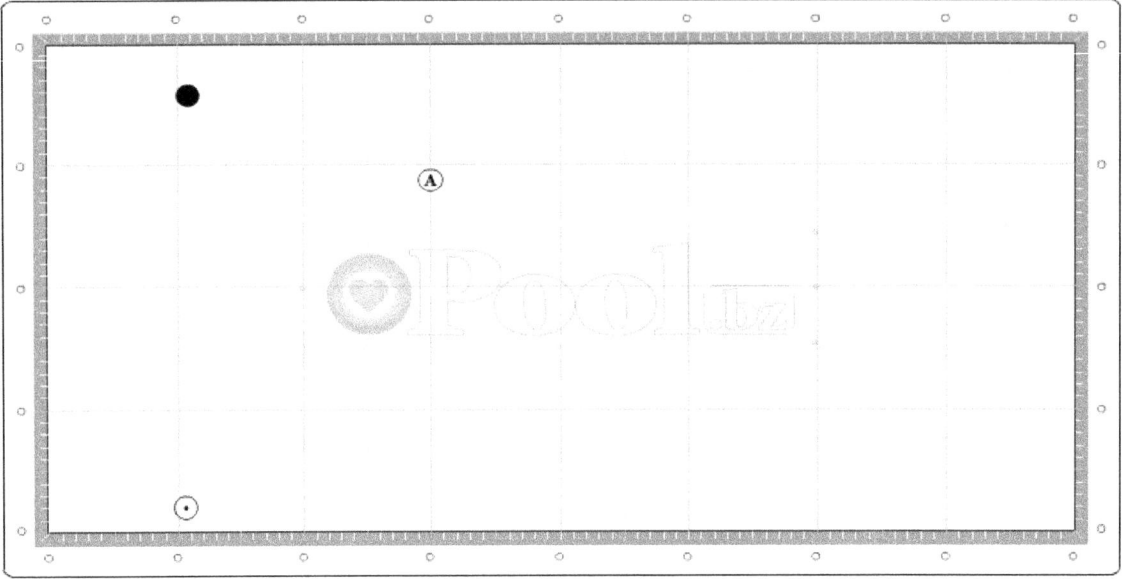

Shot Pattern

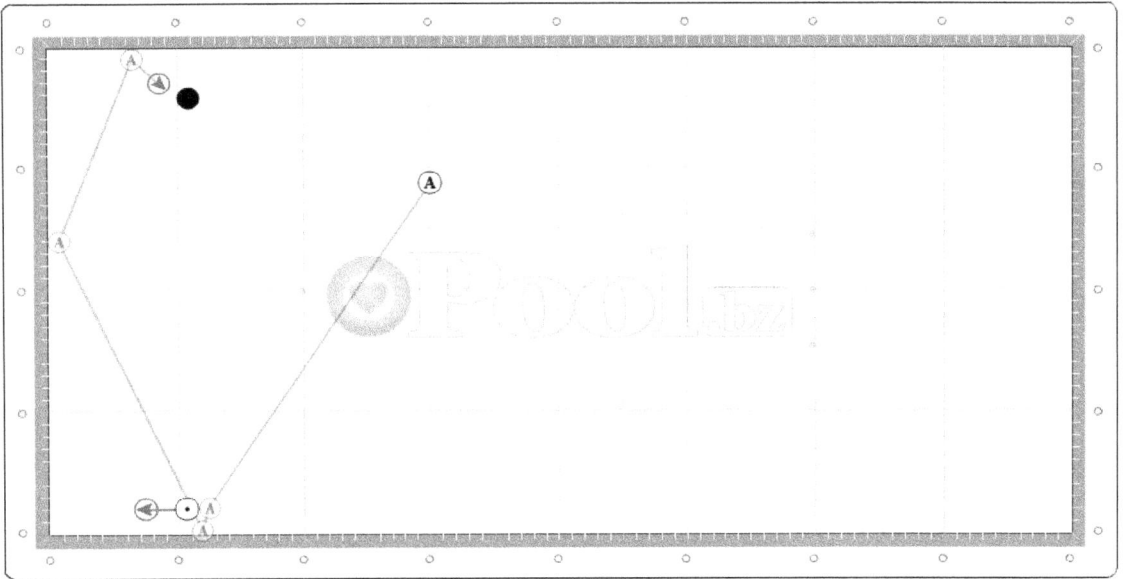

A:5d – Setup

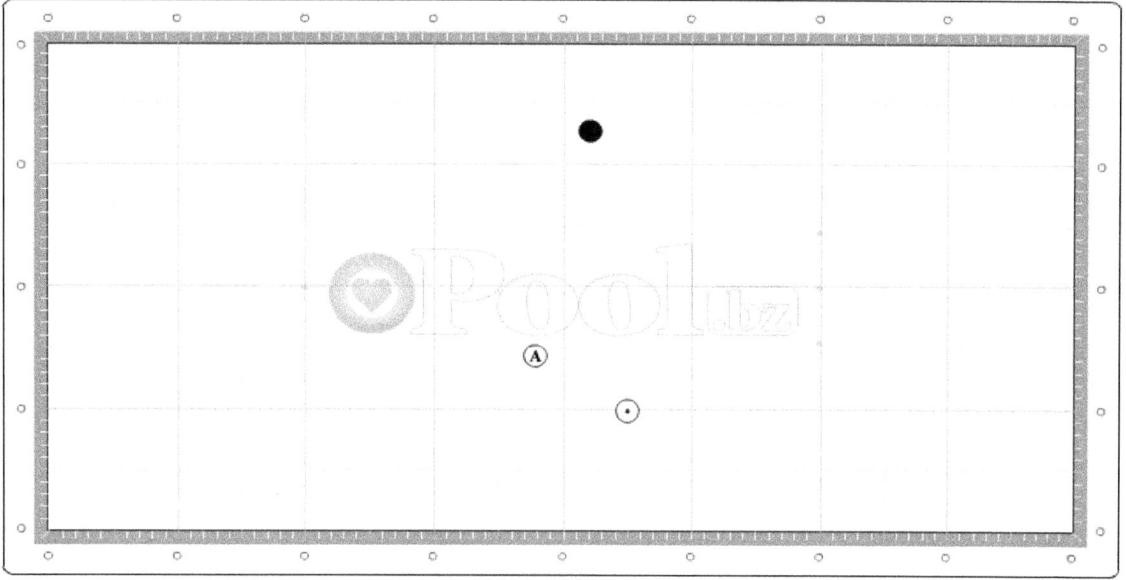

Shot Pattern

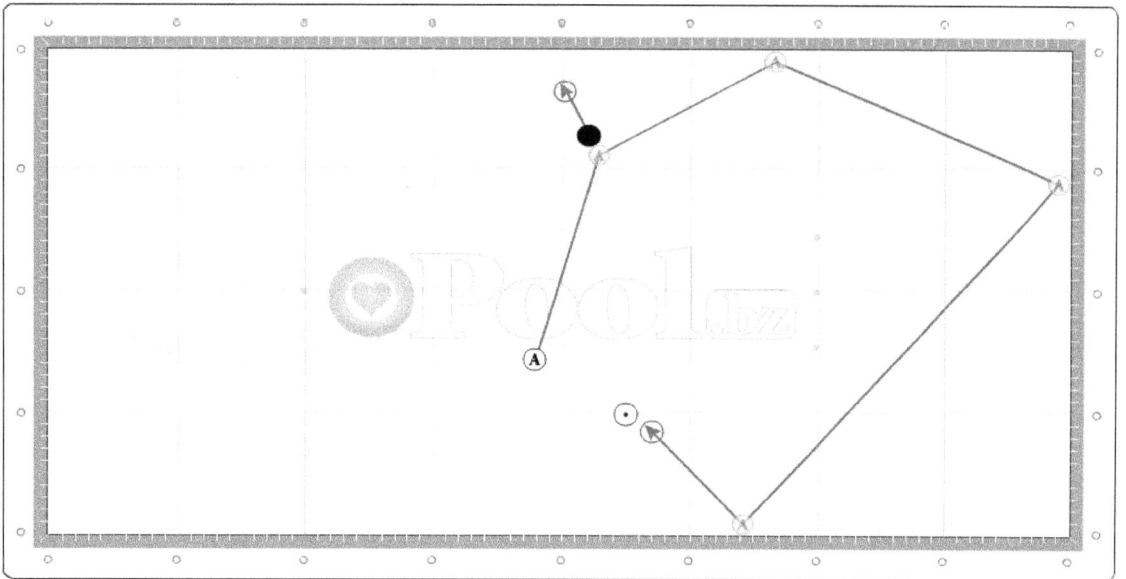

A: Group 6

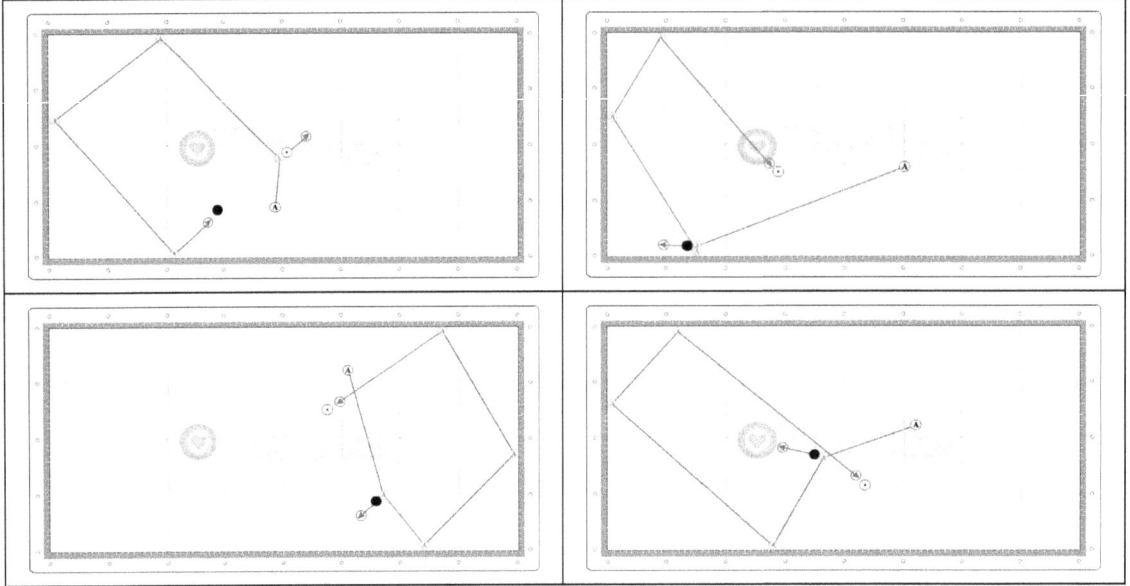

Analysis:

A:6a. _____

A:6b. _____

A:6c. _____

A:6d. _____

A:6a – Setup

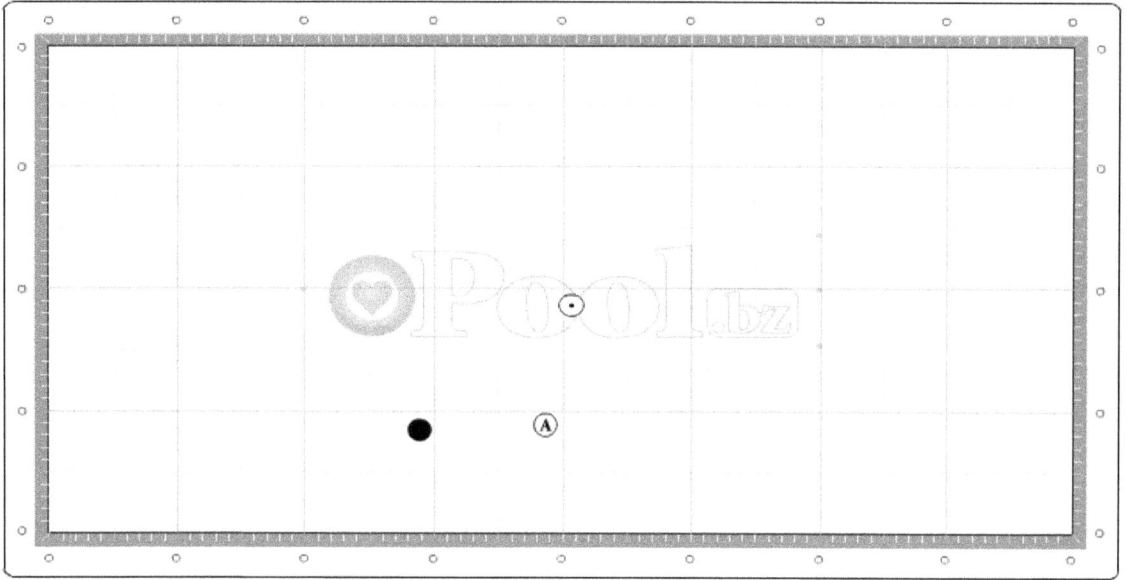

Shot Pattern

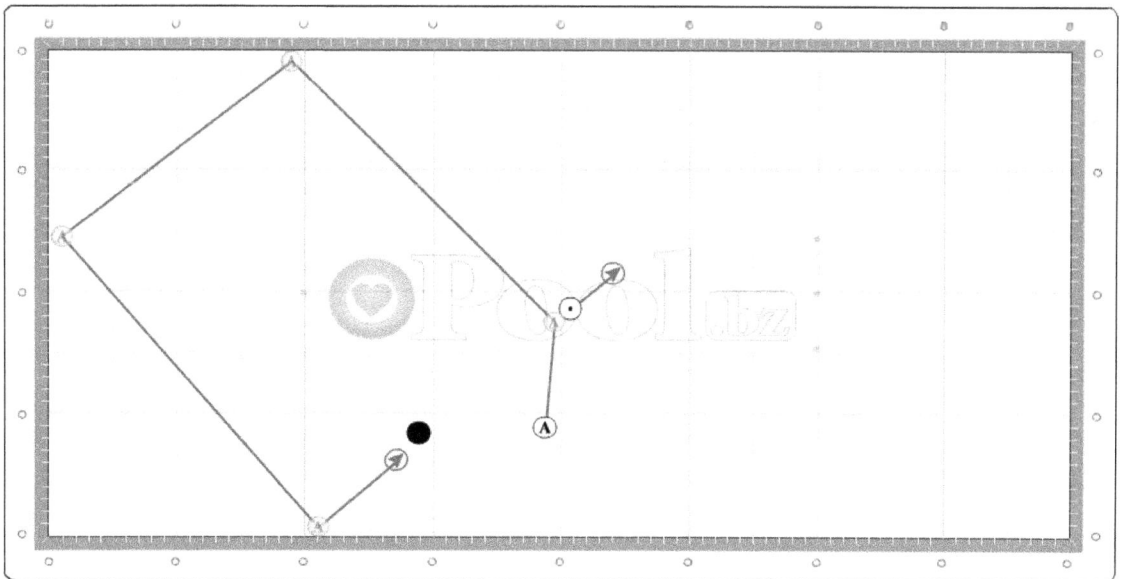

A:6b – Setup

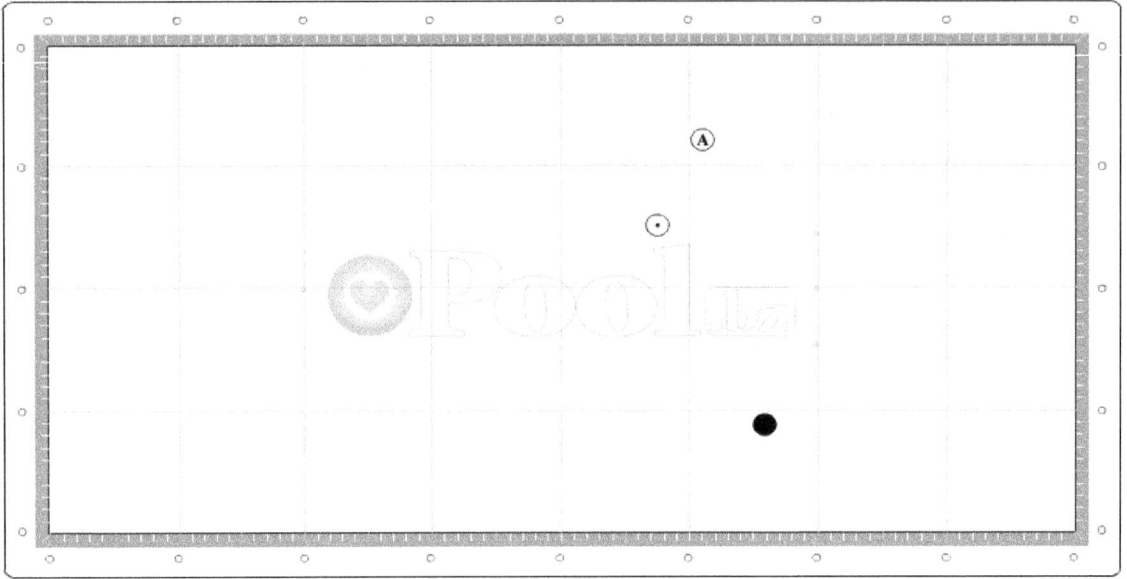

Shot Pattern

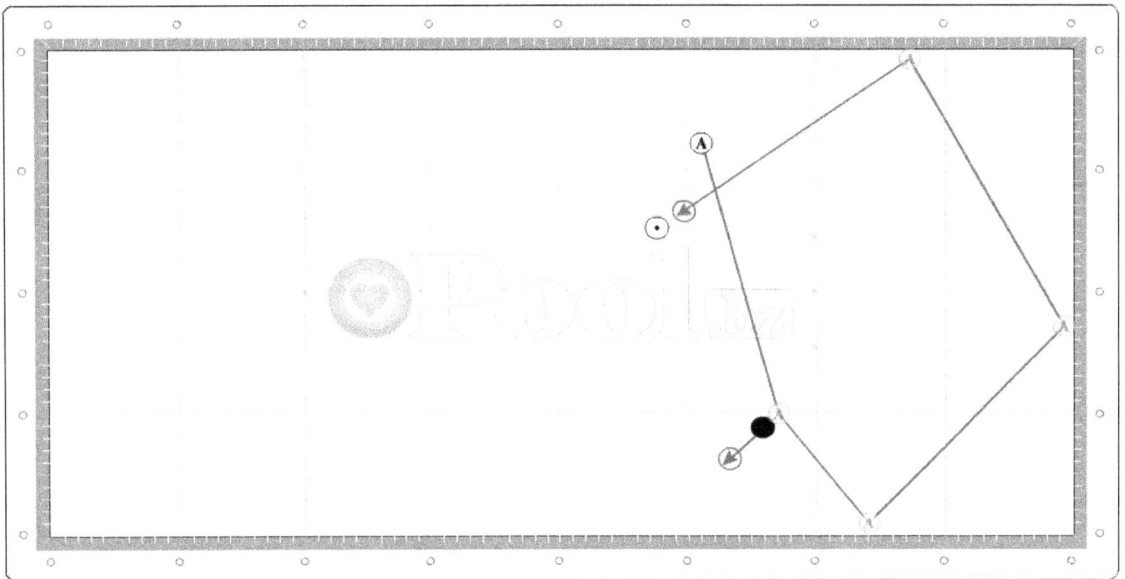

A:6c – Setup

Shot Pattern

A:6d – Setup

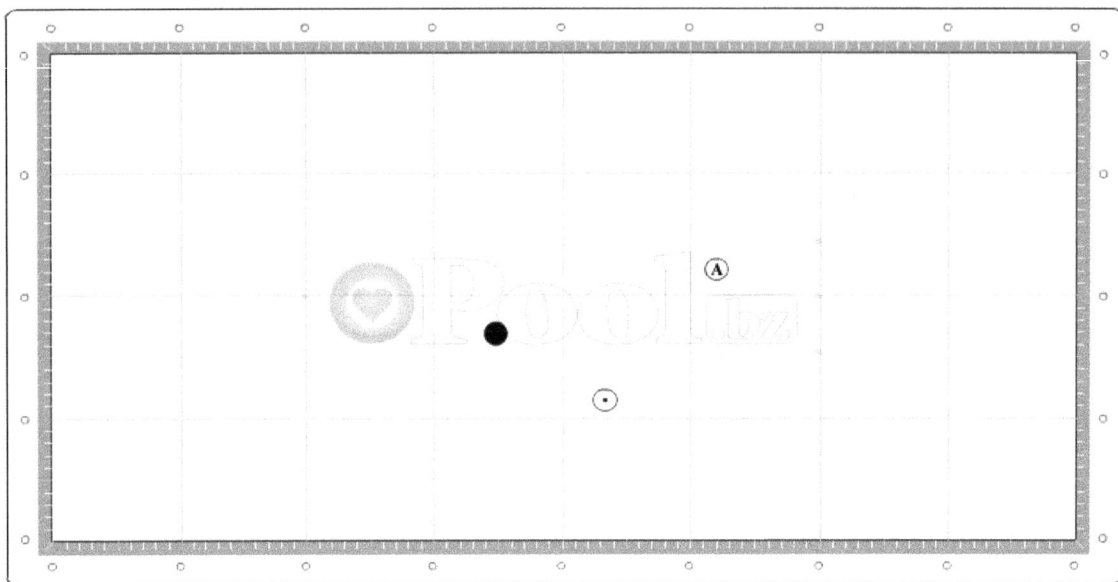

Shot Pattern

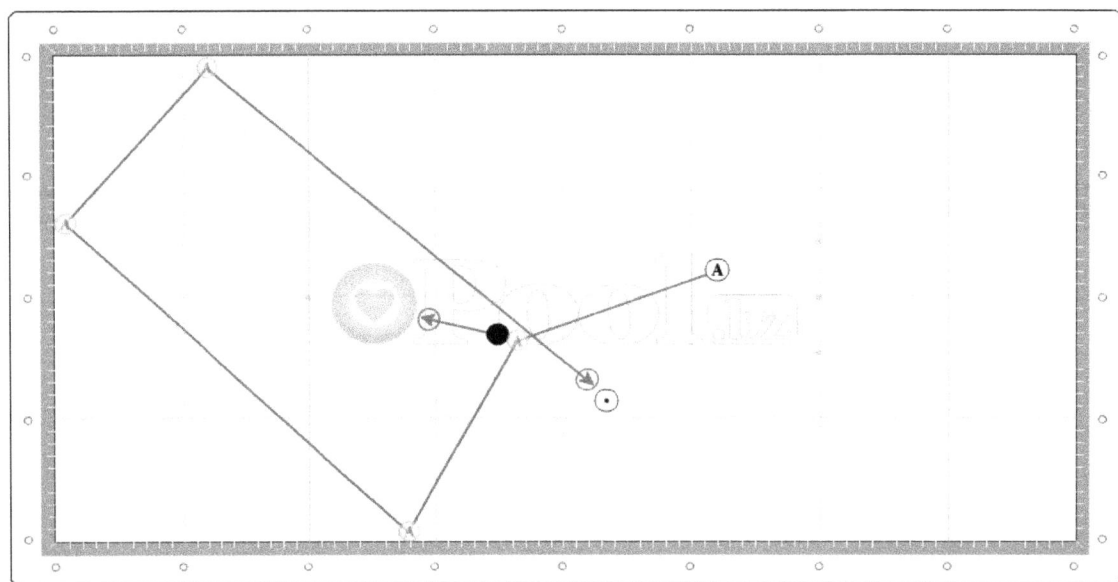

A: Group 7

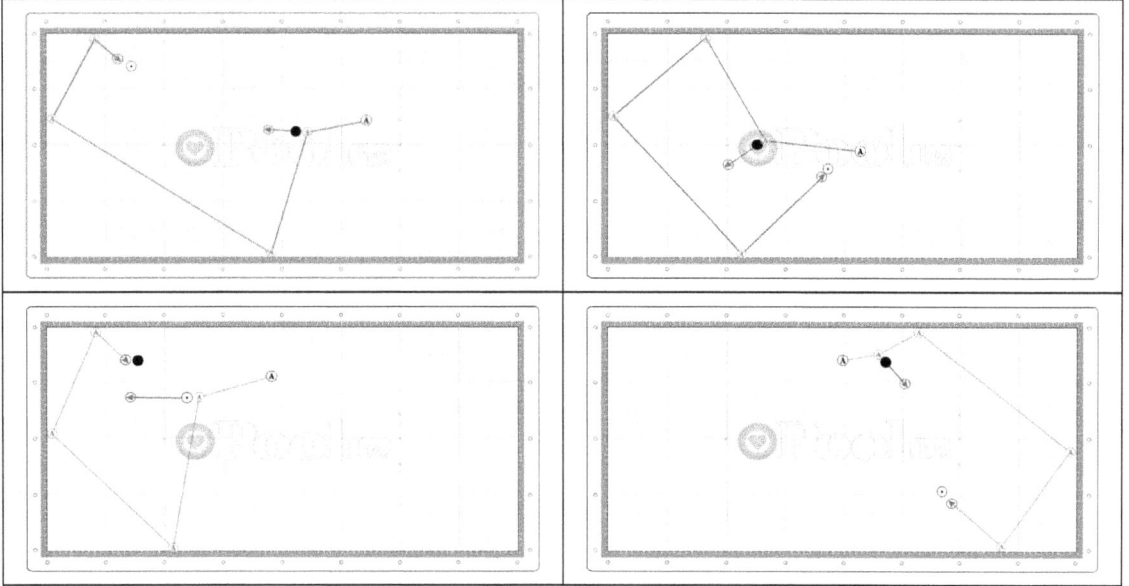

Analysis:

A:7a. _____

A:7b. _____

A:7c. _____

A:7d. _____

A:7a – Setup

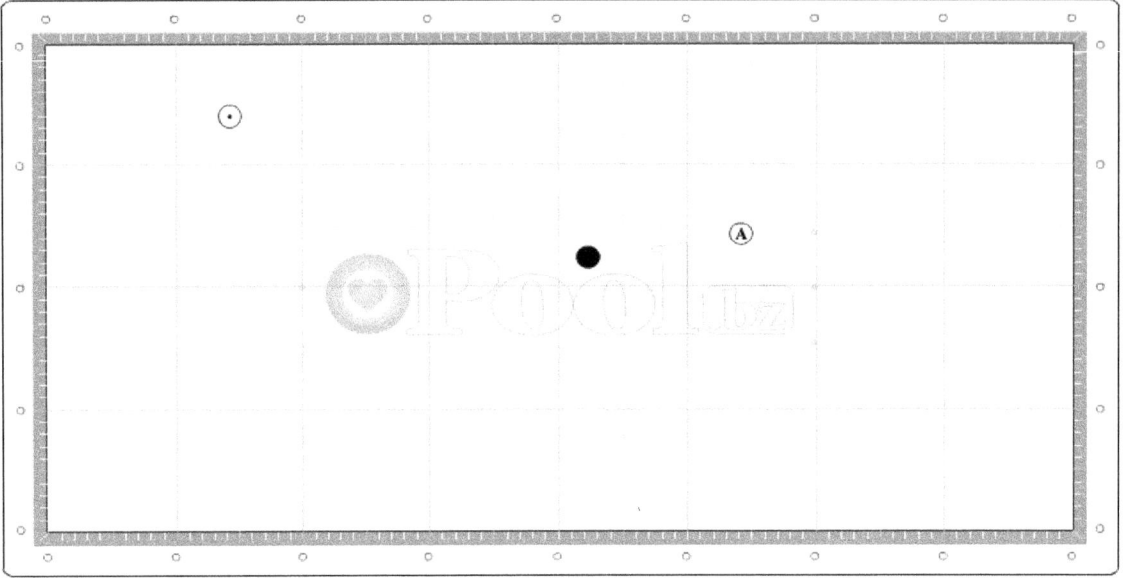

Shot Pattern

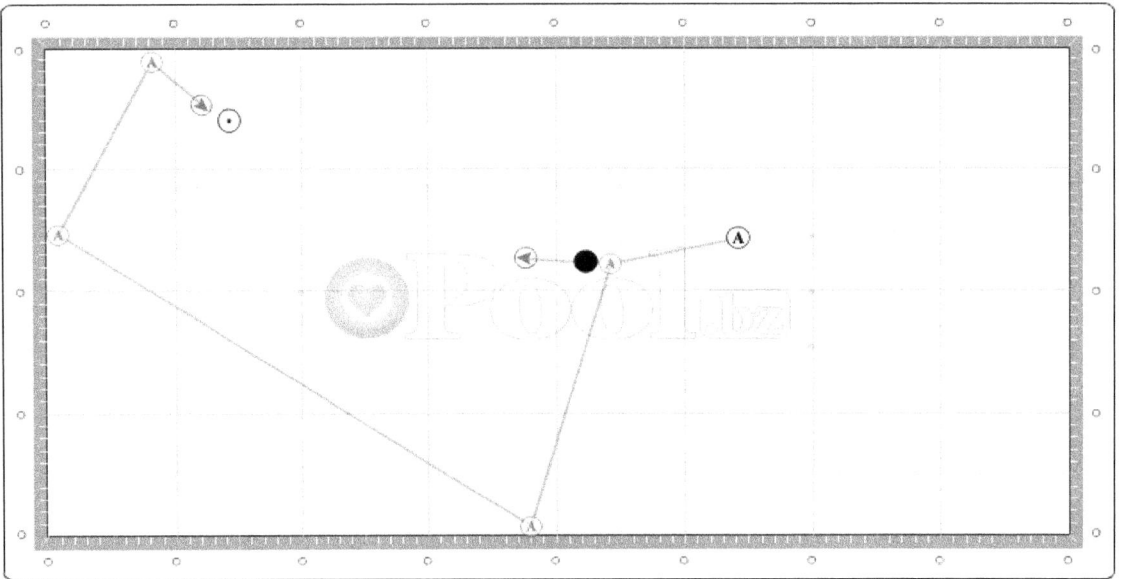

A:7b – Setup

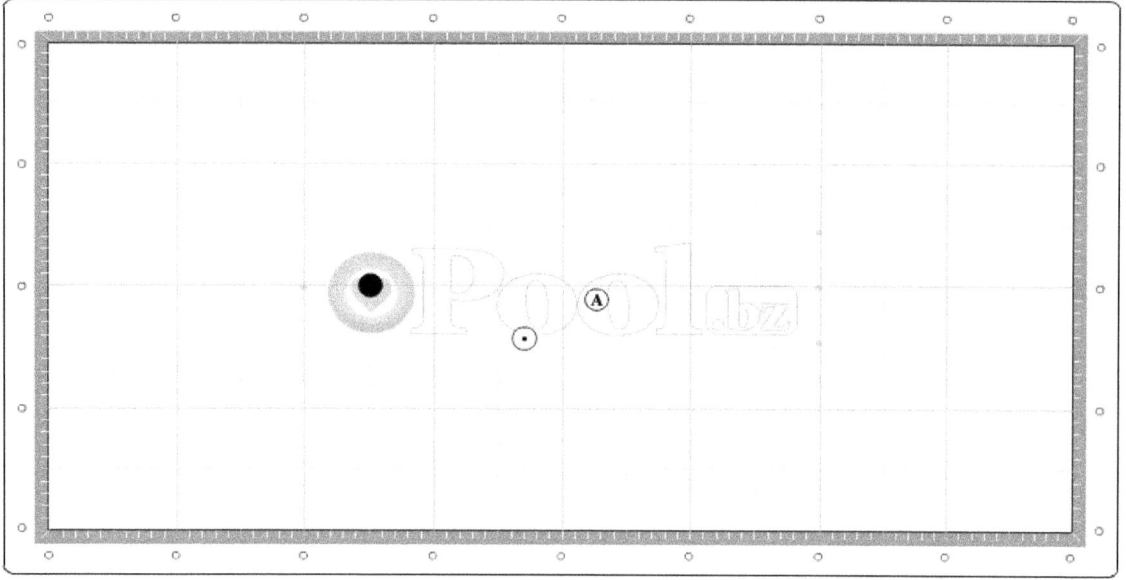

Shot Pattern

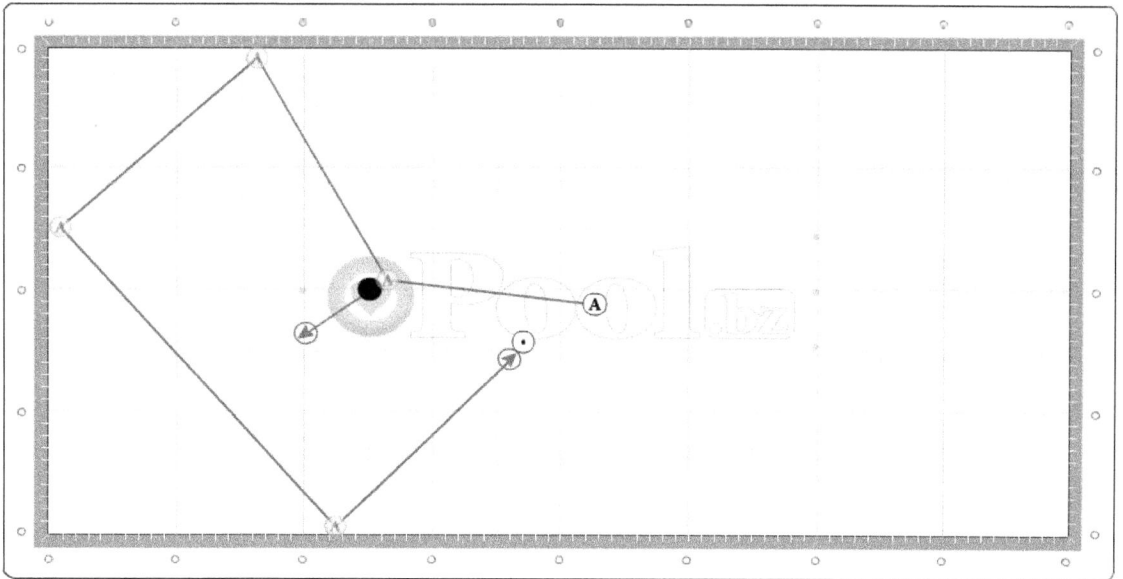

A:7c – Setup

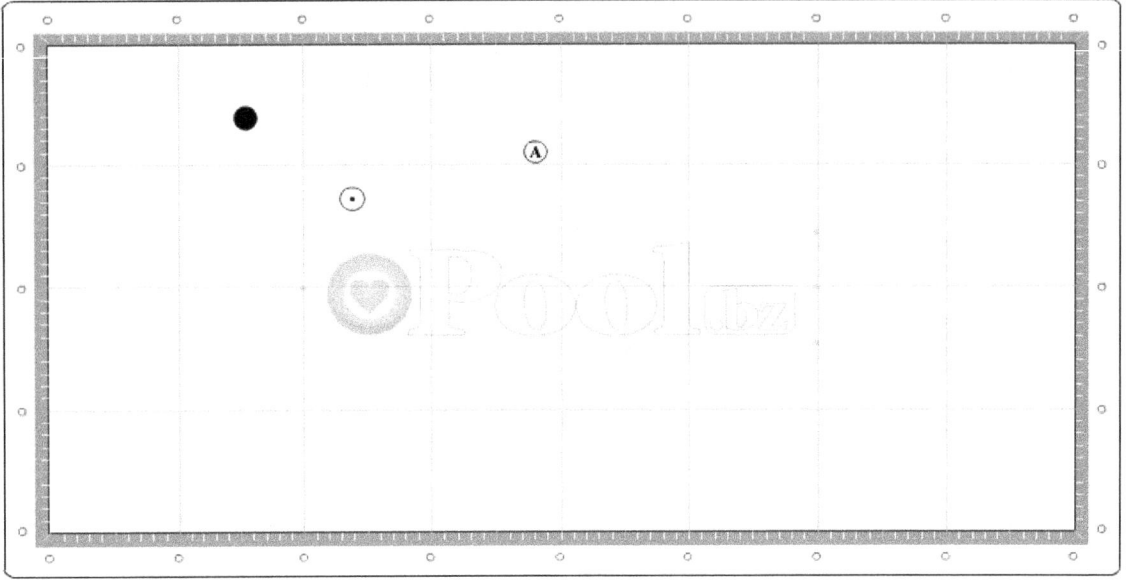

Shot Pattern

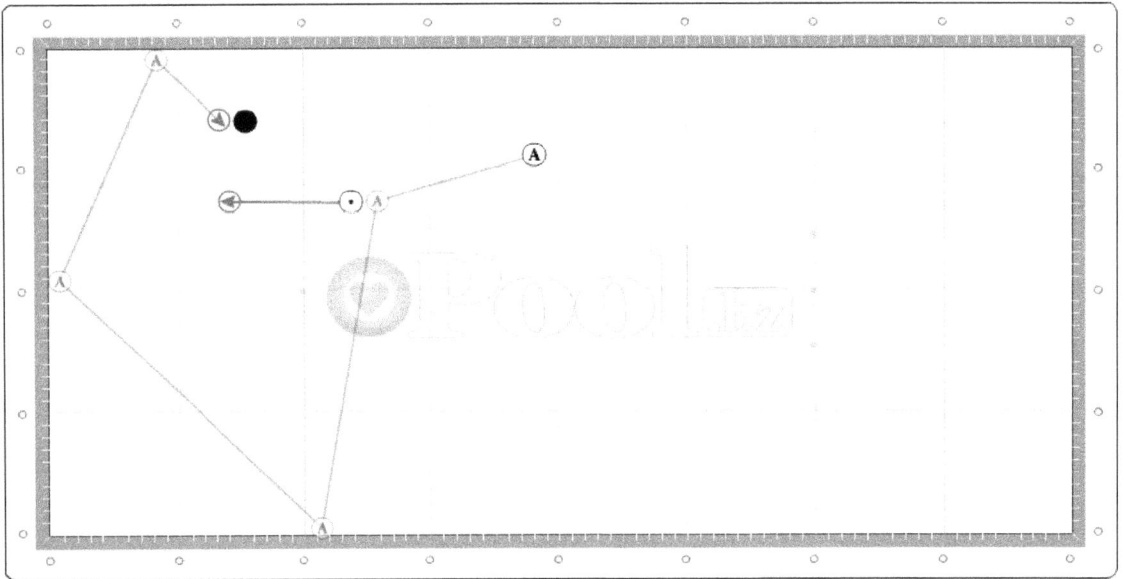

A:7d – Setup

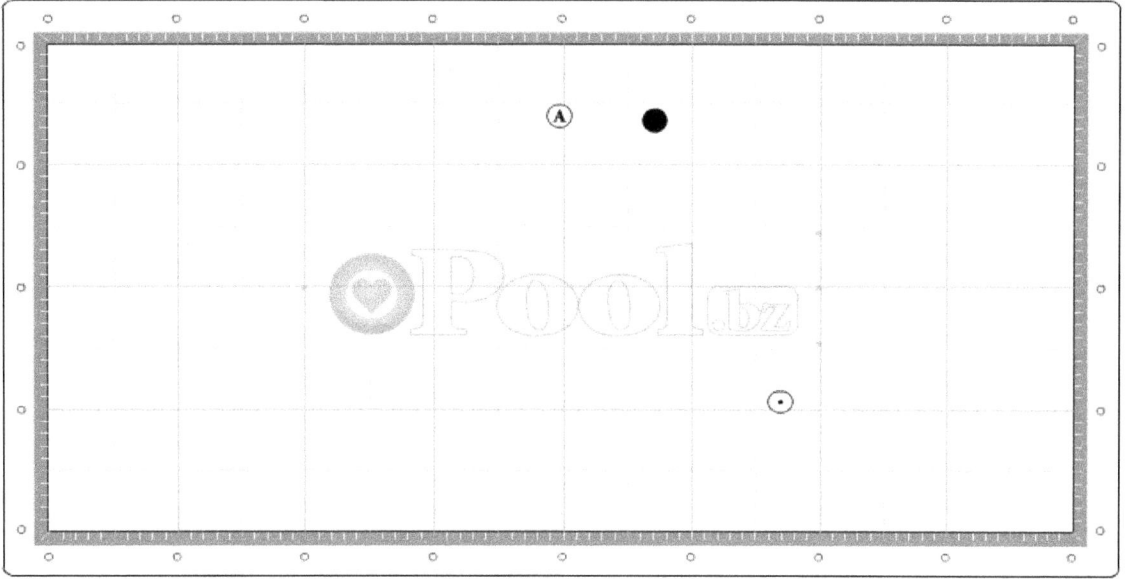

Shot Pattern

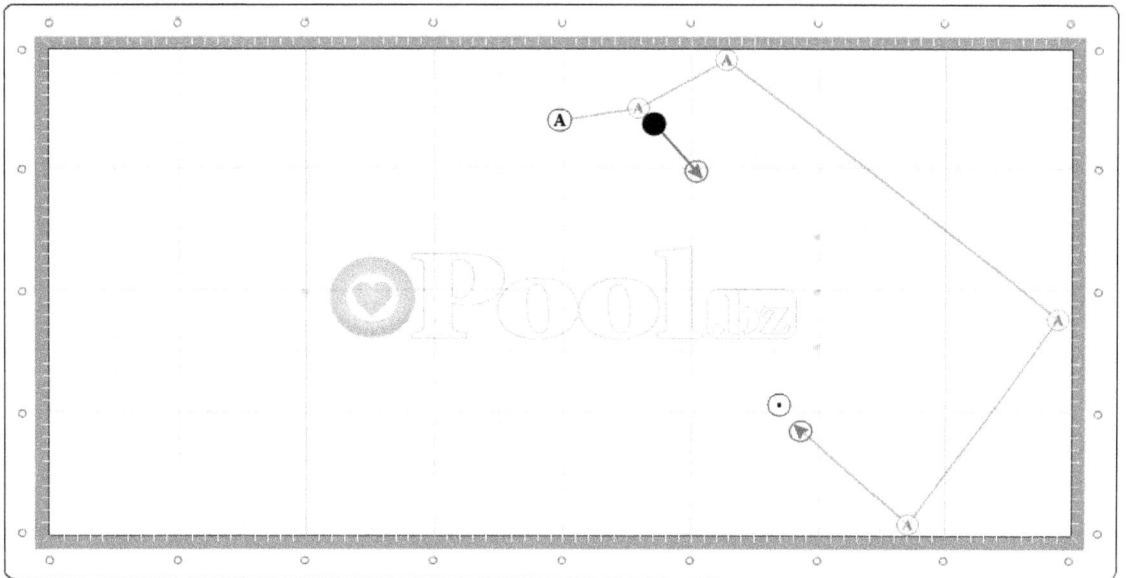

A: Group 8

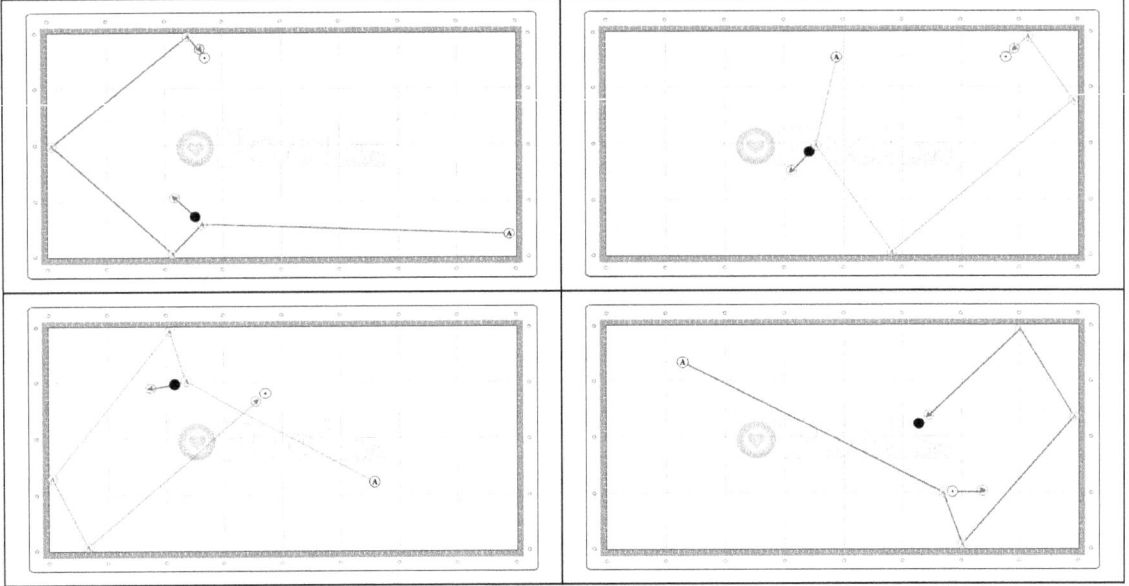

Analysis:

A:8a. _____

A:8b. _____

A:8c. _____

A:8d. _____

A:8a – Setup

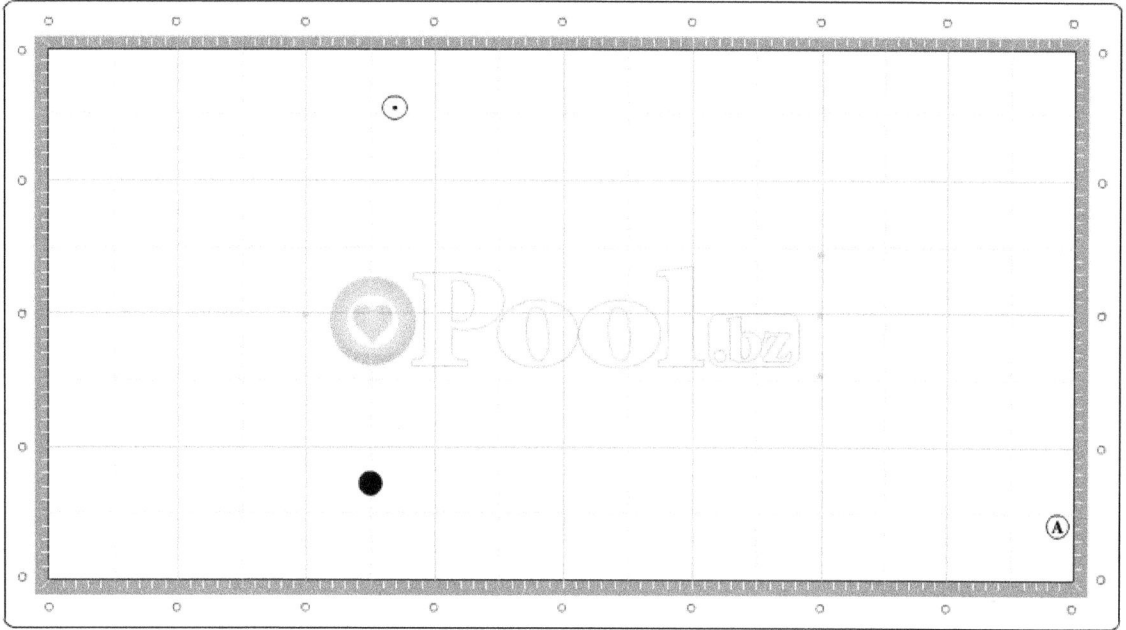

Shot Pattern

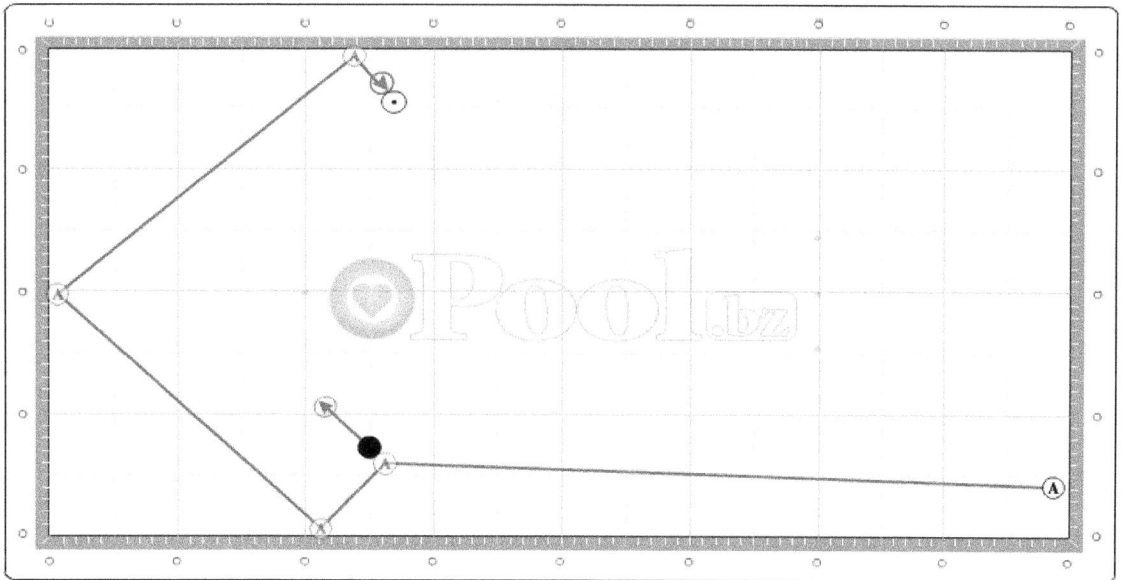

A:8b – Setup

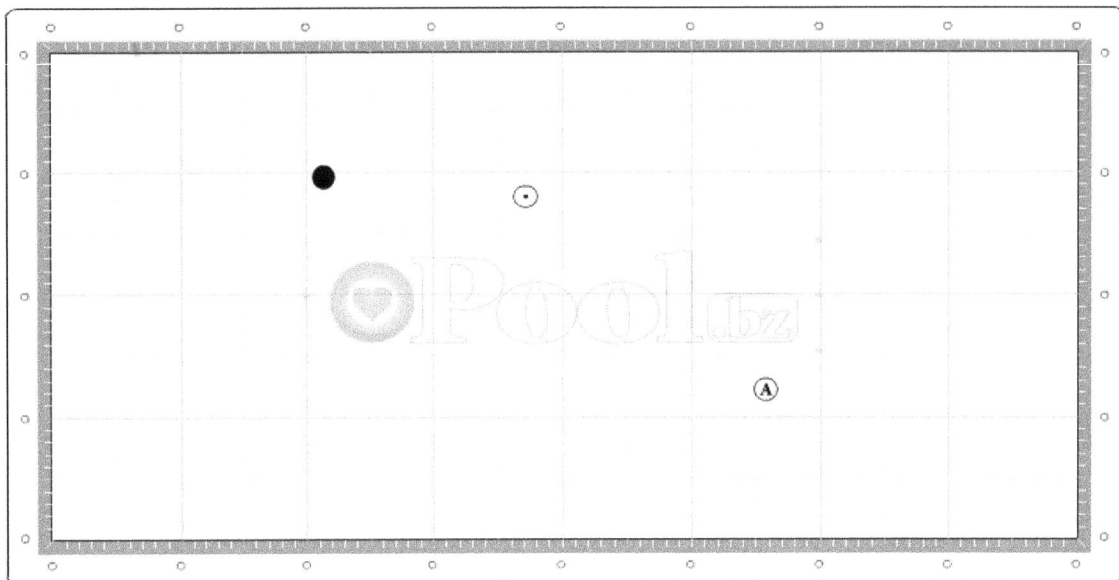

Shot Pattern

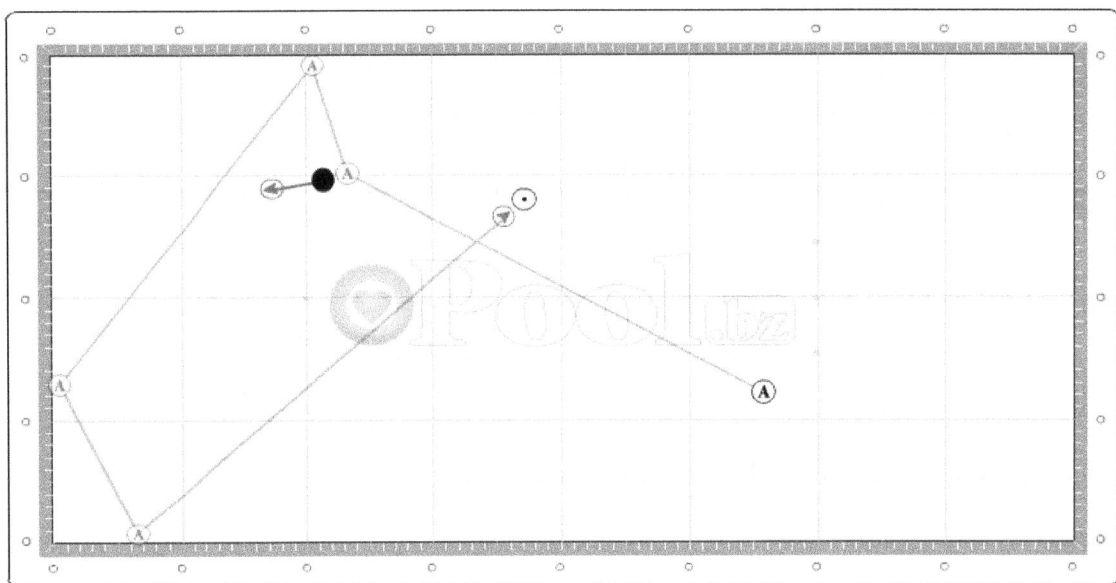

A:8c – Setup

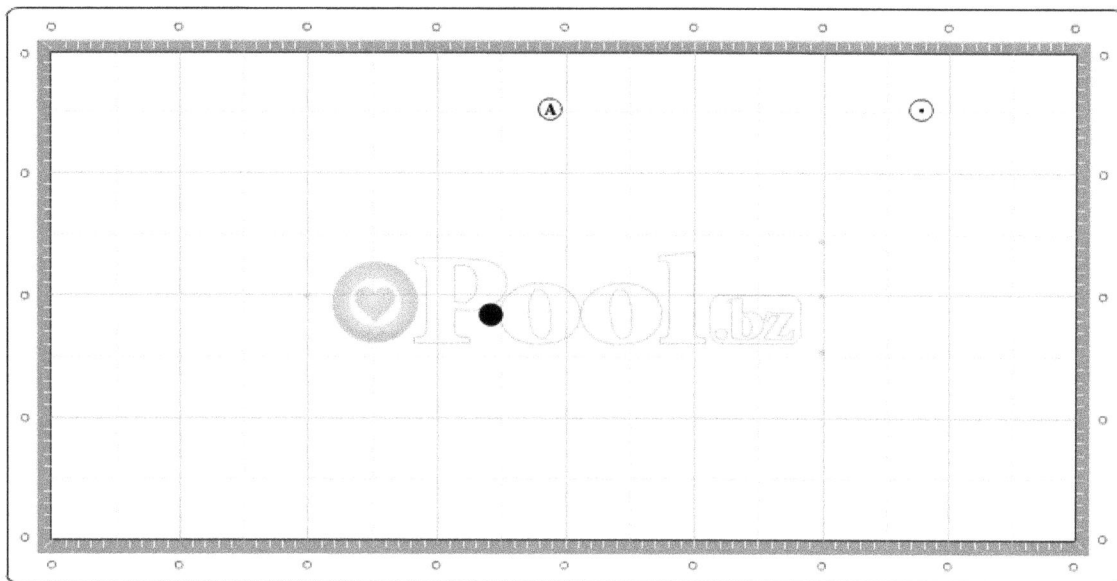

Shot Pattern

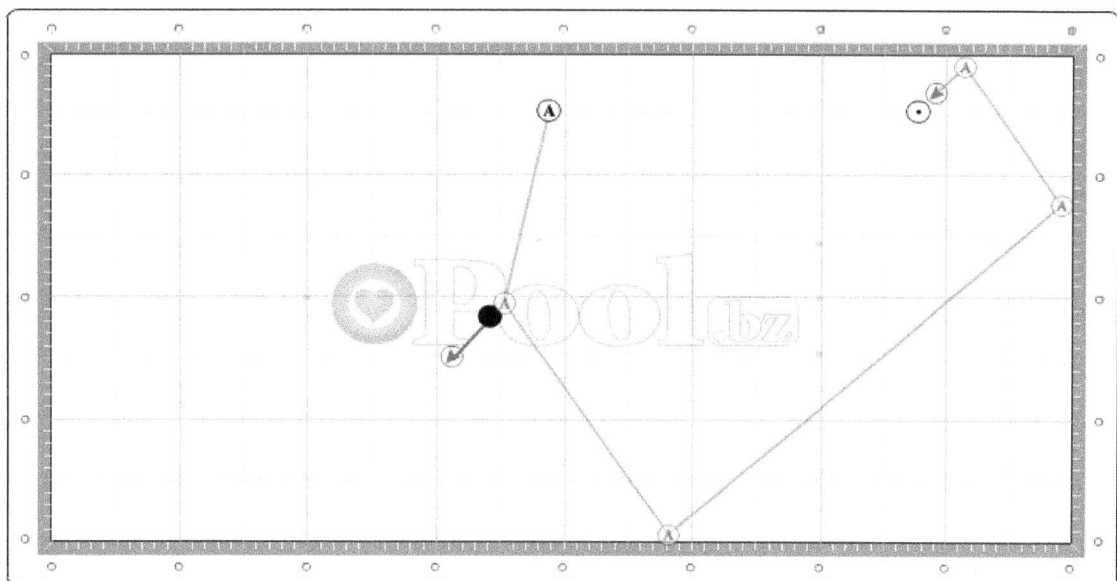

A:8d – Setup

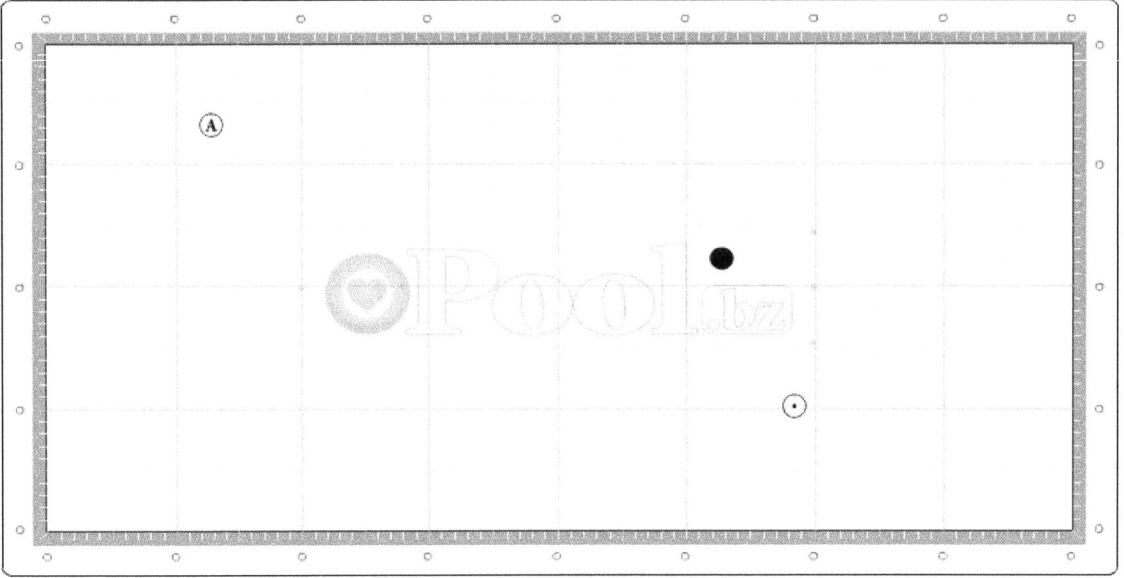

Shot Pattern

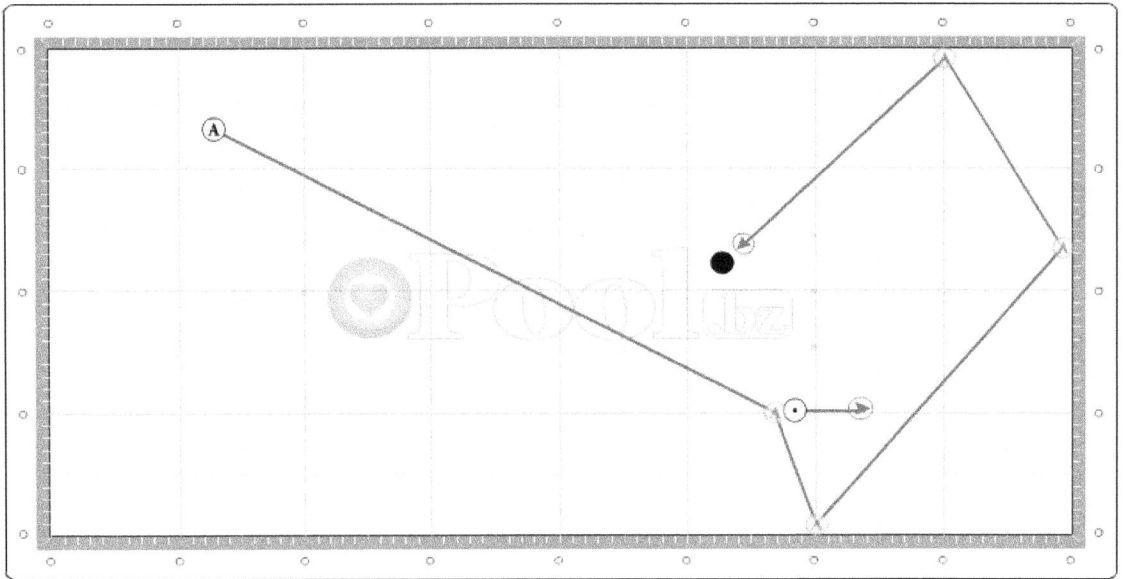

B: Out of a Small Corner

On these shots, the CB comes off the first OB into the long rail. It comes off the long rail and into the corner for the next two cushions. When the CB comes out of the corner, it contacts the second OB for the score.

B: Group 1

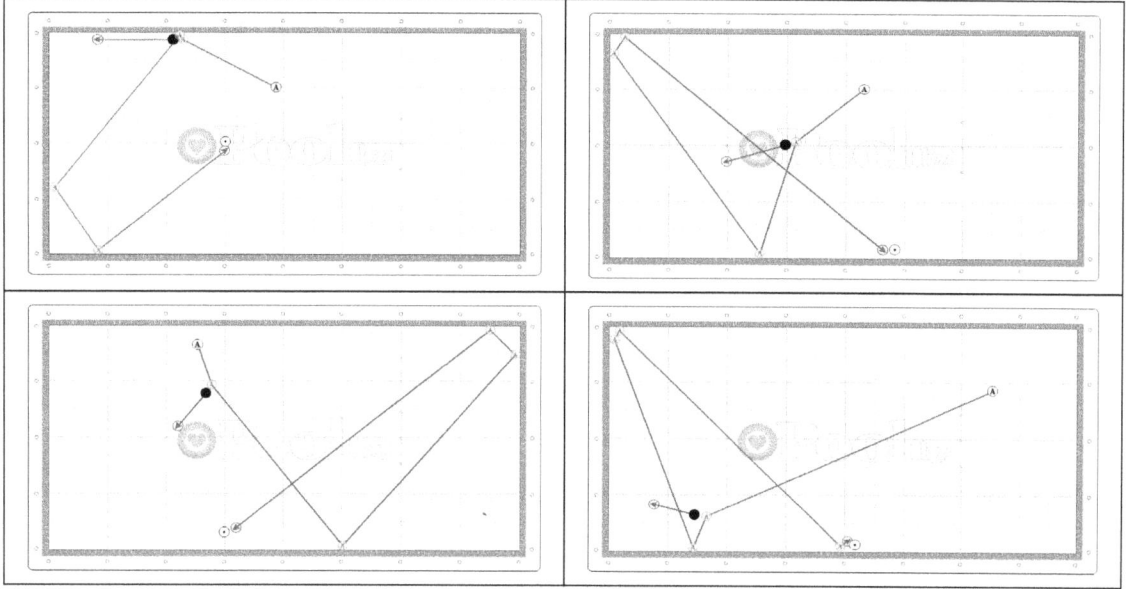

Analysis:

B:1a. _____

B:1b. _____

B:1c. _____

B:1d. _____

B:1a – Setup

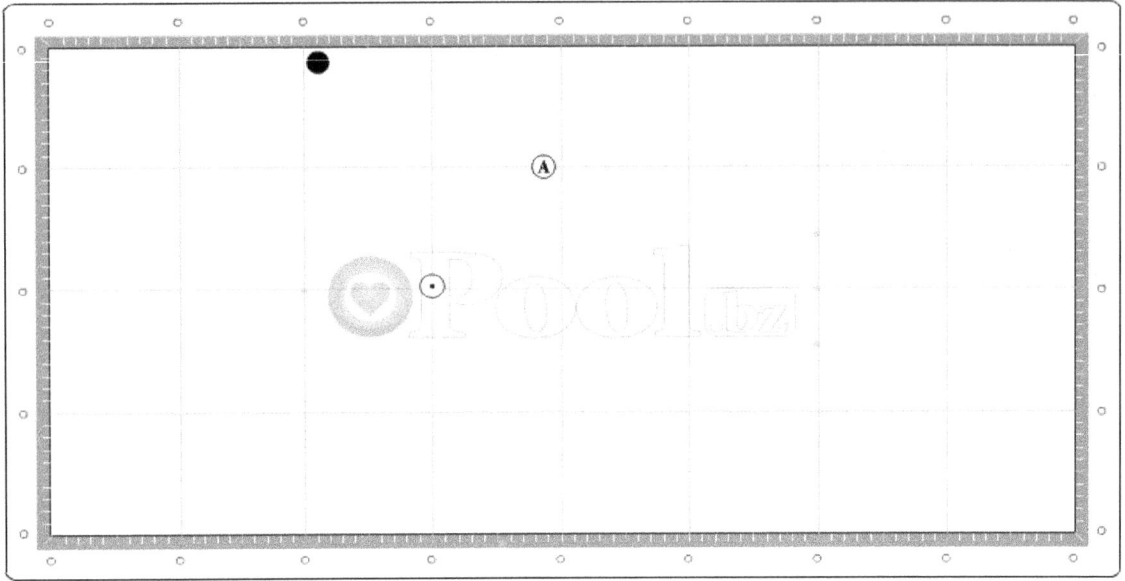

Shot Pattern

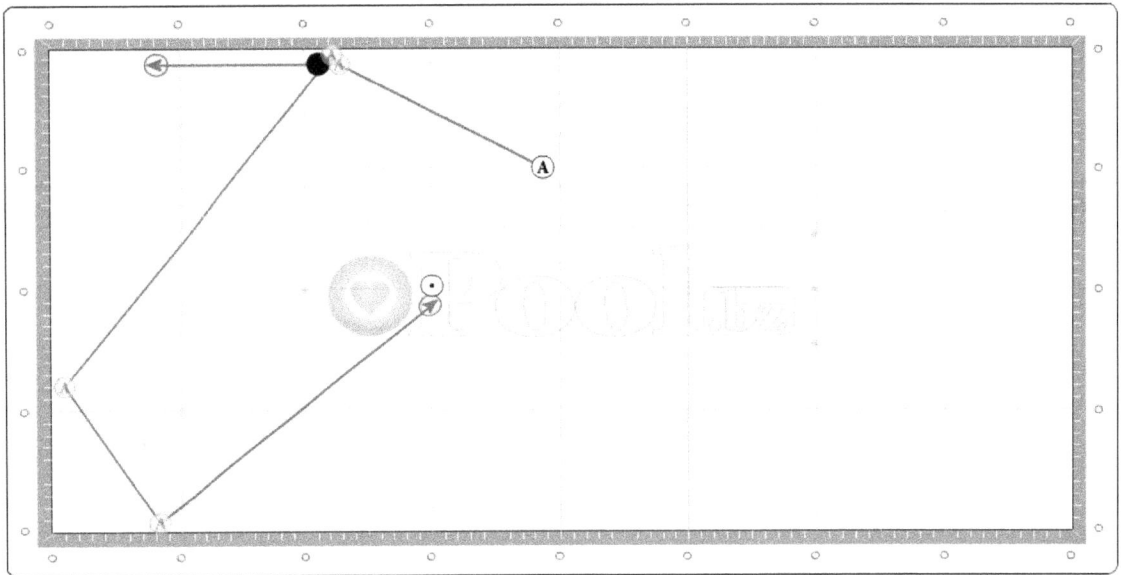

B:1b – Setup

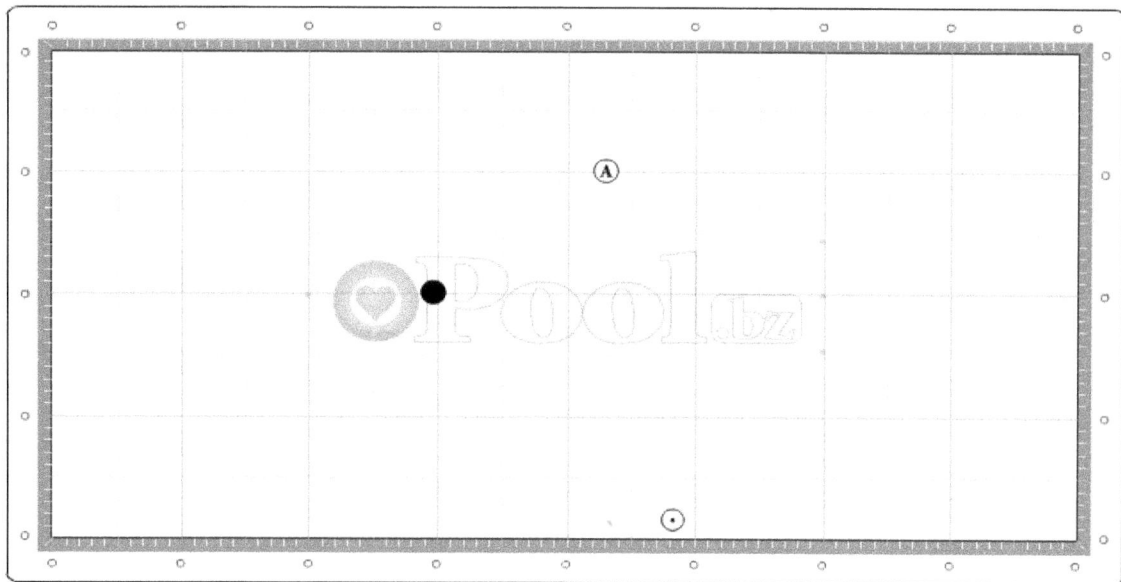

Shot Pattern

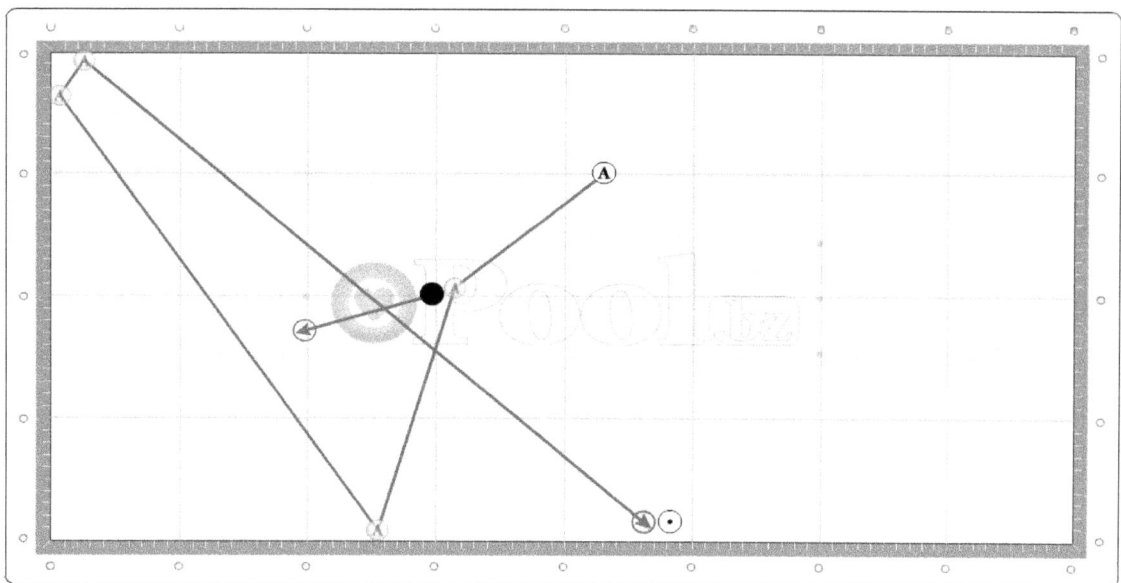

B:1c – Setup

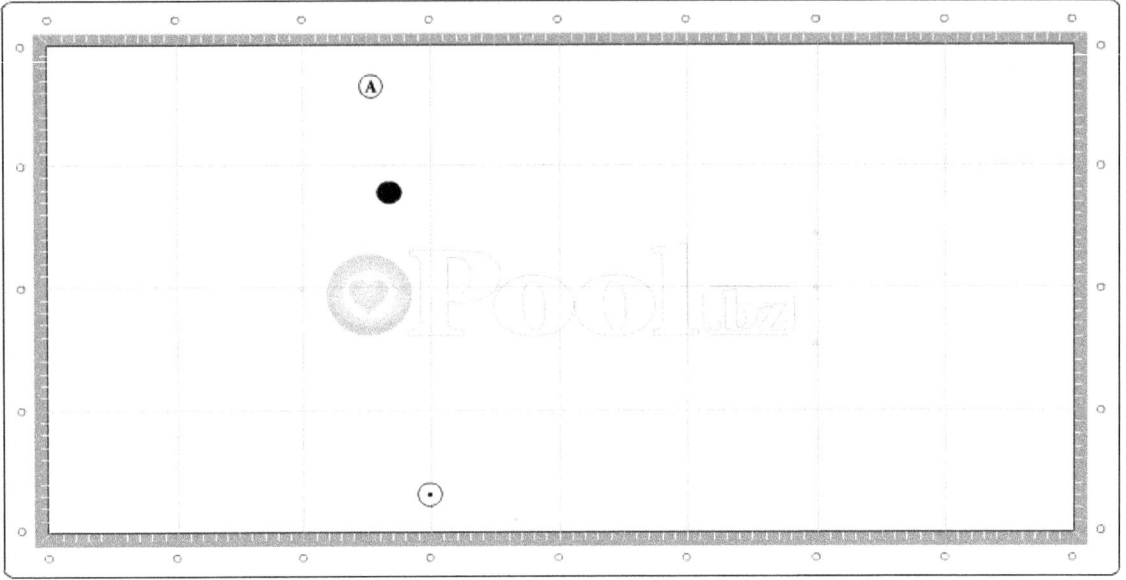

Shot Pattern

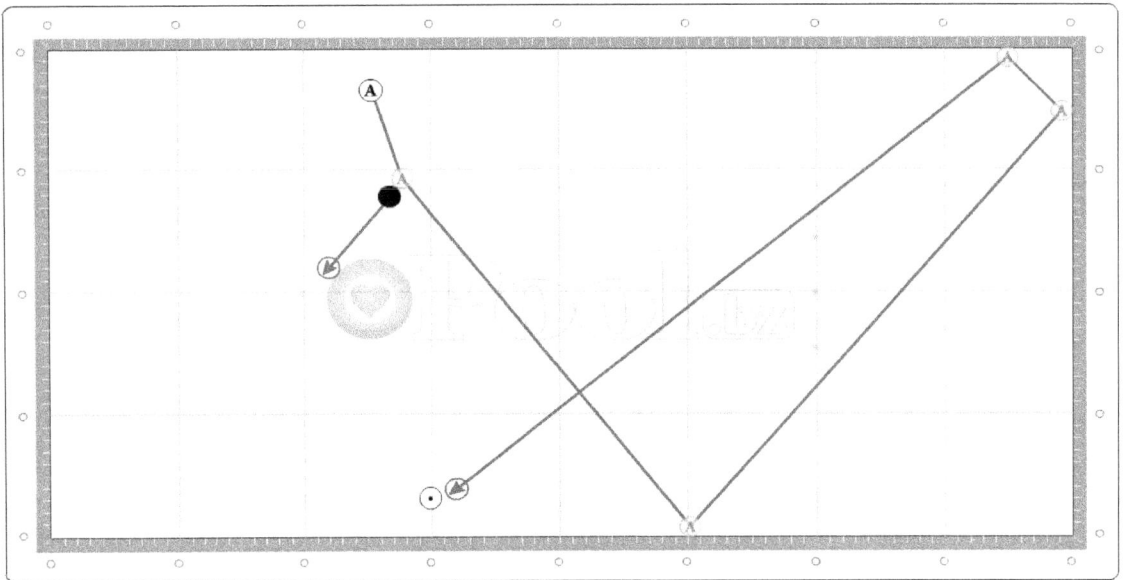

B:1d – Setup

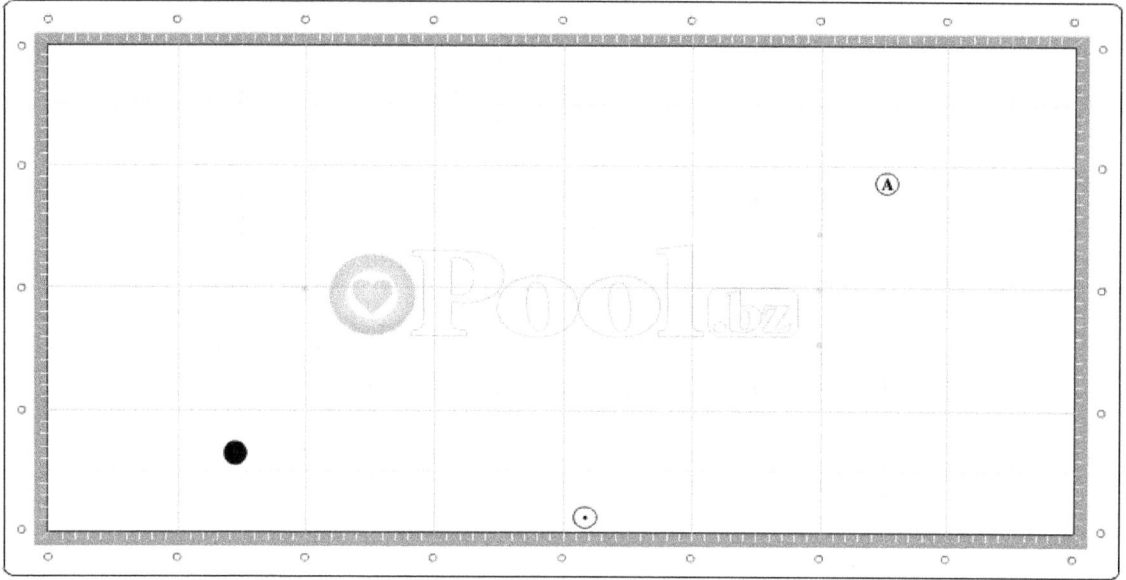

Shot Pattern

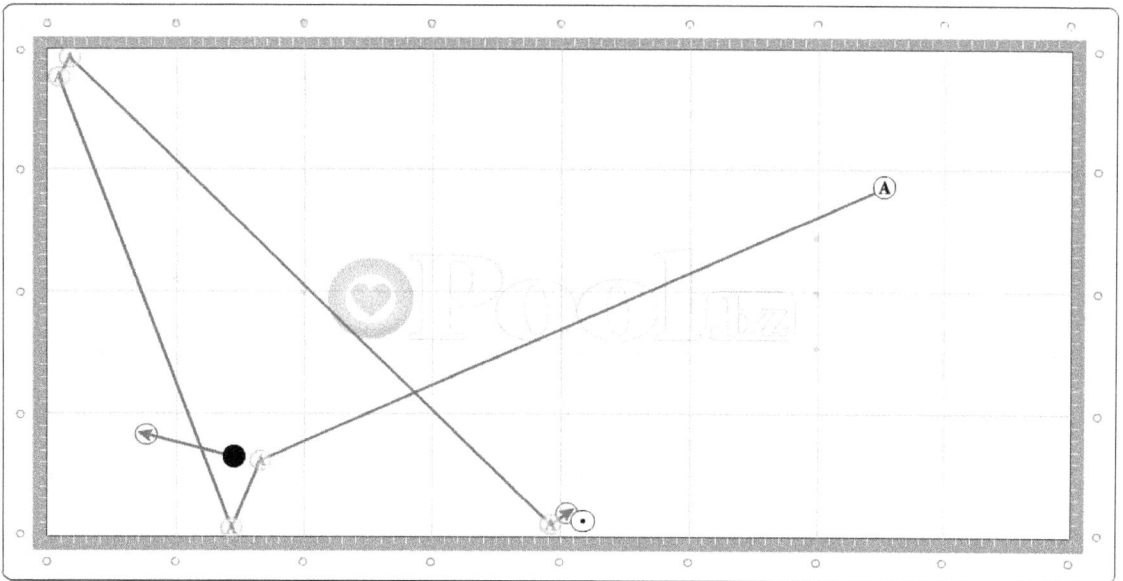

B: Group 2

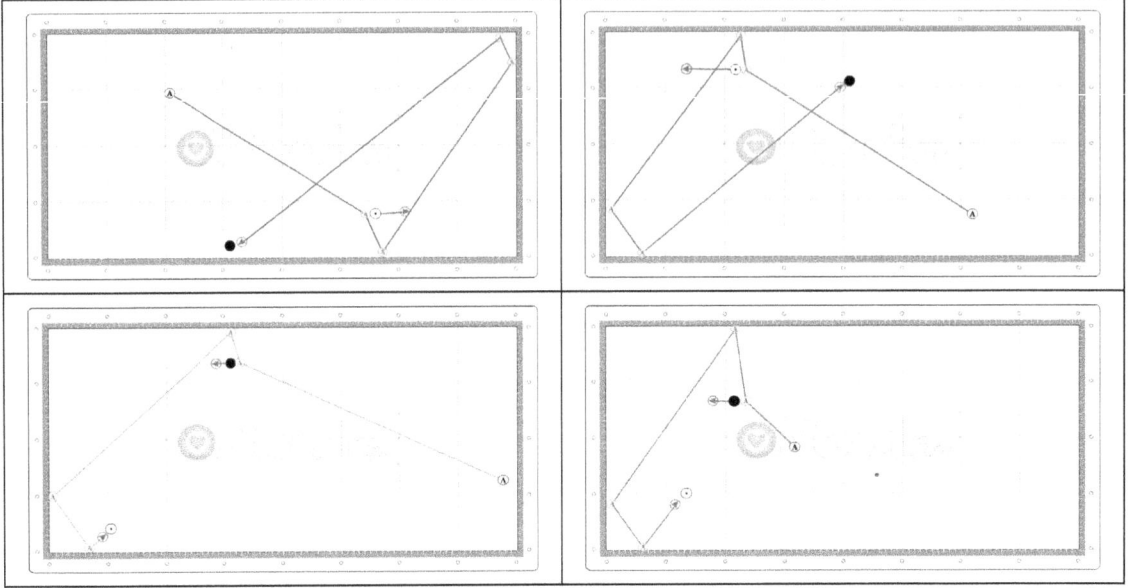

Analysis:

B:2a. _____

B:2b. _____

B:2c. _____

B:2d. _____

B:2a – Setup

Shot Pattern

B:2b – Setup

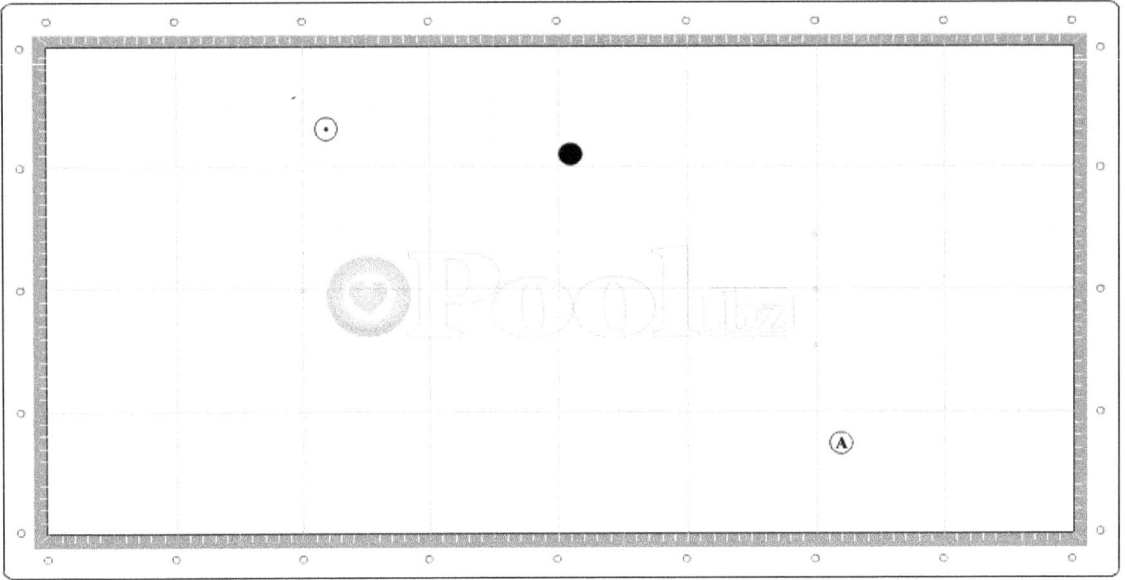

Shot Pattern

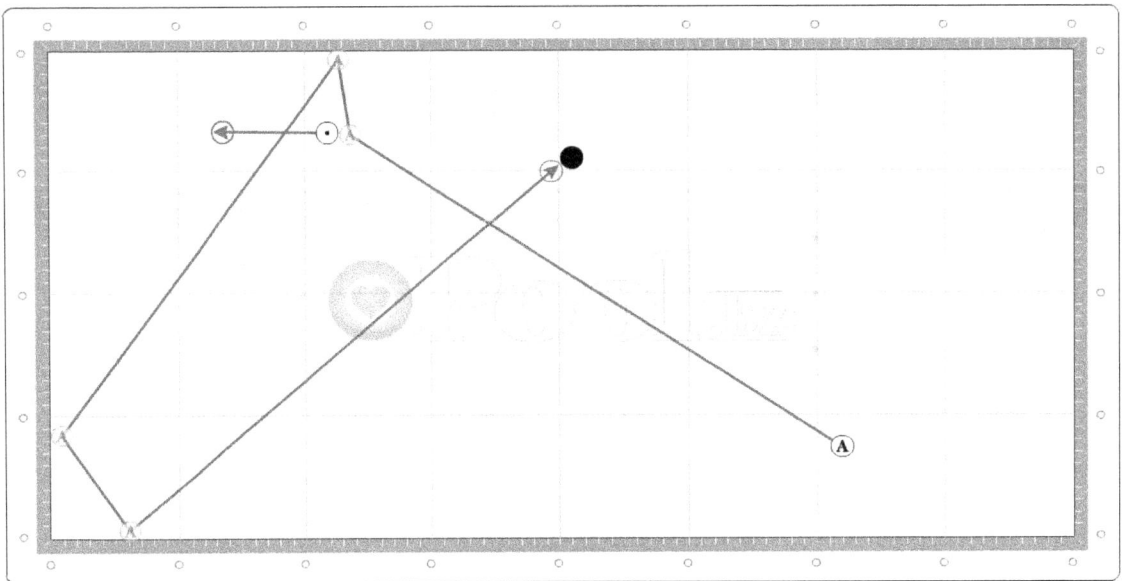

B:2c – Setup

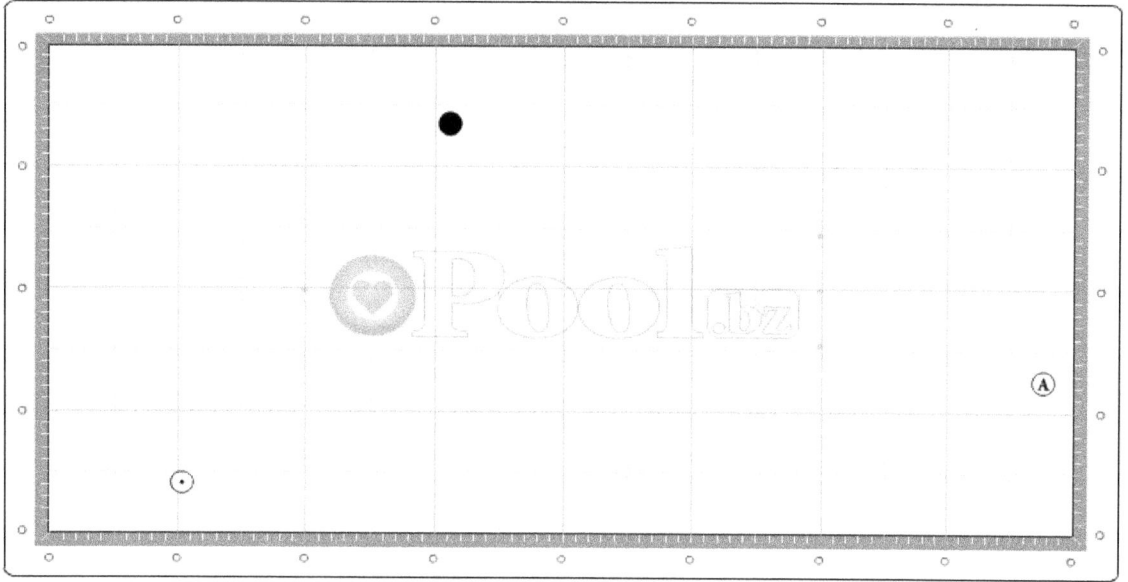

Shot Pattern

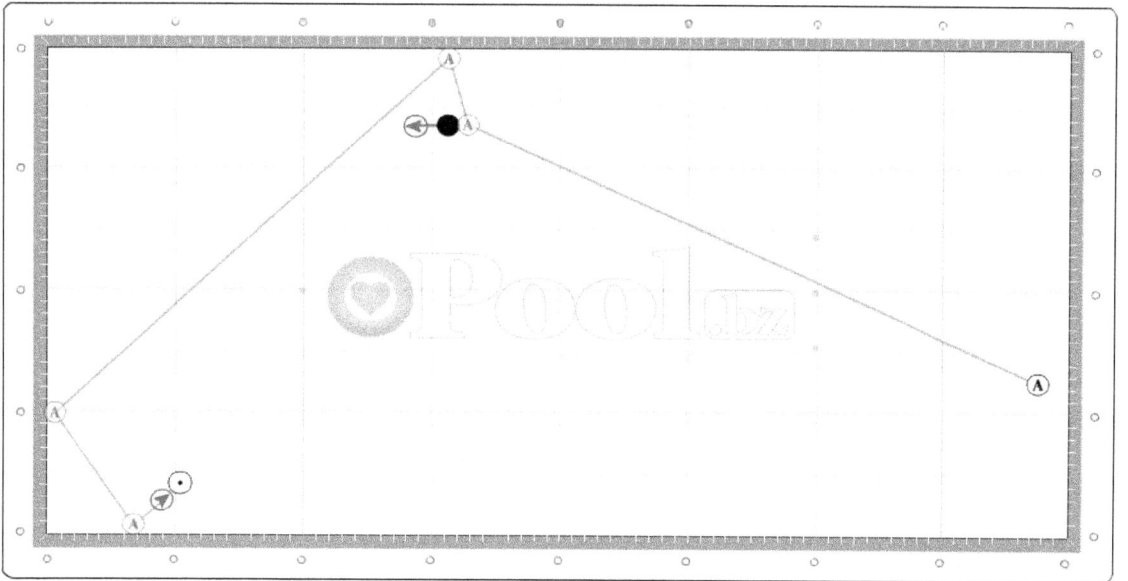

B:2d – Setup

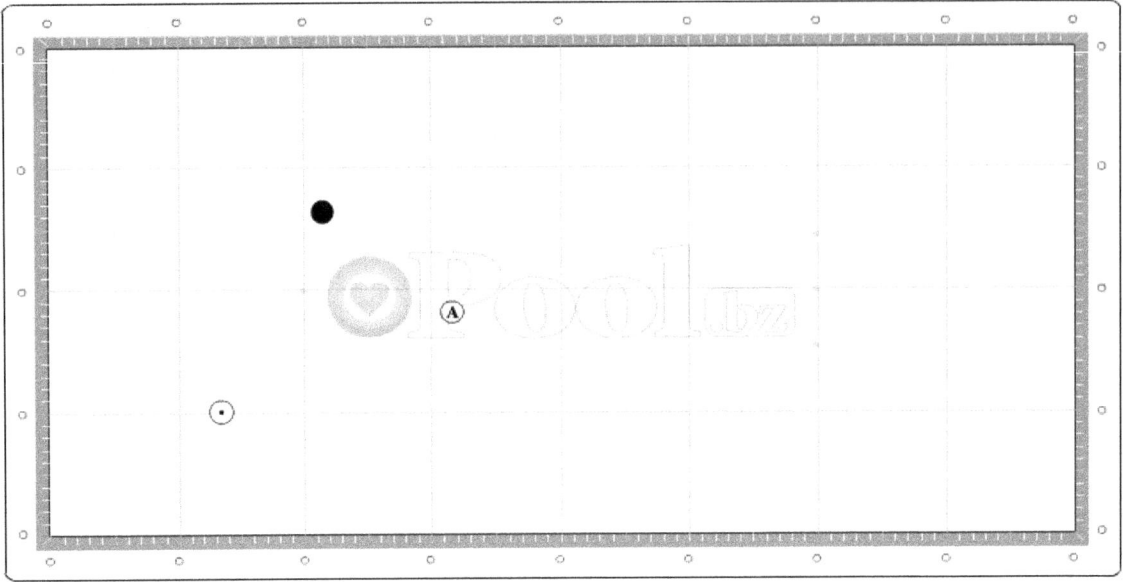

Shot Pattern

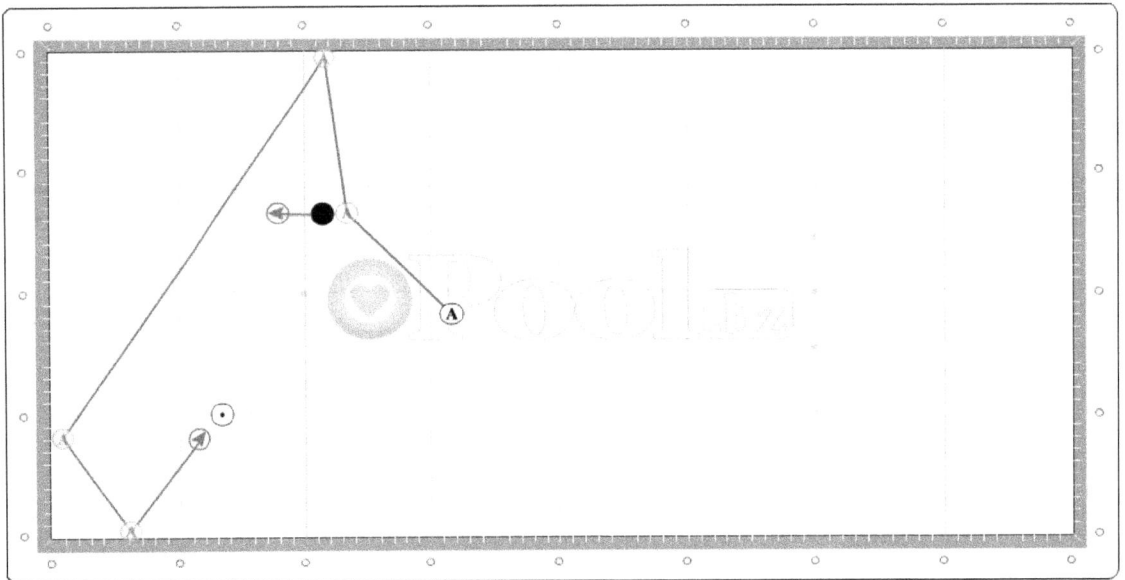

B: Group 3

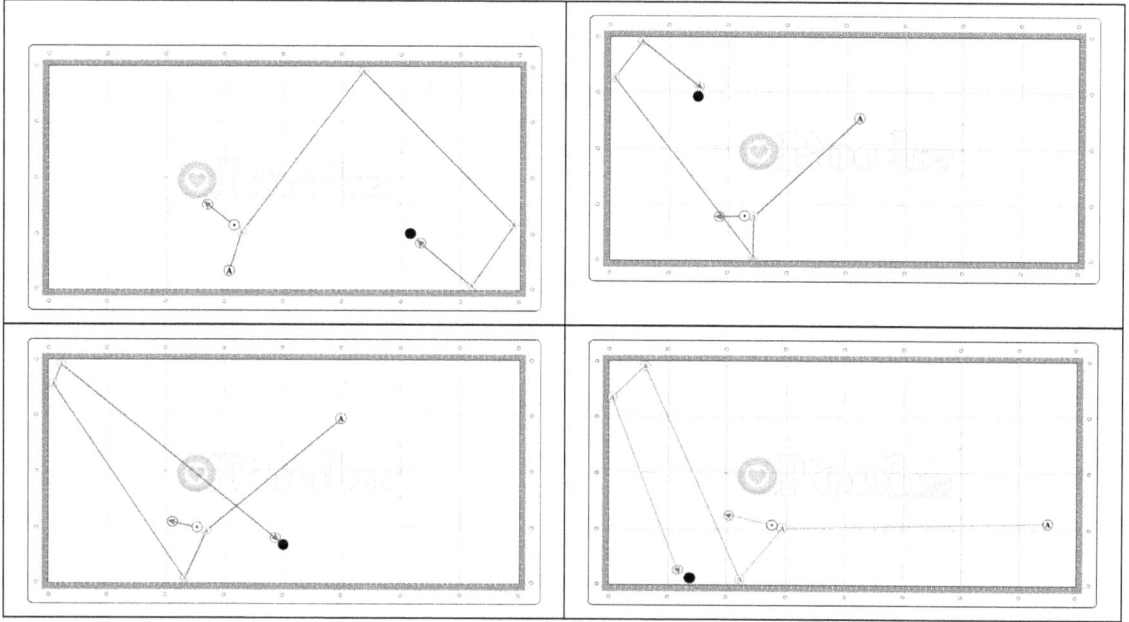

Analysis:

B:3a. _____

B:3b. _____

B:3c. _____

B:3d. _____

B:3a – Setup

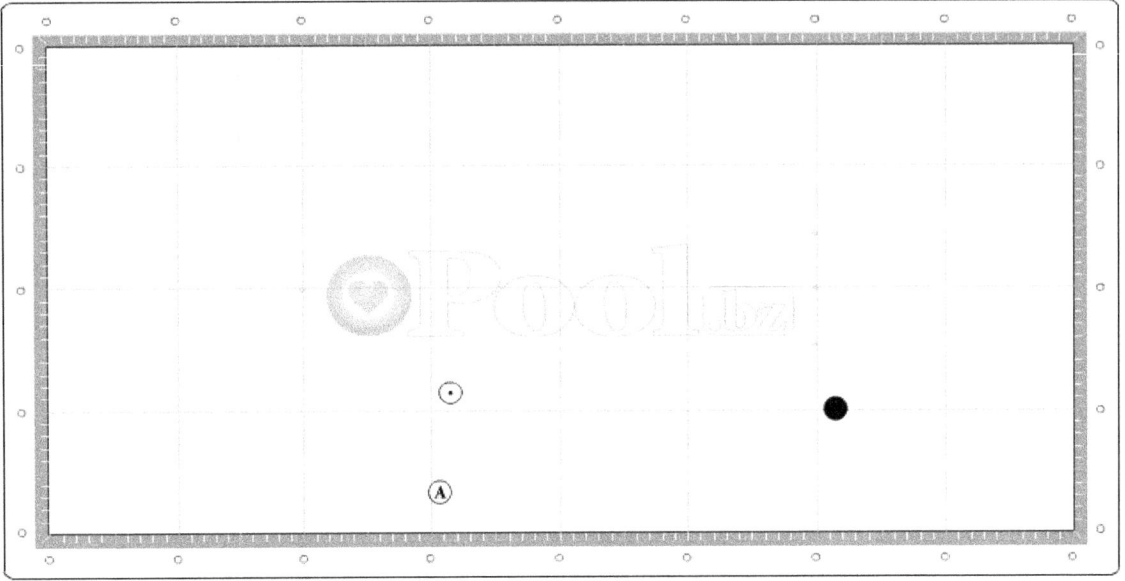

Shot Pattern

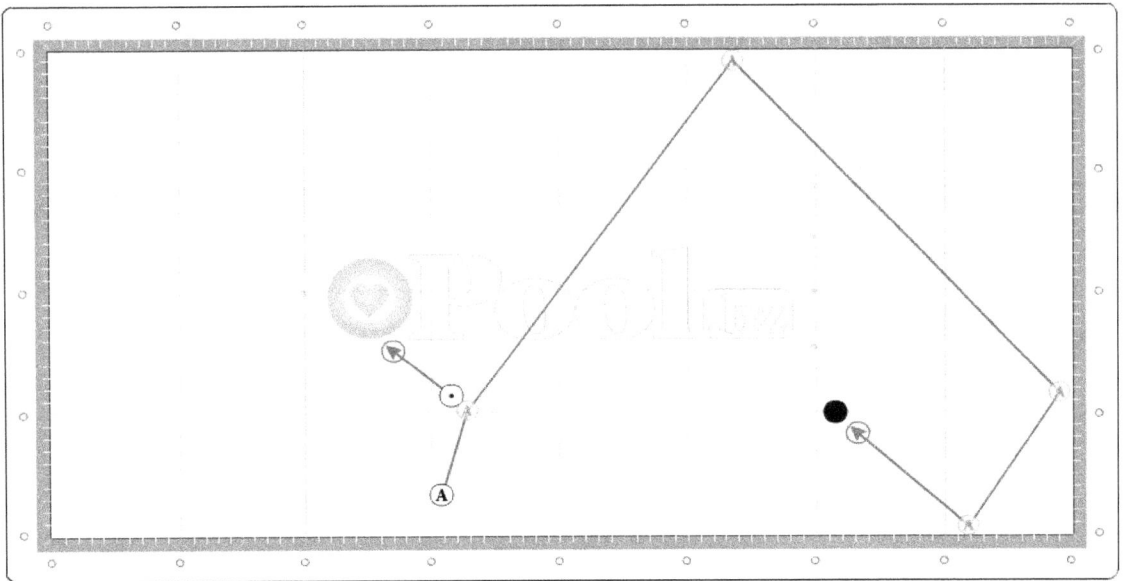

B:3b – Setup

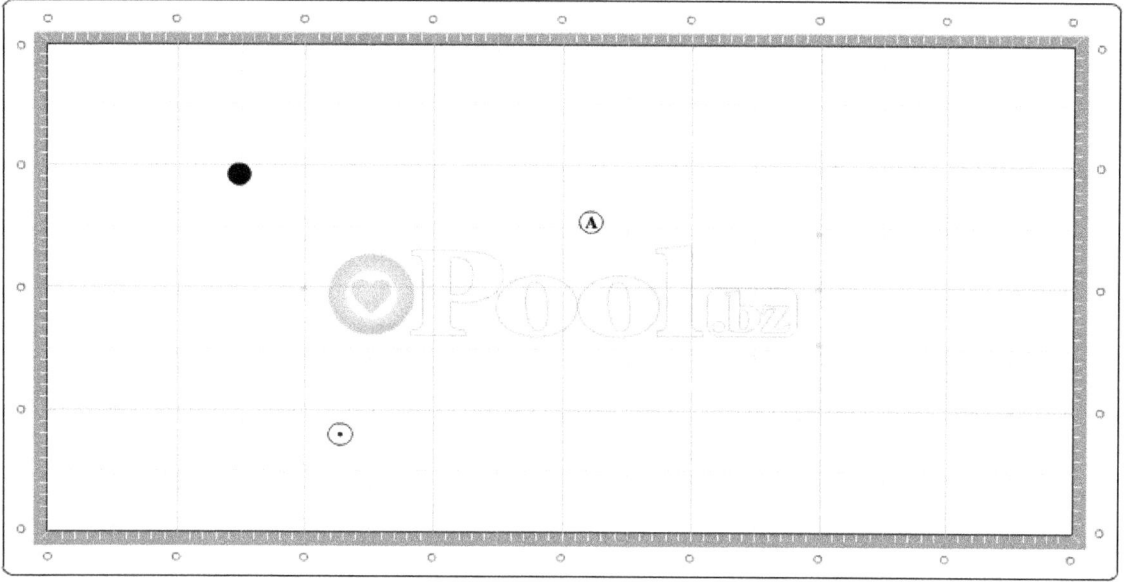

Shot Pattern

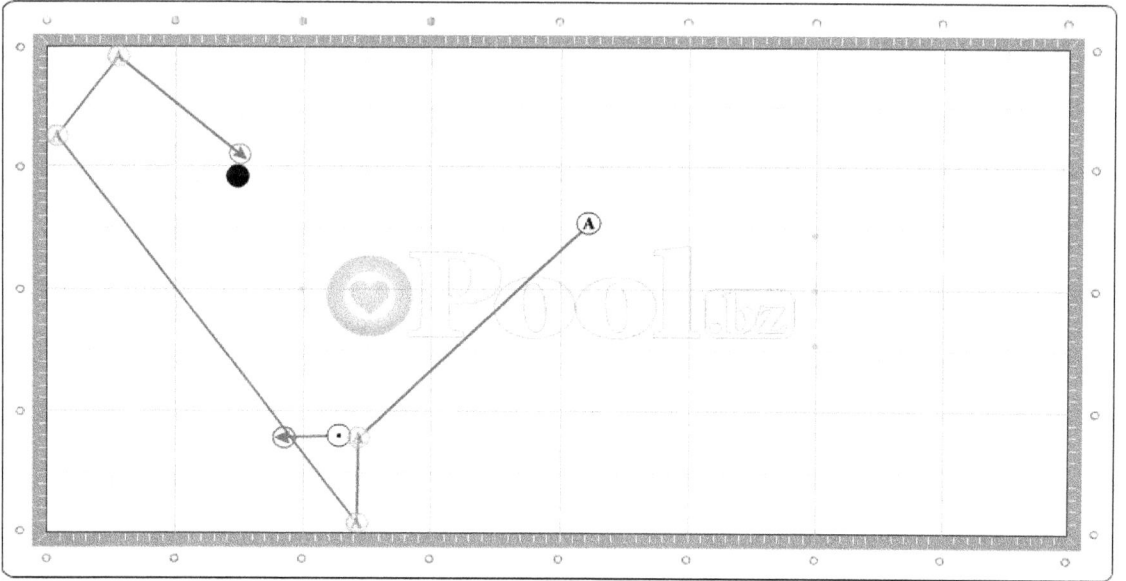

B:3c – Setup

Shot Pattern

B:3d – Setup

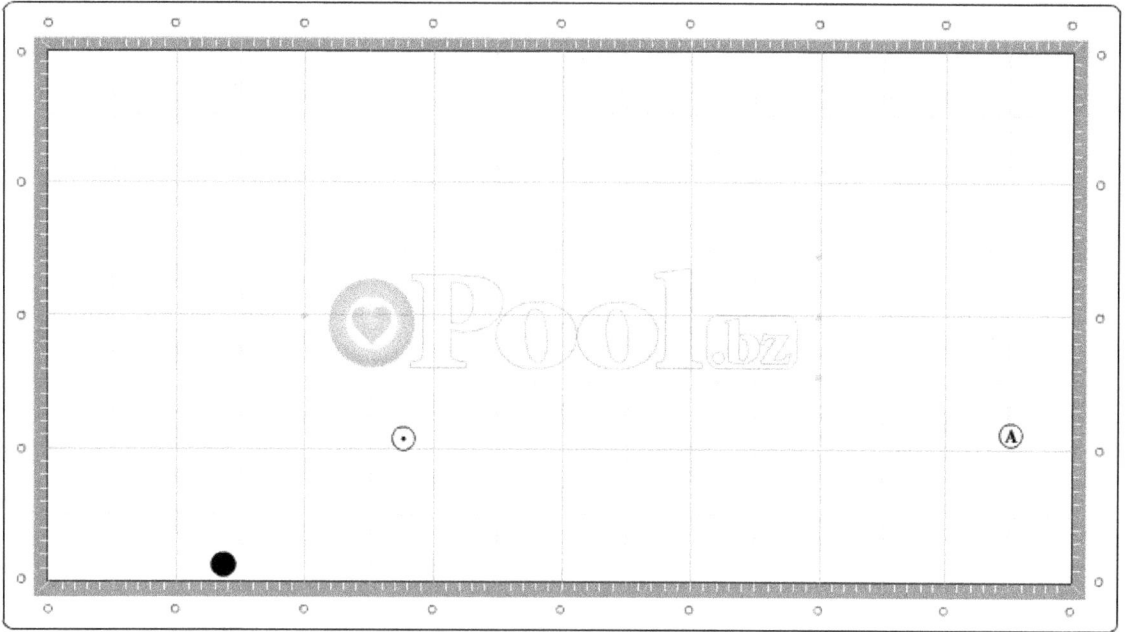

Shot Pattern

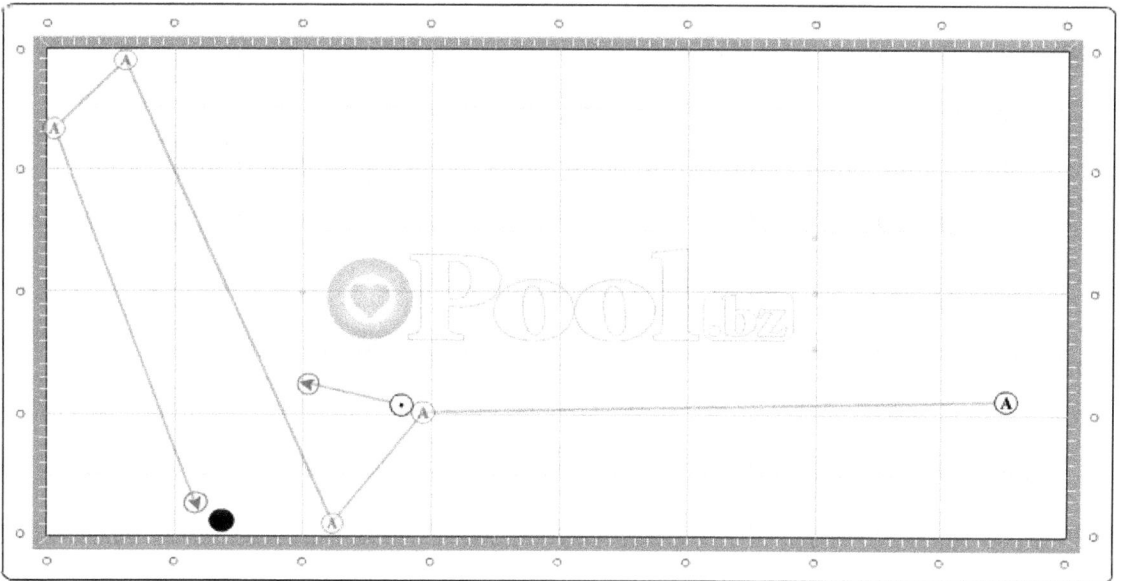

C: Into a Small Corner

On this set of shots, the CB comes off the first OB into the corner. This makes the first two cushions. When the CB comes out of the corner, it goes to the opposite long rail. The CB then comes out of the long rail and into the second OB for a point.

C: Group 1

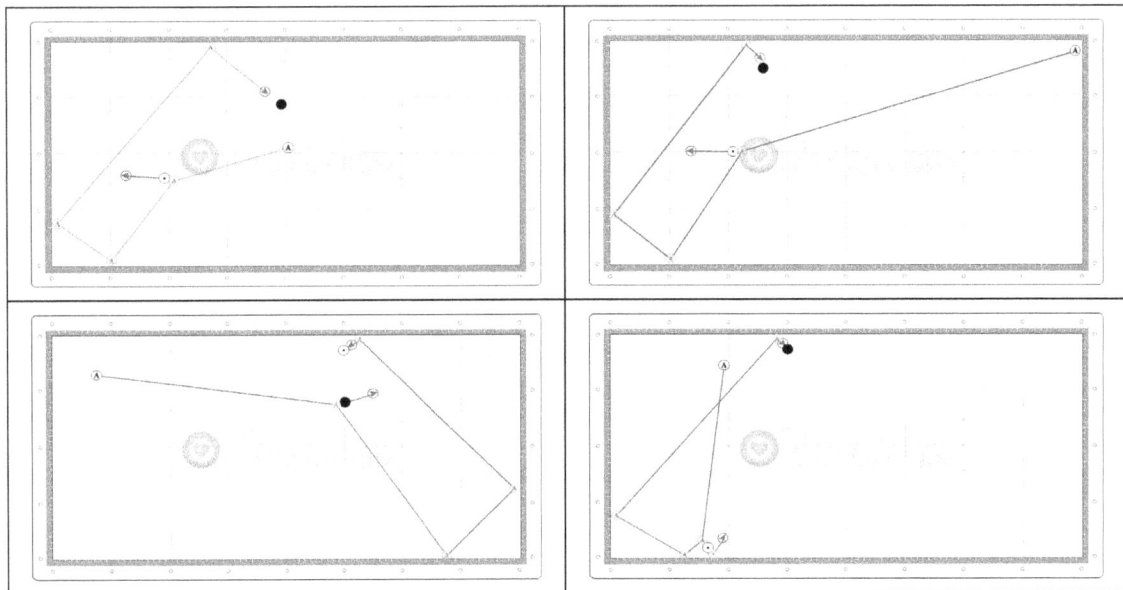

Analysis:

C:1a. _____

C:1b. _____

C:1c. _____

C:1d. _____

C:1a – Setup

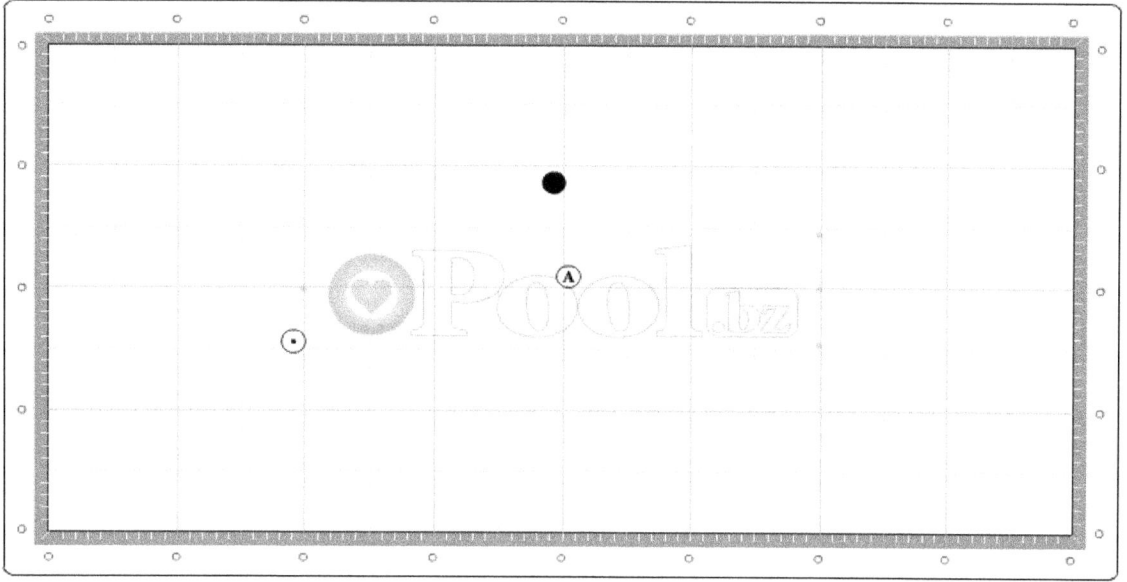

Shot Pattern

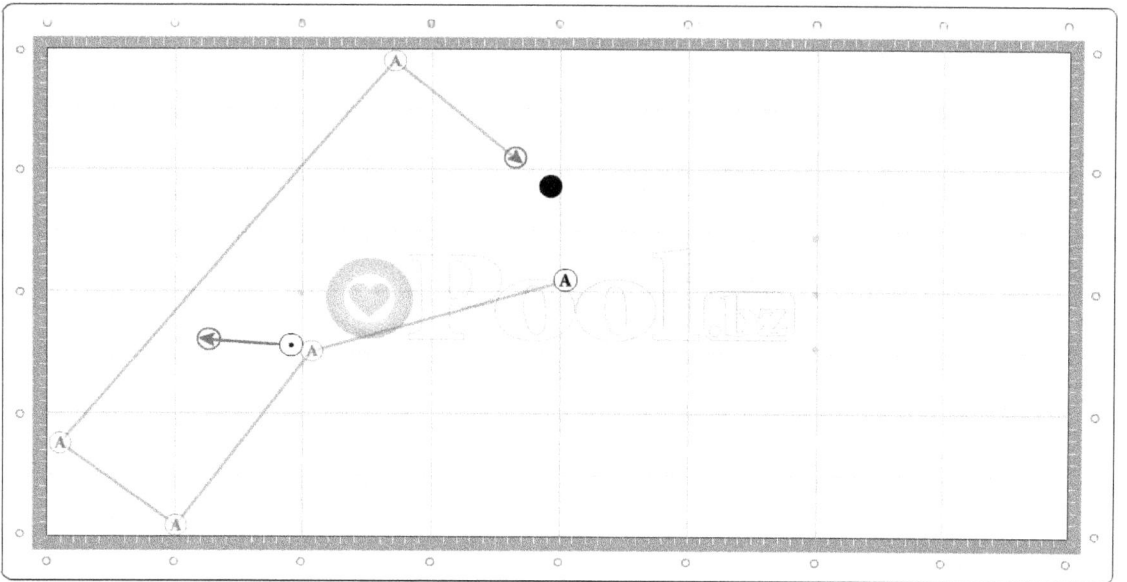

C:1b – Setup

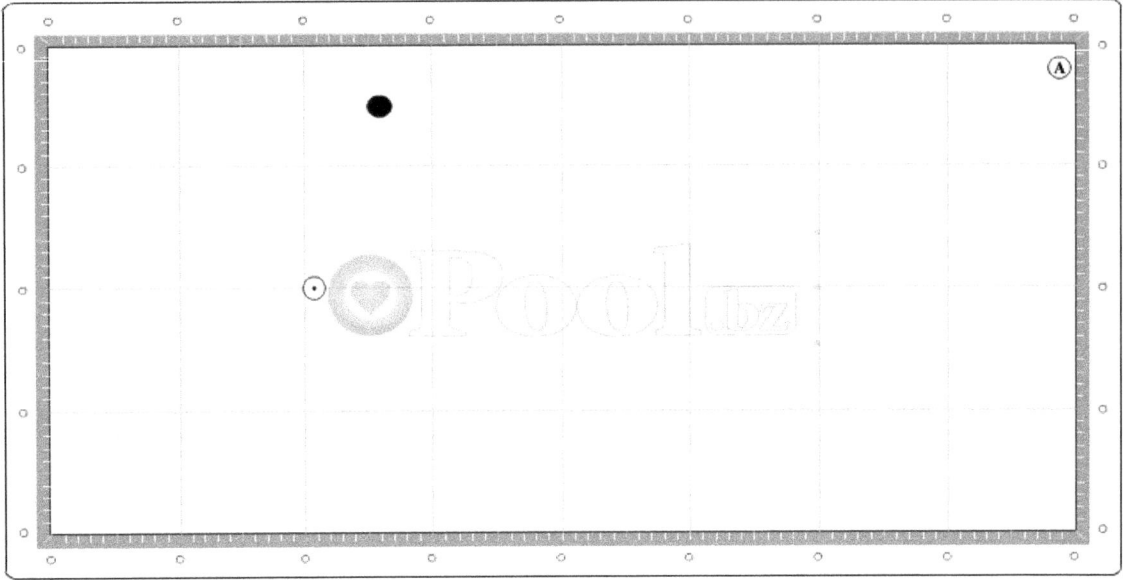

Shot Pattern

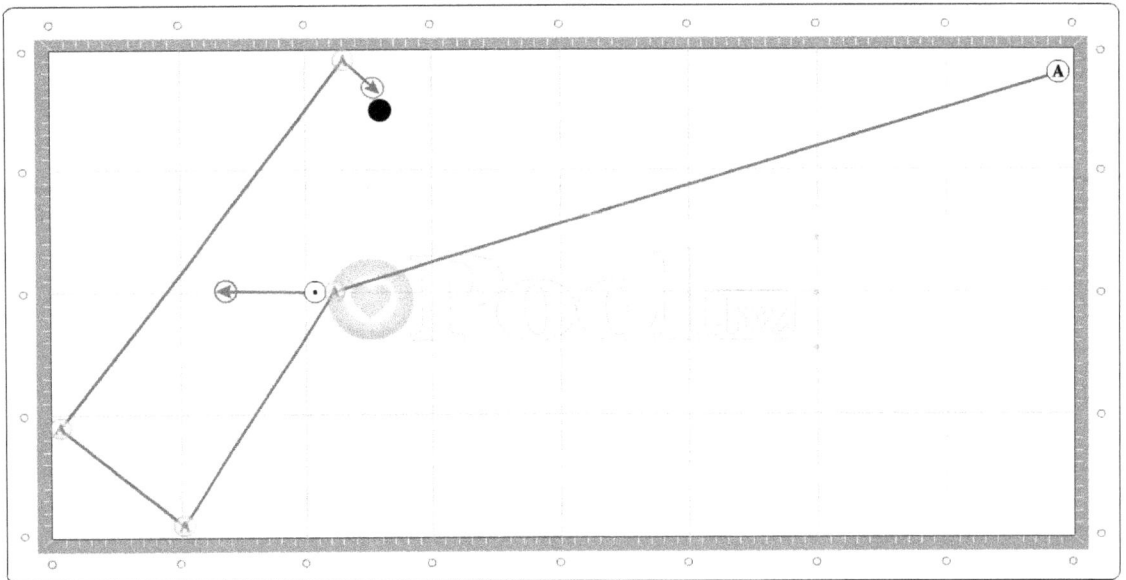

C:1c – Setup

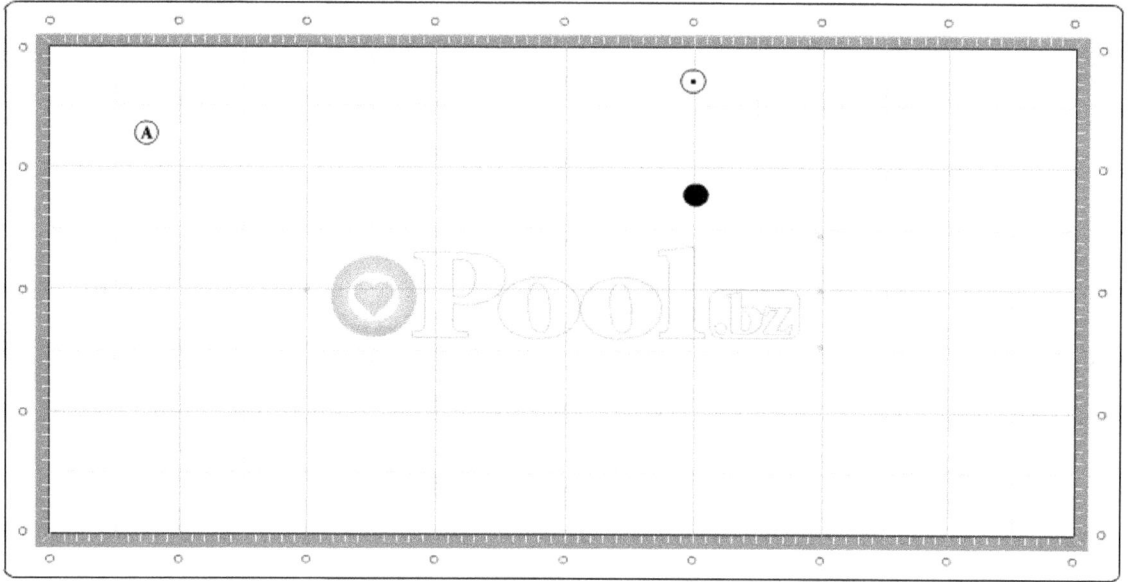

Shot Pattern

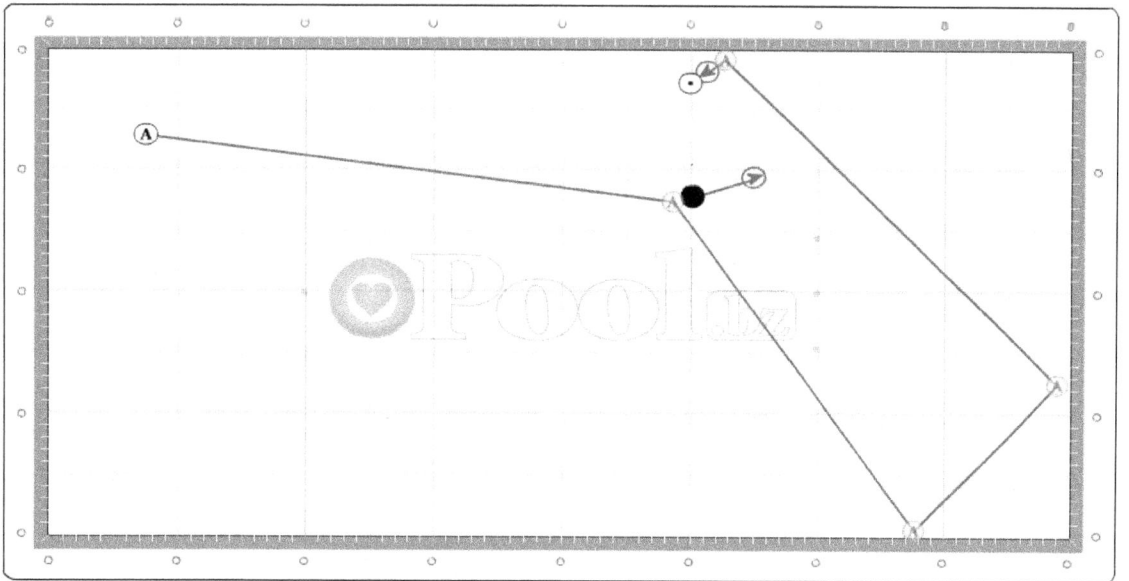

C:1d – Setup

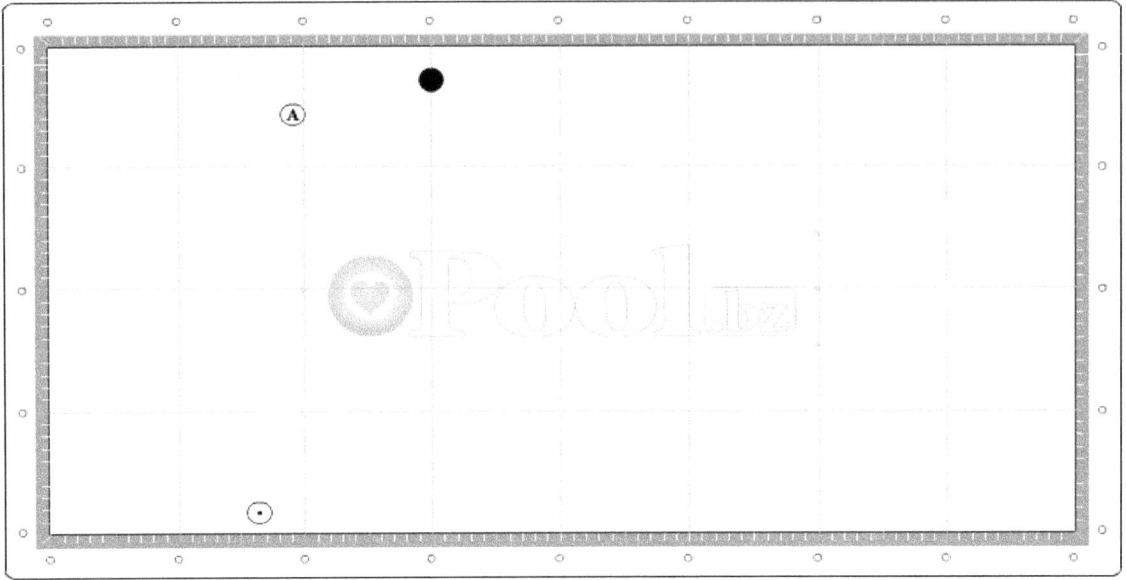

Shot Pattern

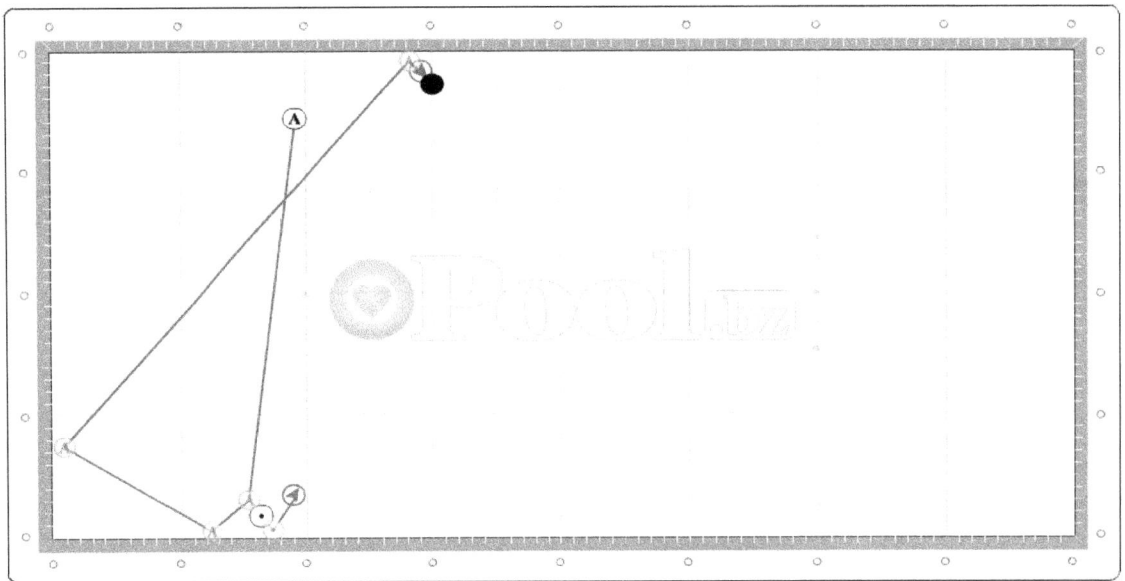

C: Group 2

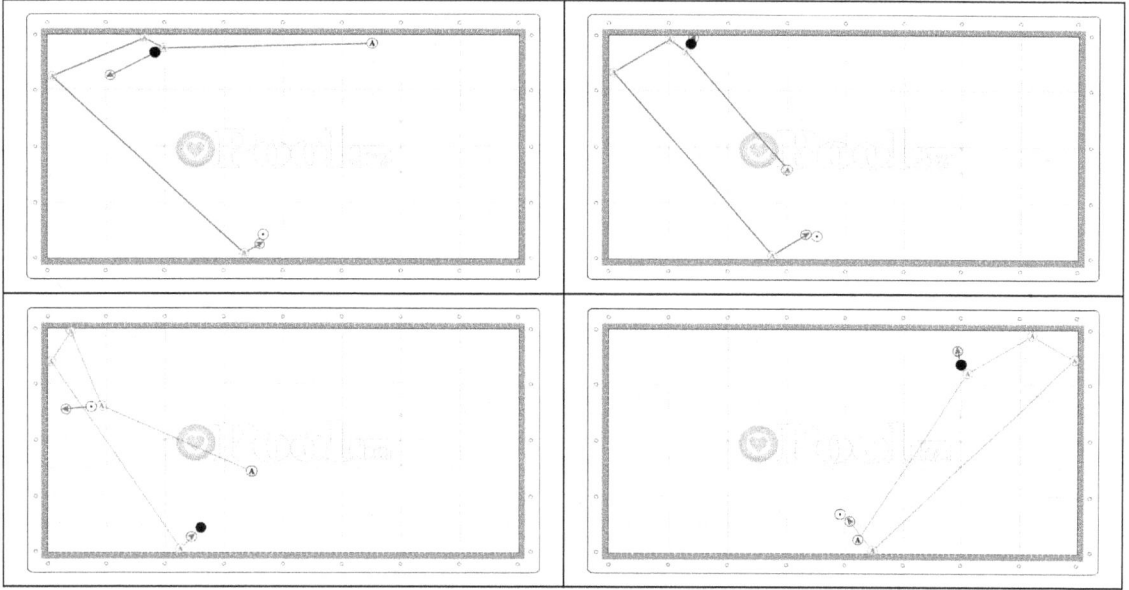

Analysis:

C:2a. _____

C:2b. _____

C:2c. _____

C:2d. _____

C:2a – Setup

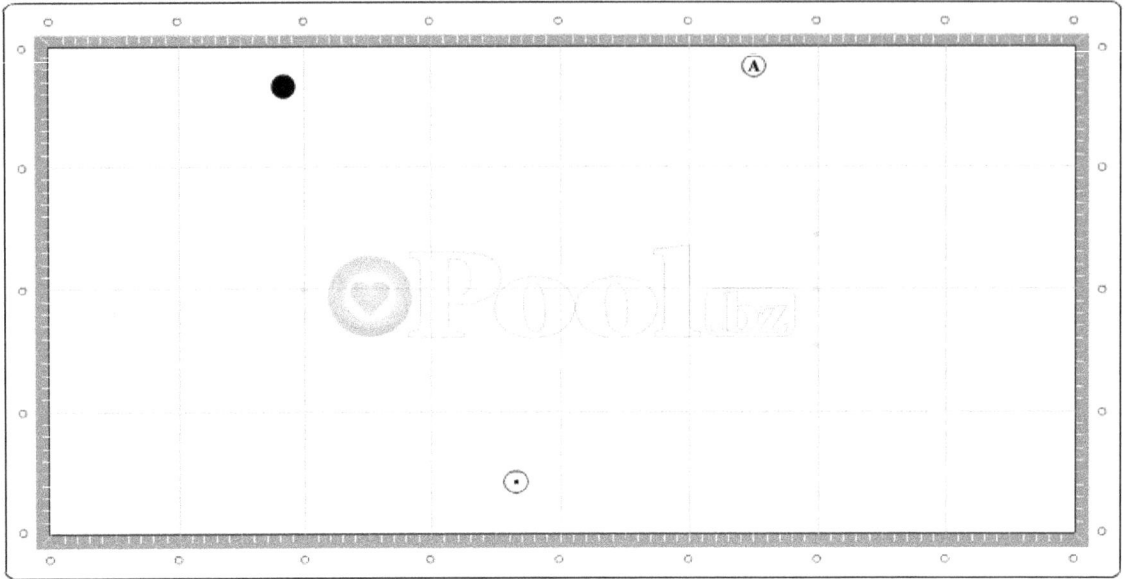

Shot Pattern

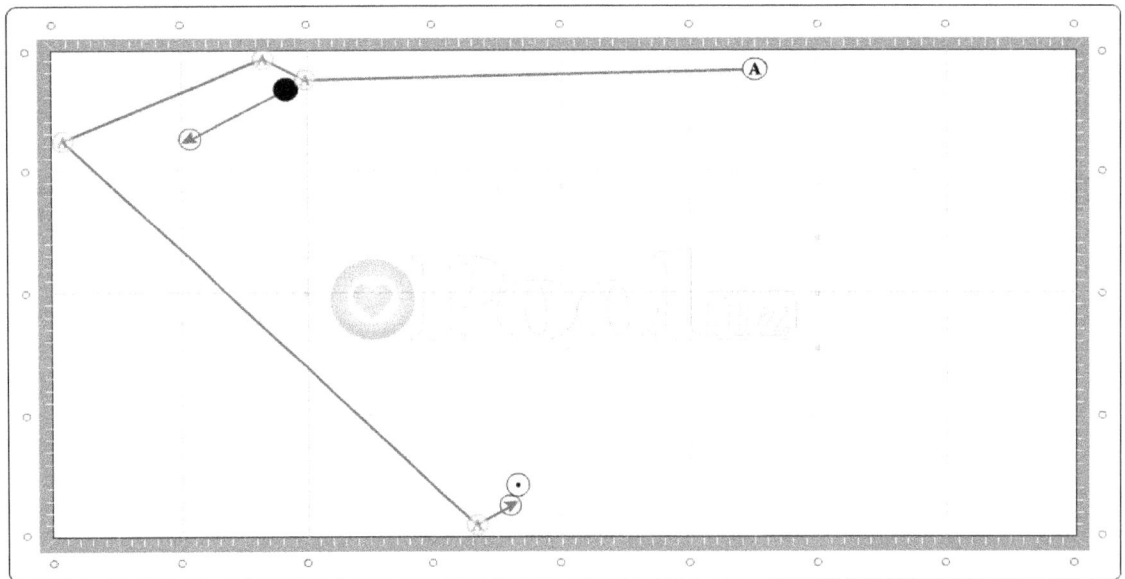

C:2b – Setup

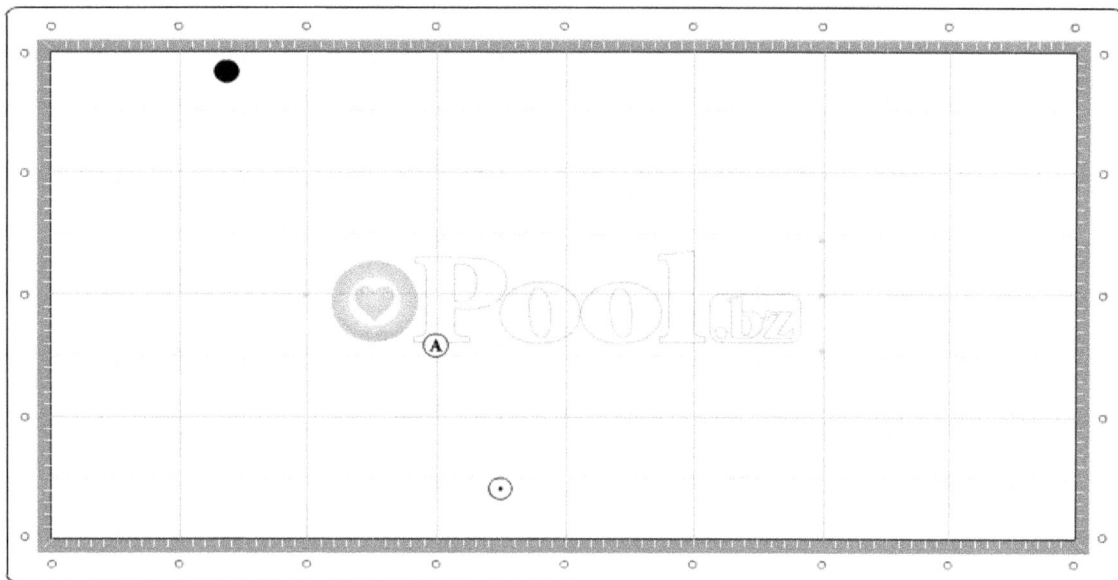

Shot Pattern

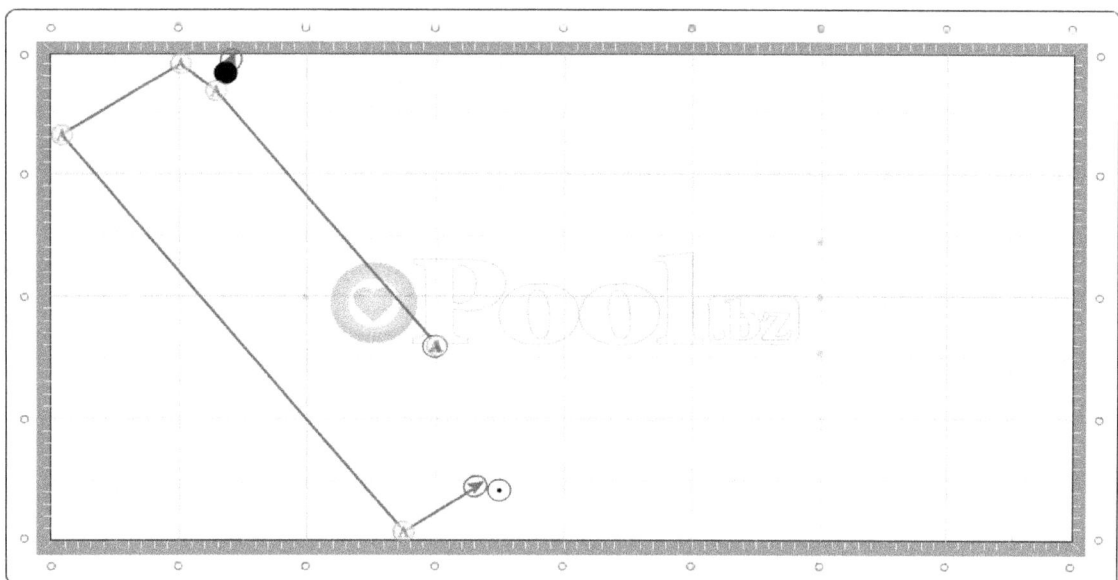

C:2c – Setup

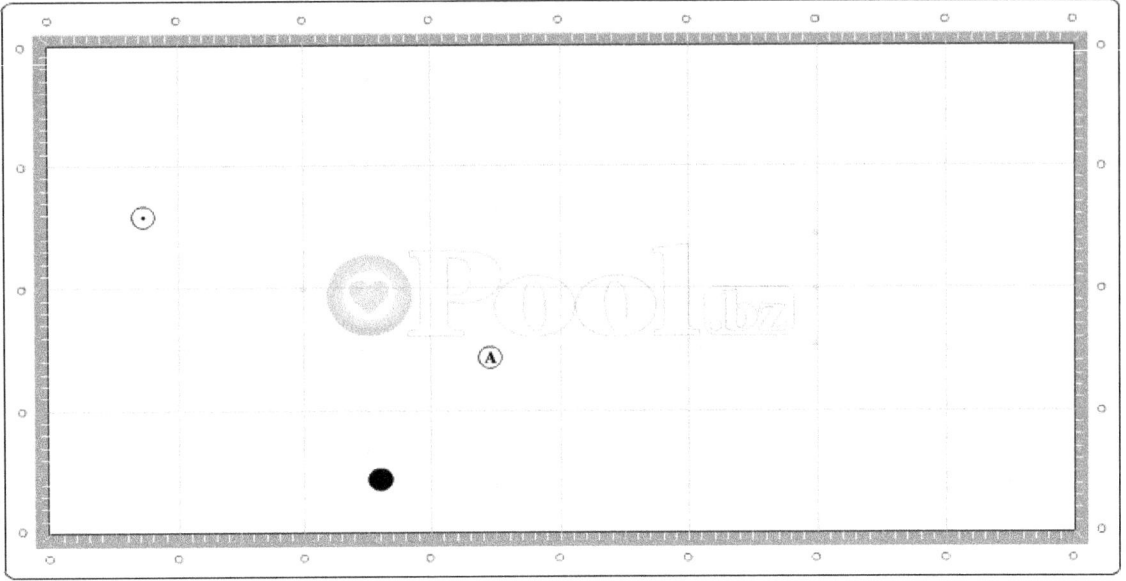

Shot Pattern

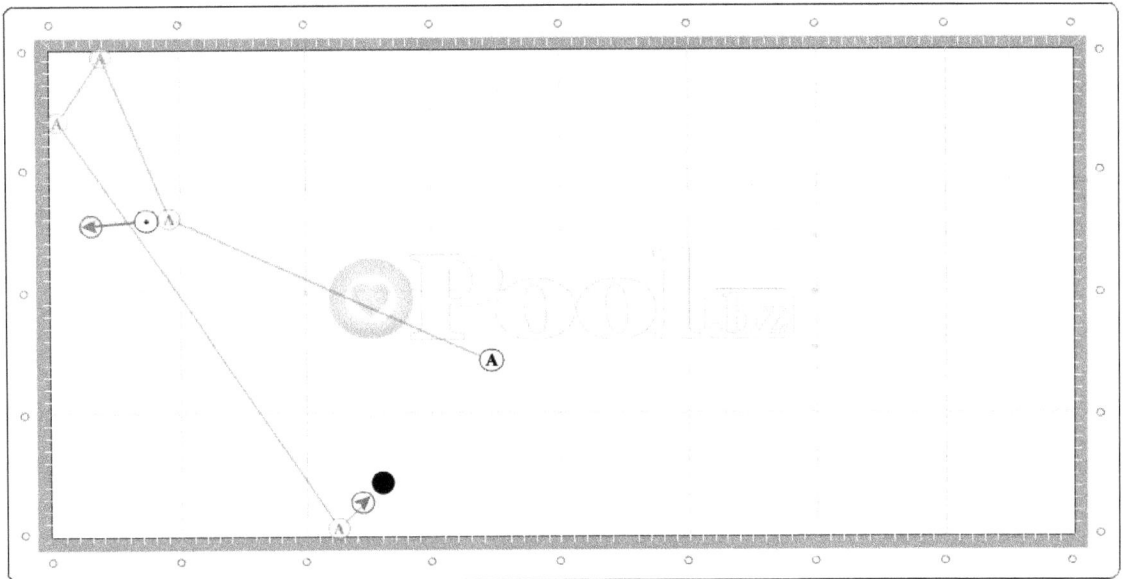

C:2d – Setup

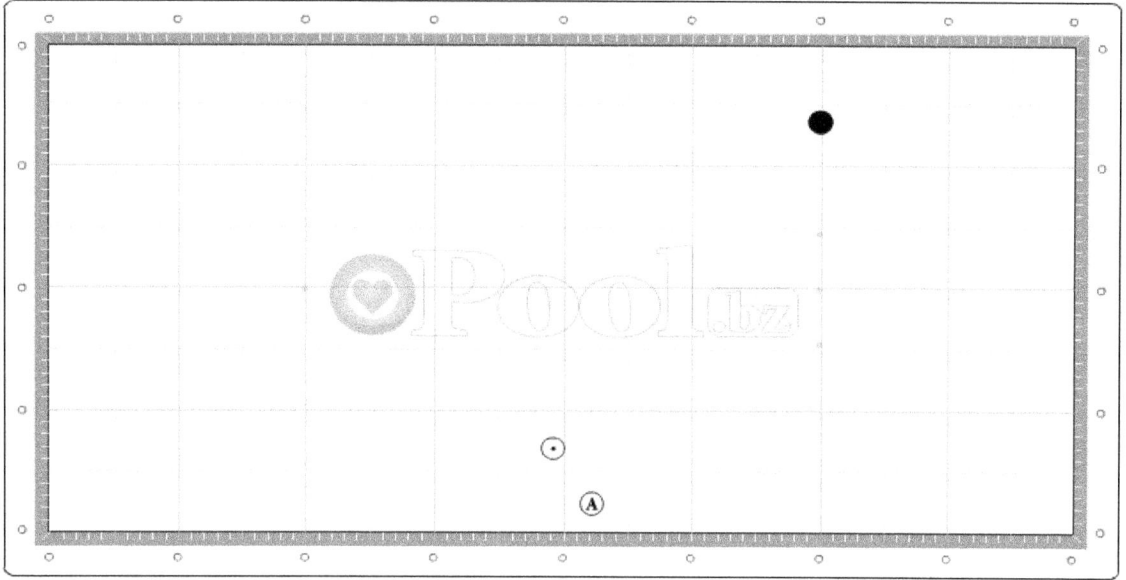

Shot Pattern

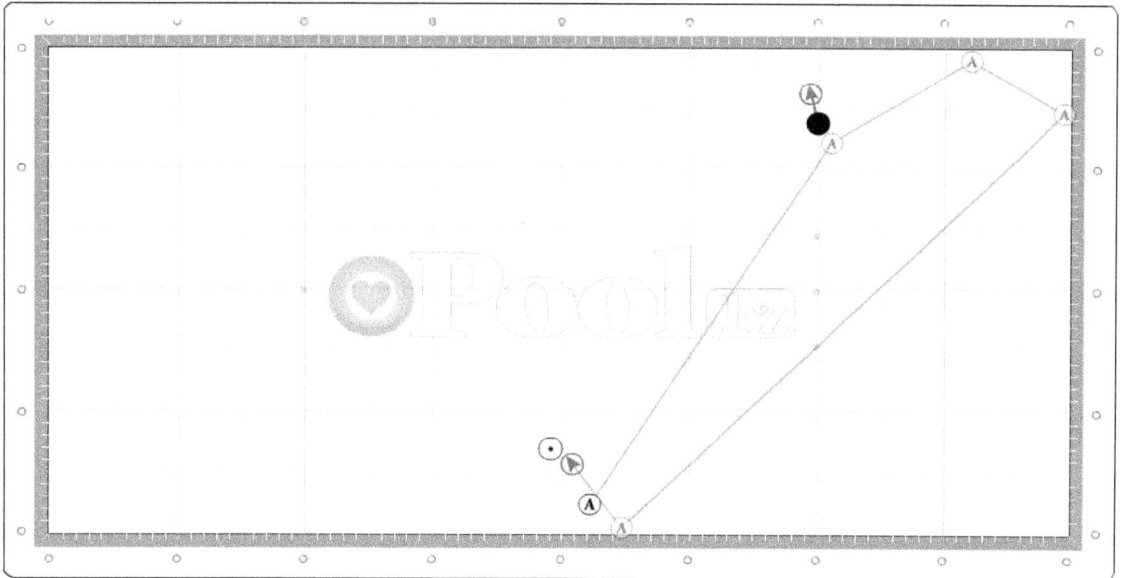

D: Reverse Pattern

On this set of shots, the CB comes off the first OB towards the first rail. The CB has to be pulled back from the first OB and then continues to connect with the pattern. These shots require a combination of reverse and side spin.

D: Group 1

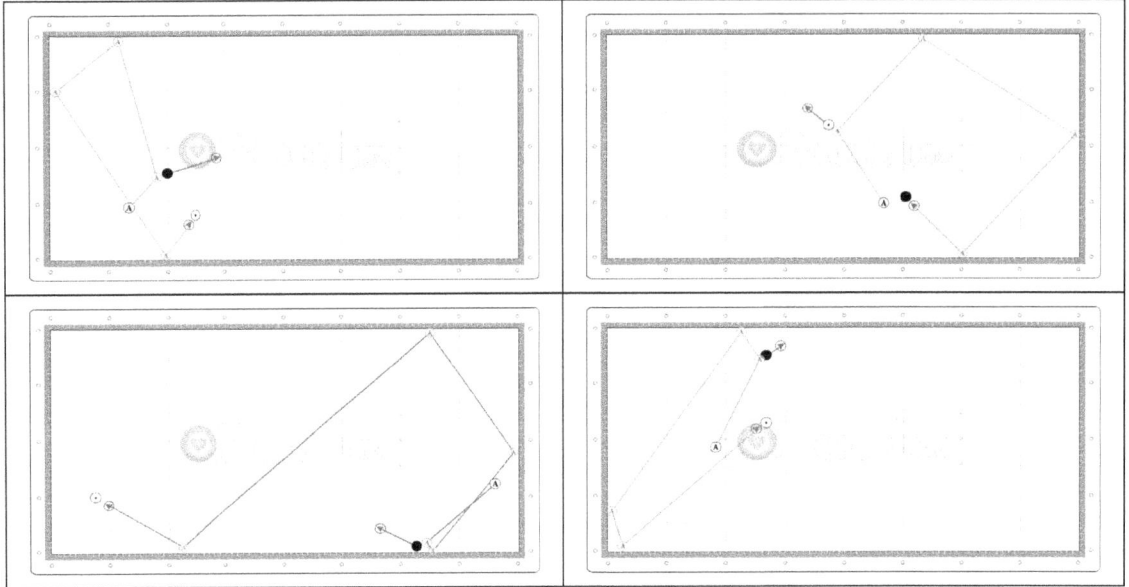

Analysis:

D:1a. _____

D:1b. _____

D:1c. _____

D:1d. _____

D:1a – Setup

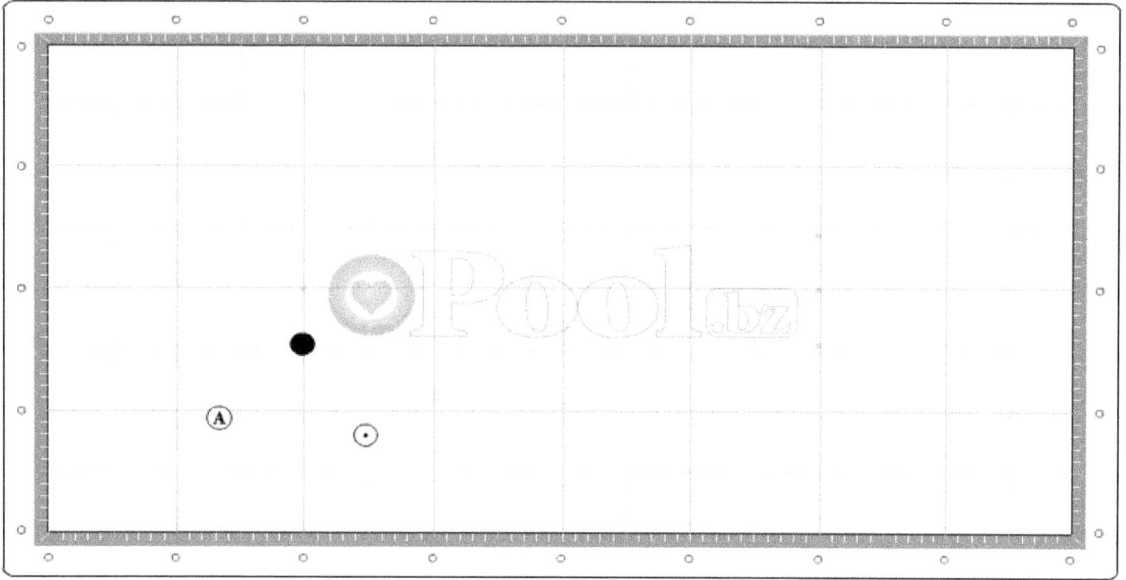

Shot Pattern

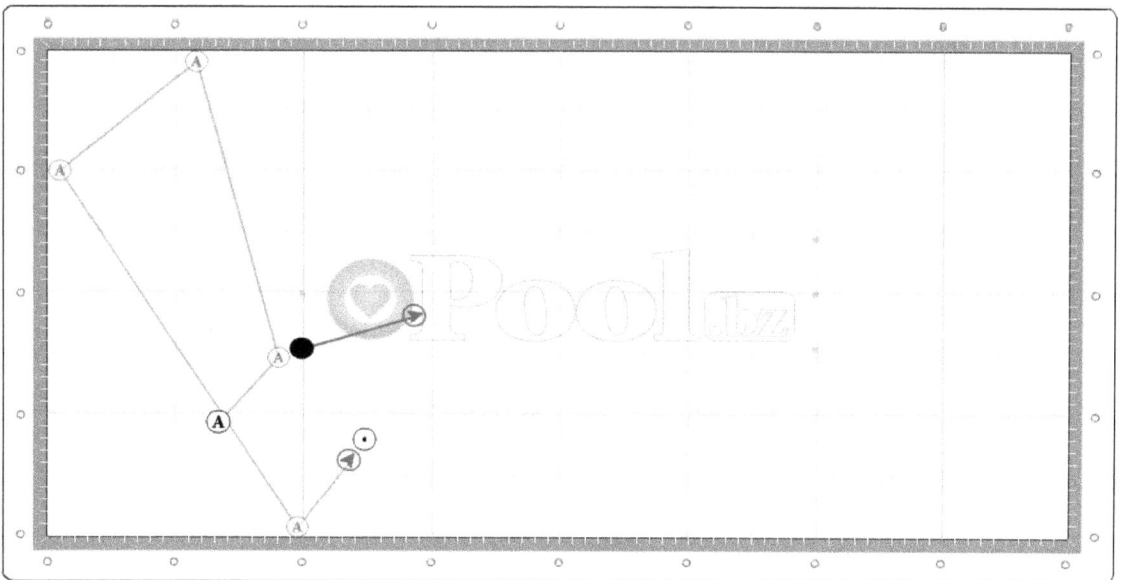

D:1b – Setup

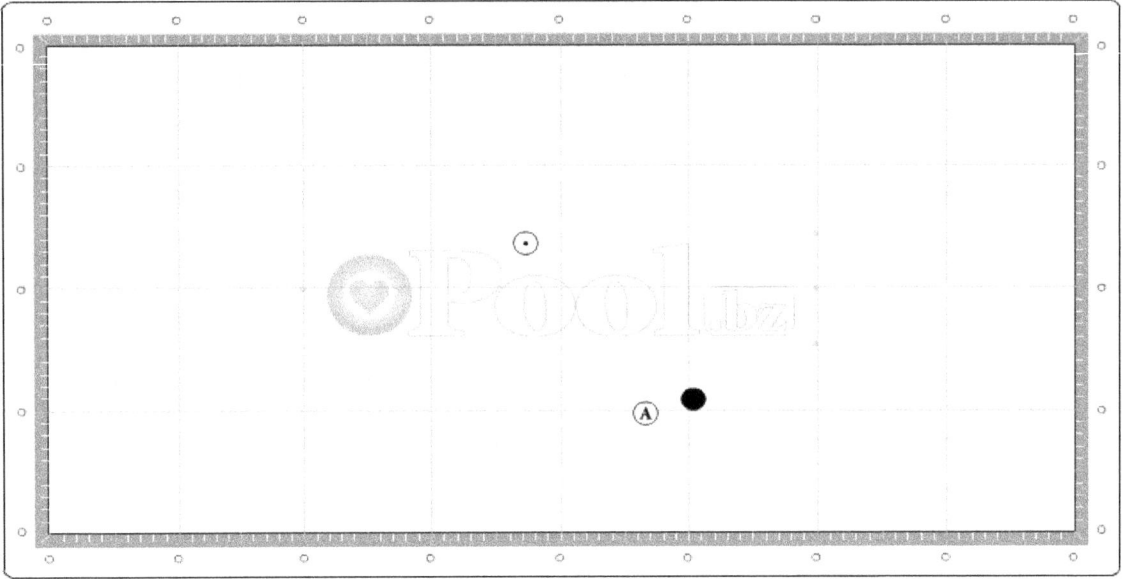

Shot Pattern

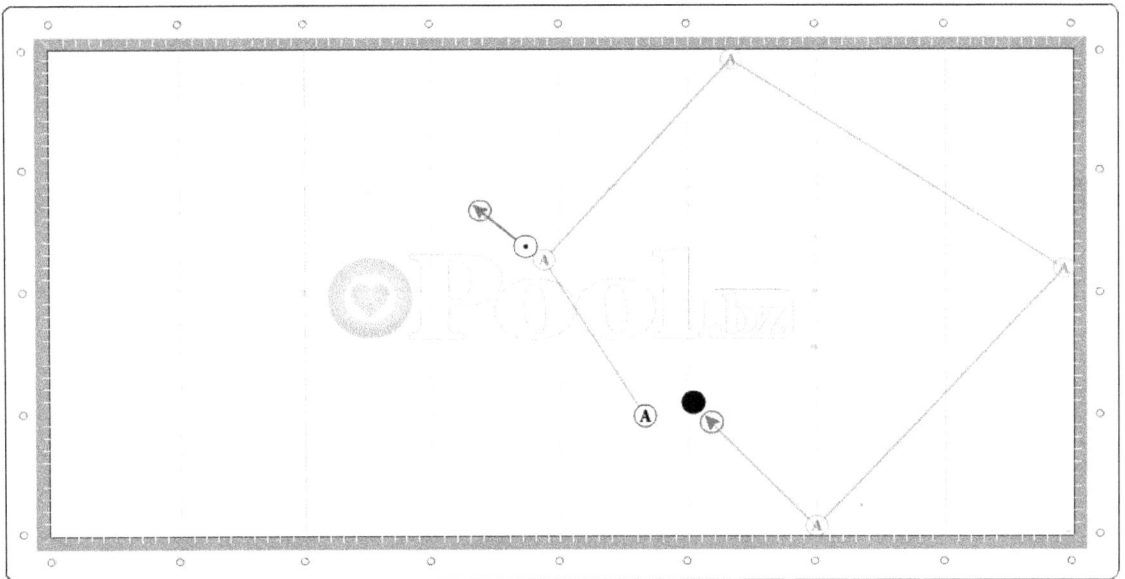

D:1c – Setup

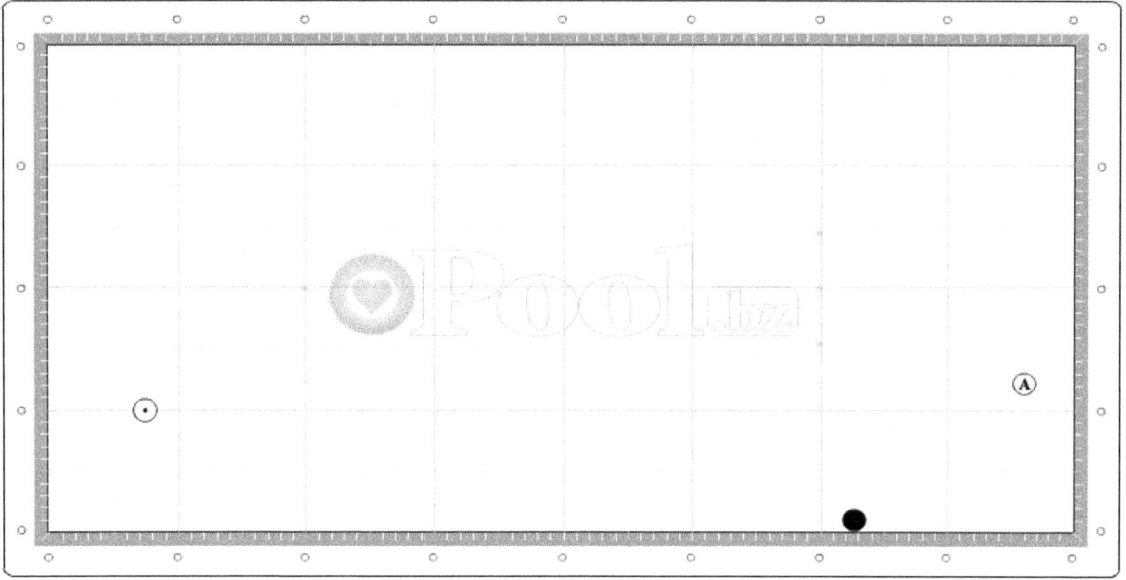

Shot Pattern

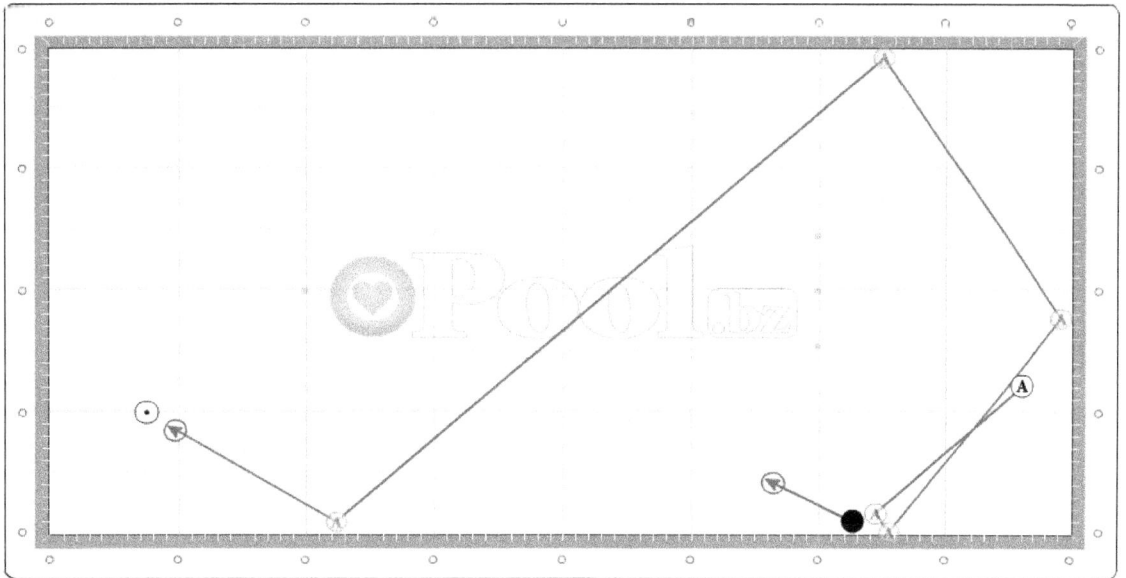

D:1d – Setup

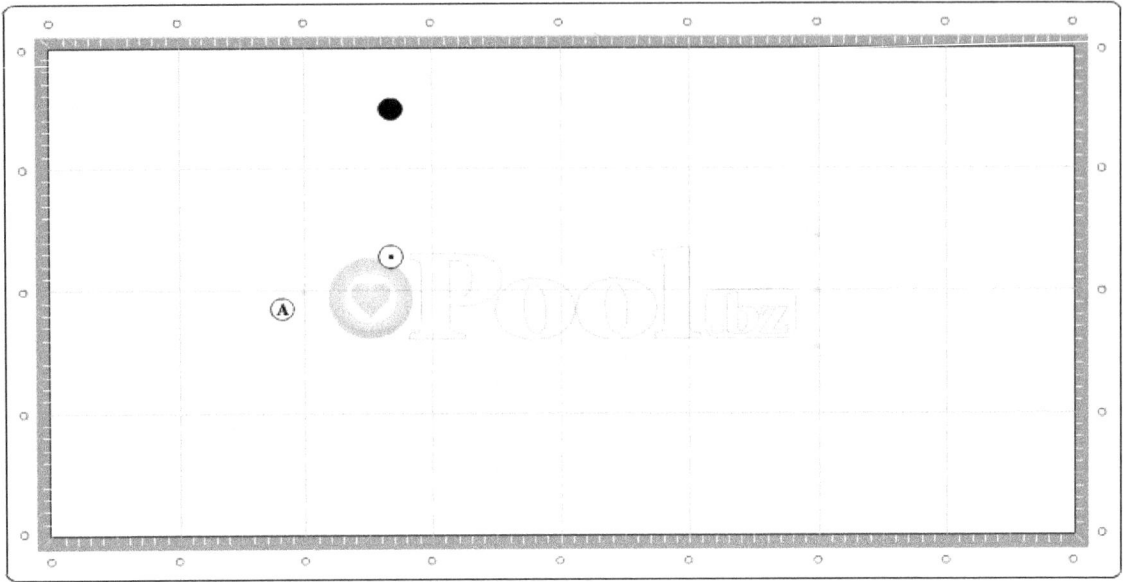

Shot Pattern

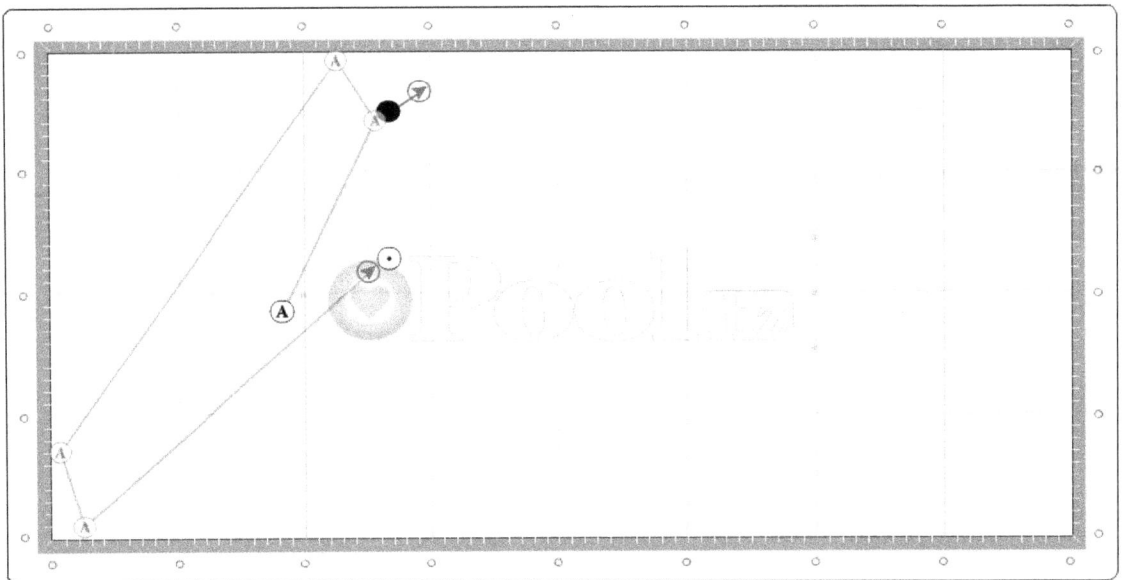

D: Group 2

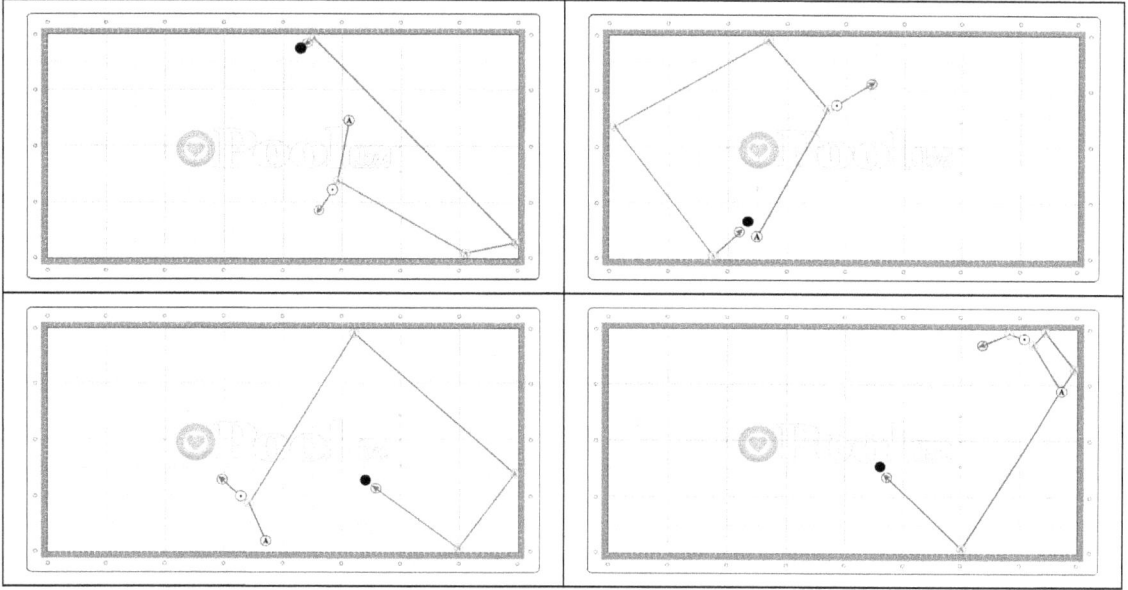

Analysis:

D:2a. _____

D:2b. _____

D:2c. _____

D:2d. _____

D:2a – Setup

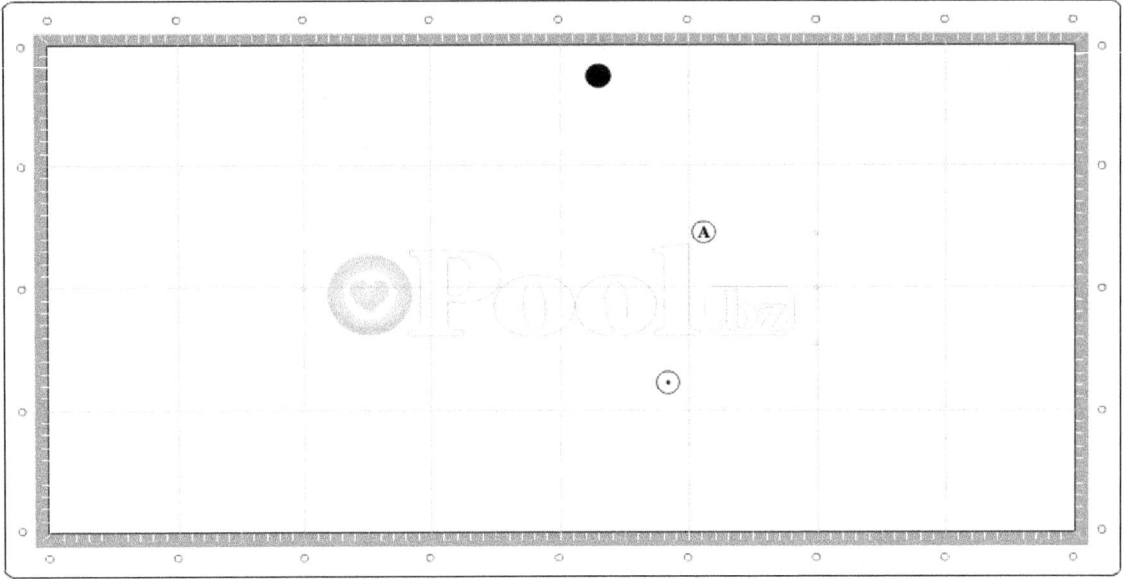

Shot Pattern

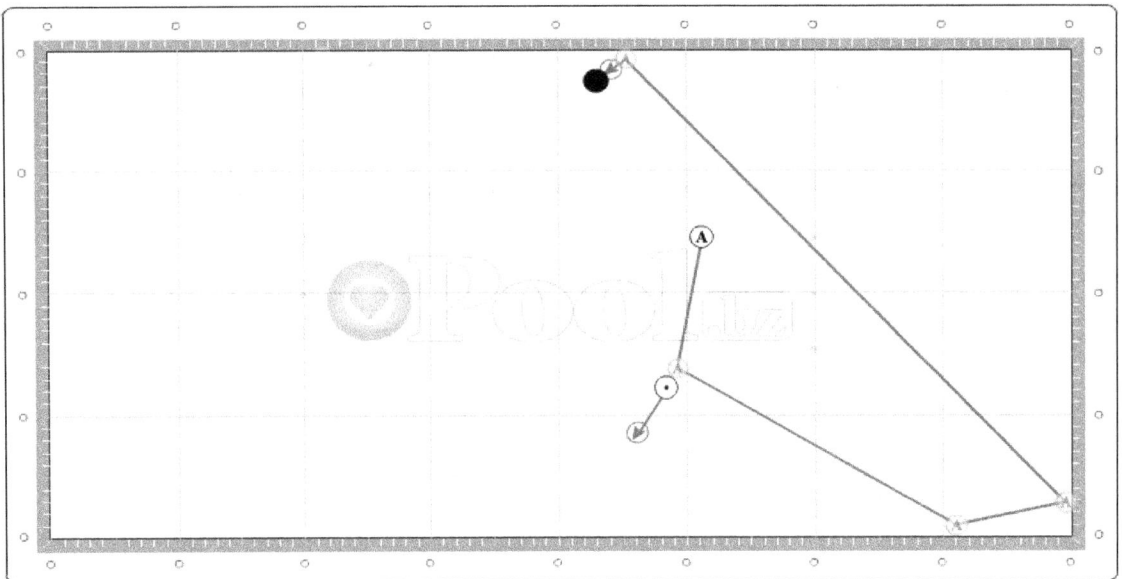

D:2b – Setup

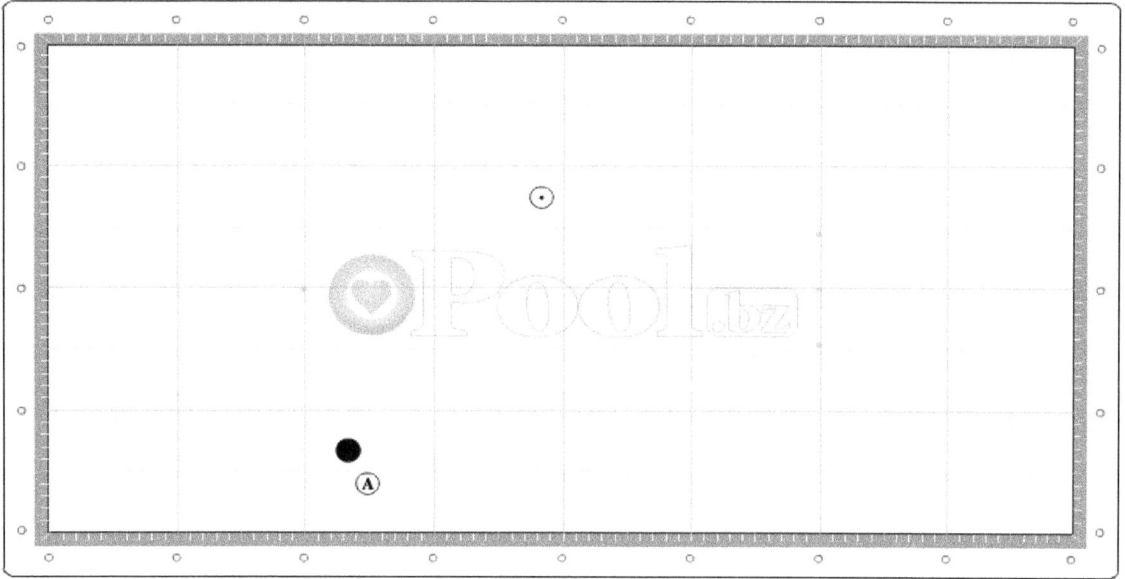

Shot Pattern

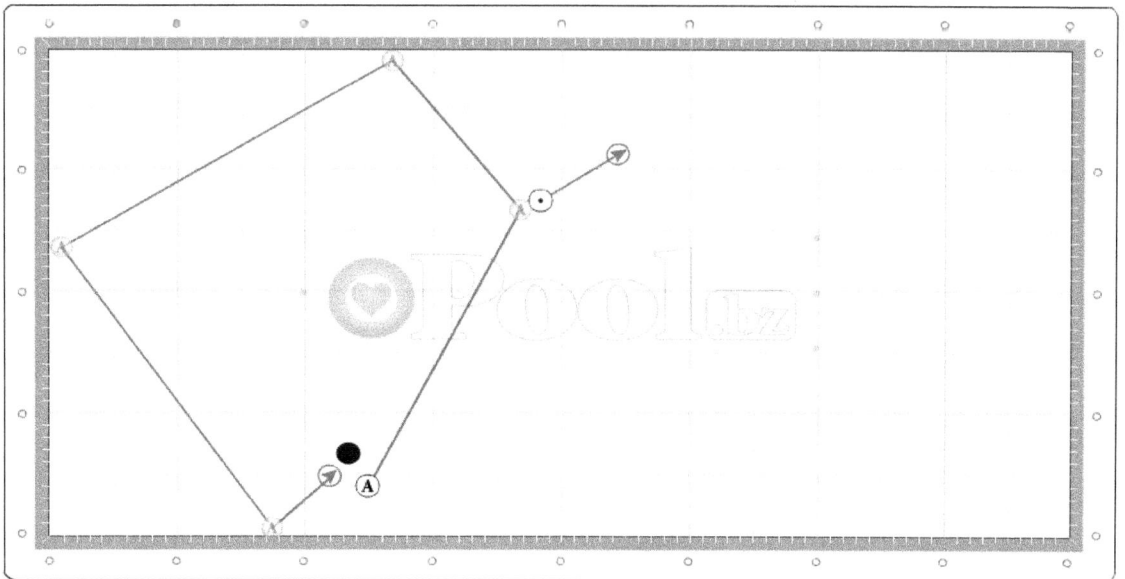

D:2c – Setup

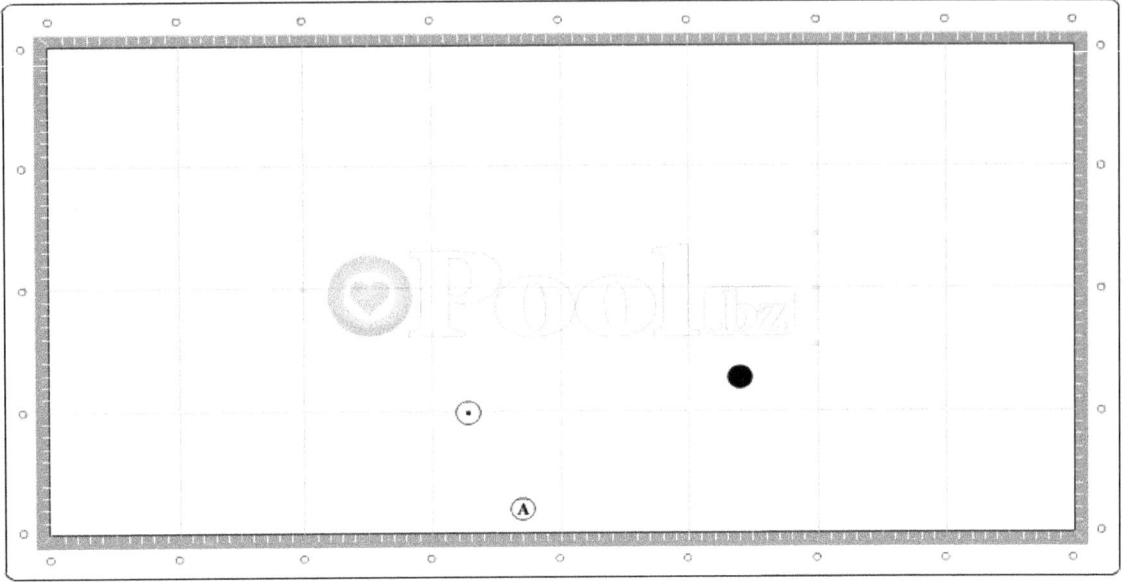

Shot Pattern

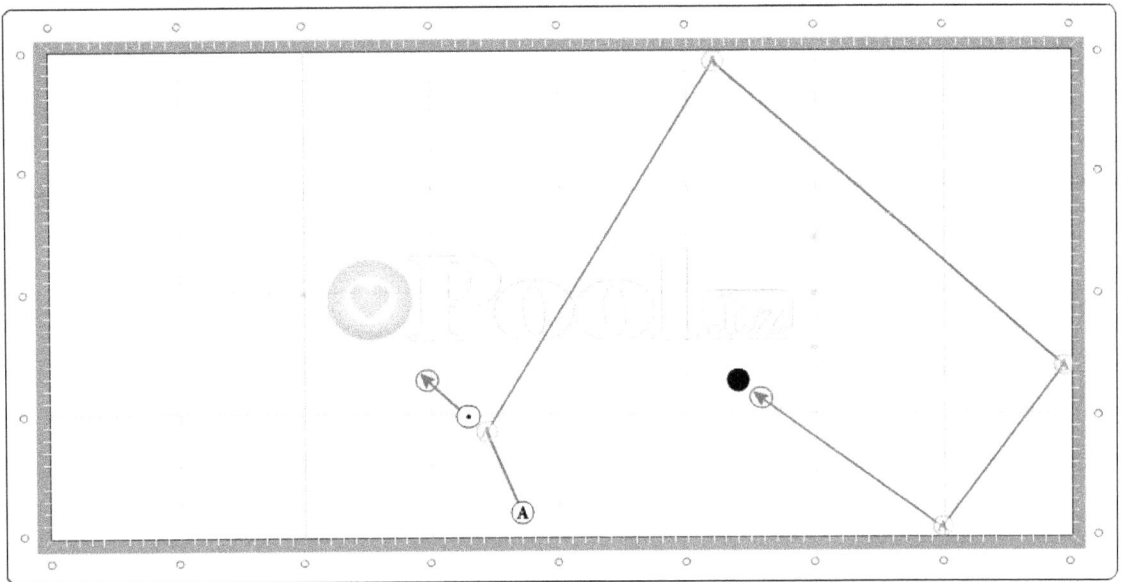

D:2d – Setup

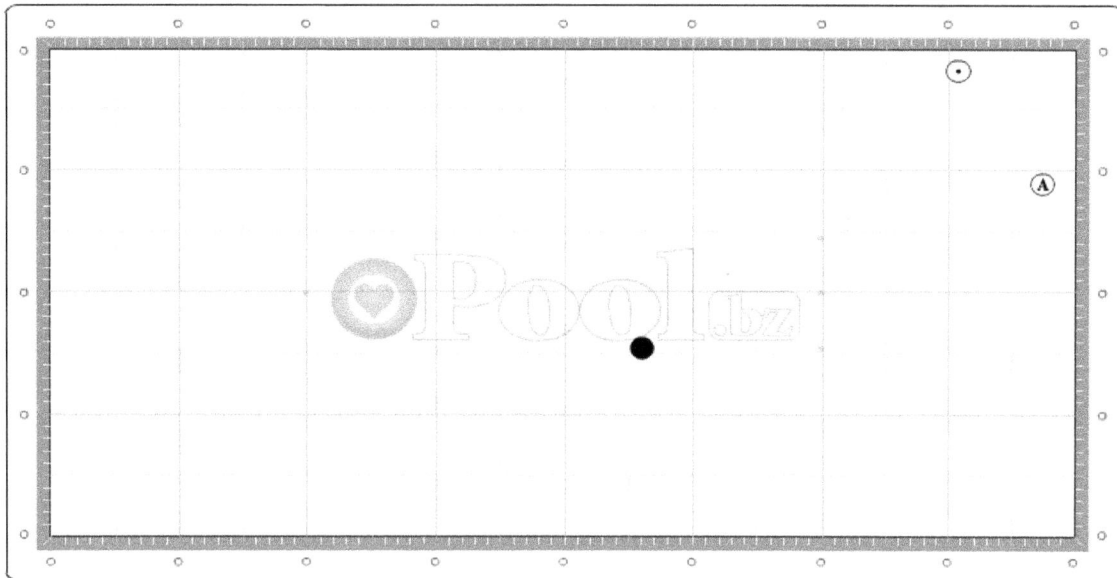

Shot Pattern

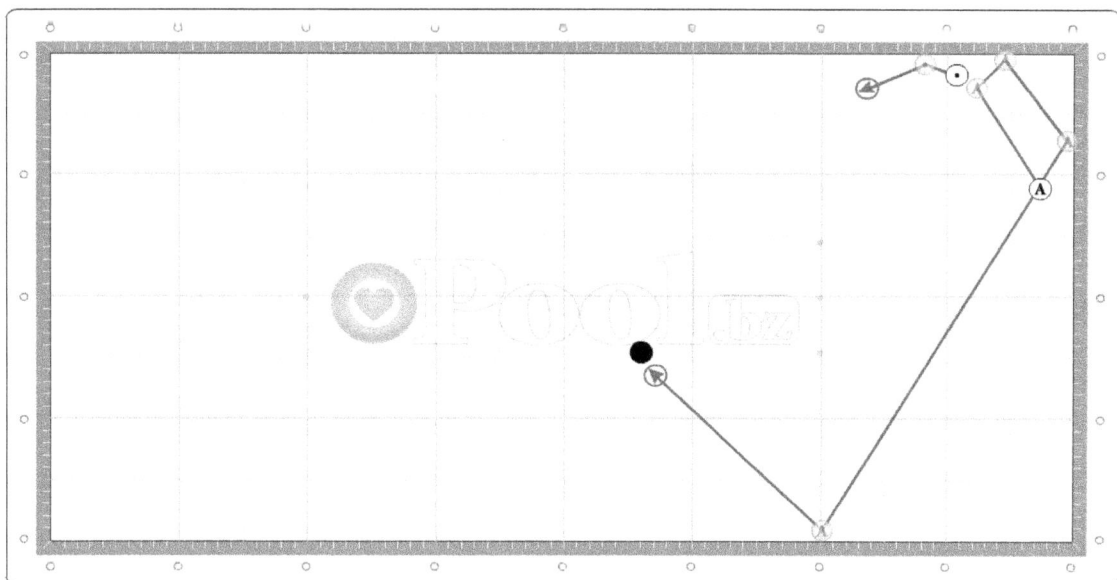

D: Group 3

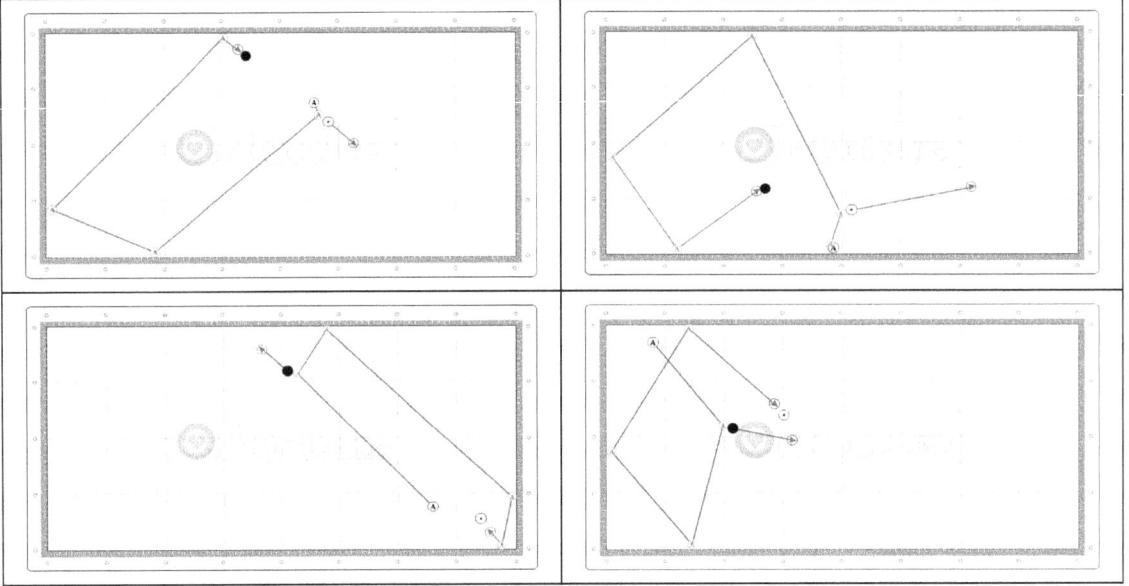

Analysis:

D:3a. _____

D:3b. _____

D:3c. _____

D:3d. _____

D:3a – Setup

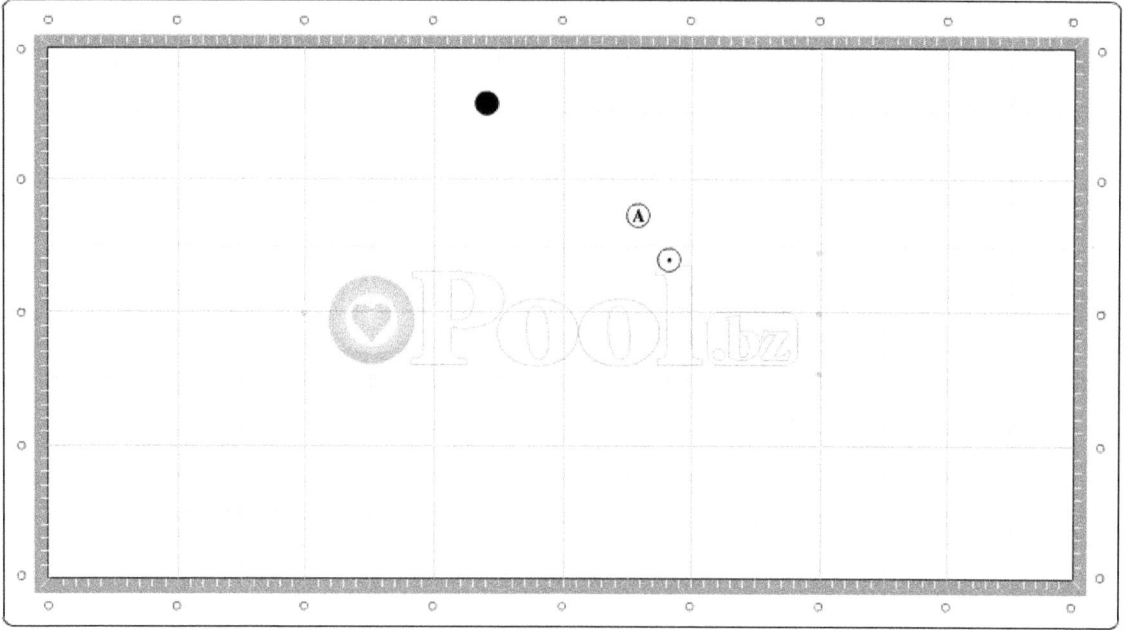

Shot Pattern

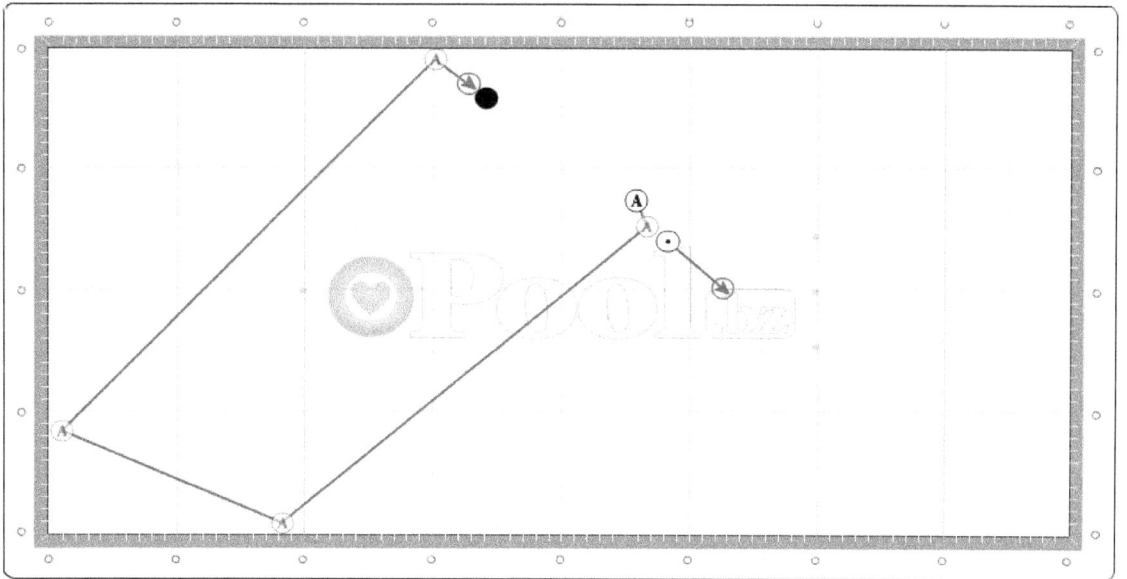

D:3b – Setup

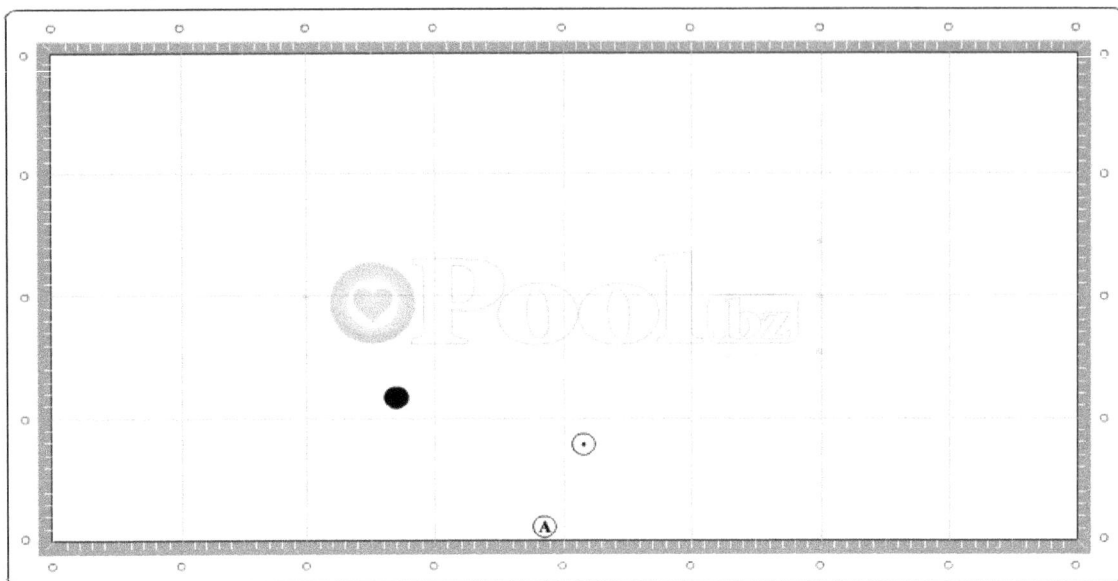

Shot Pattern

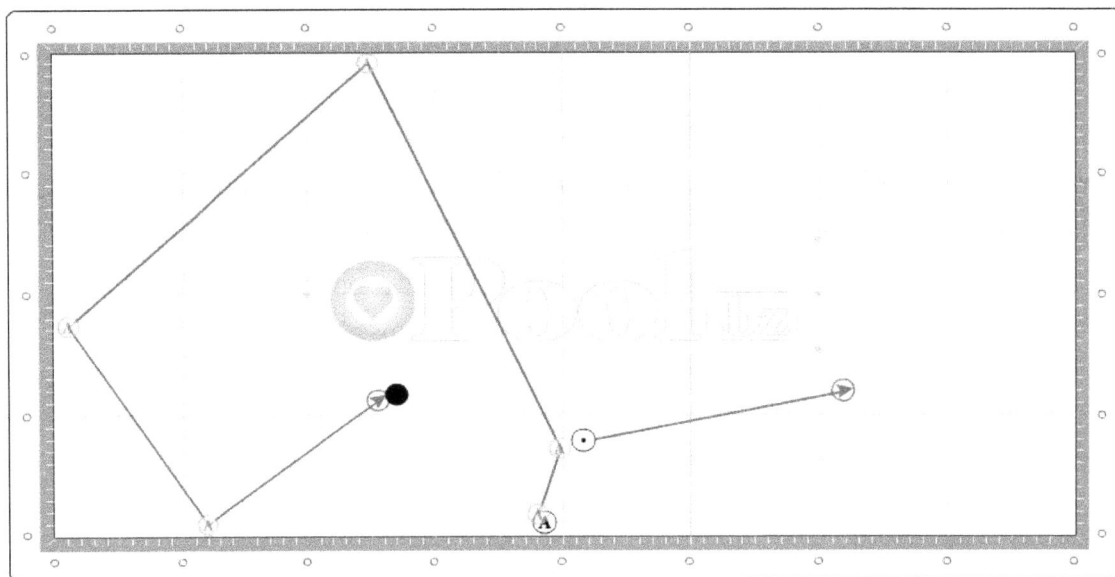

D:3c – Setup

Shot Pattern

D:3d – Setup

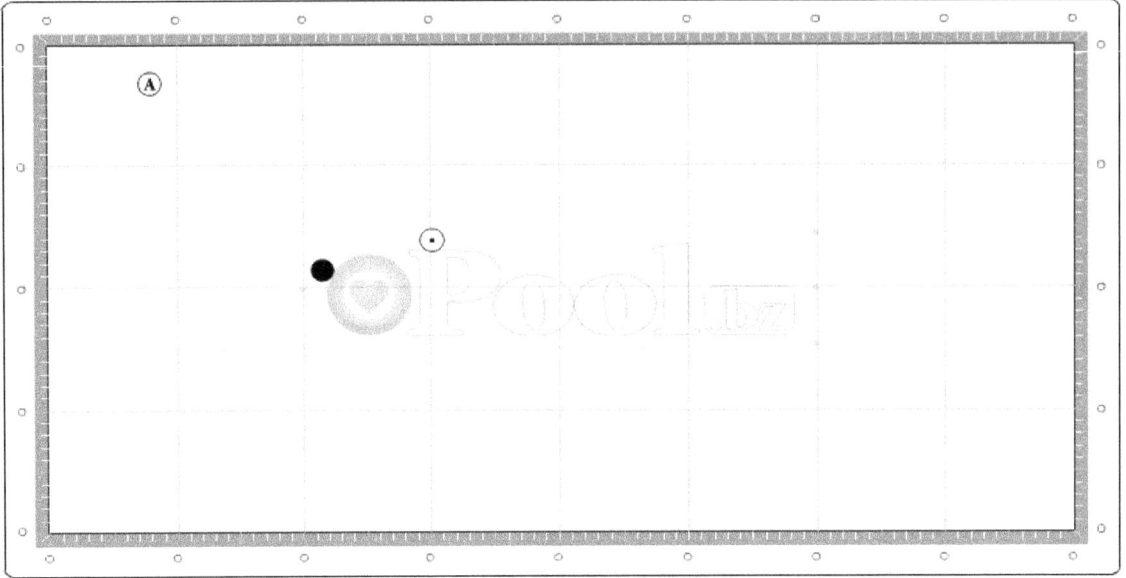

Shot Pattern

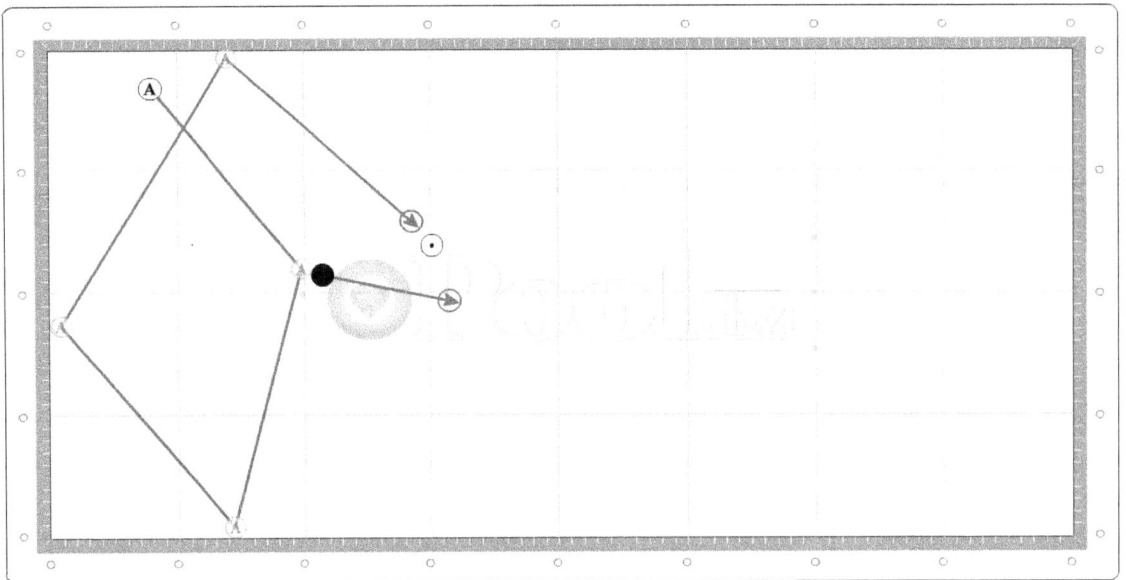

D: Group 4

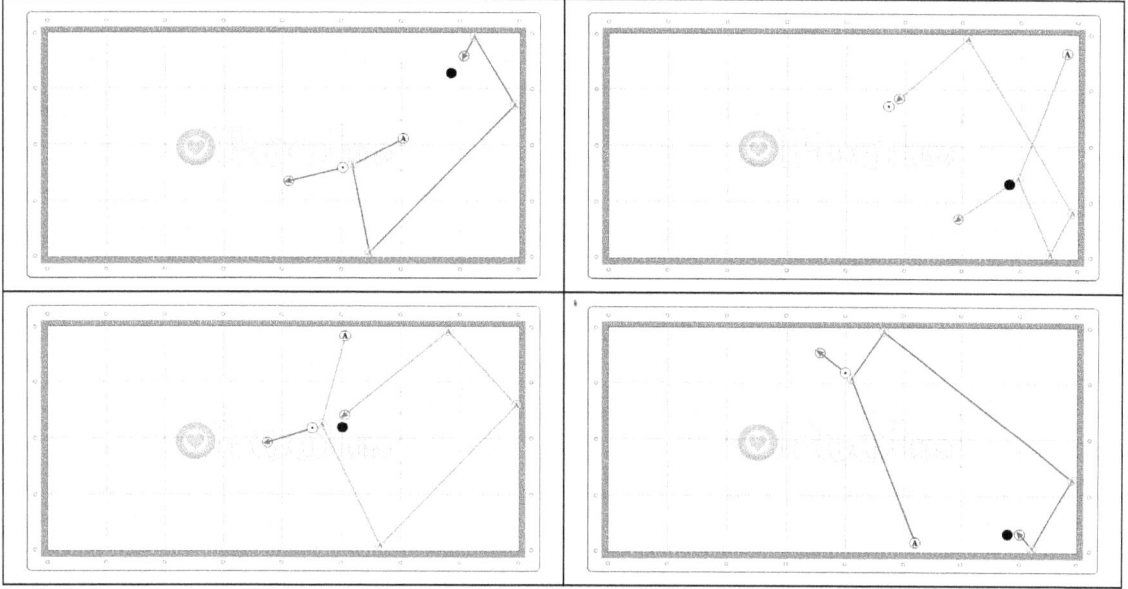

Analysis:

D:4a. _____

D:4b. _____

D:4c. _____

D:4d. _____

D:4a – Setup

Shot Pattern

D:4b – Setup

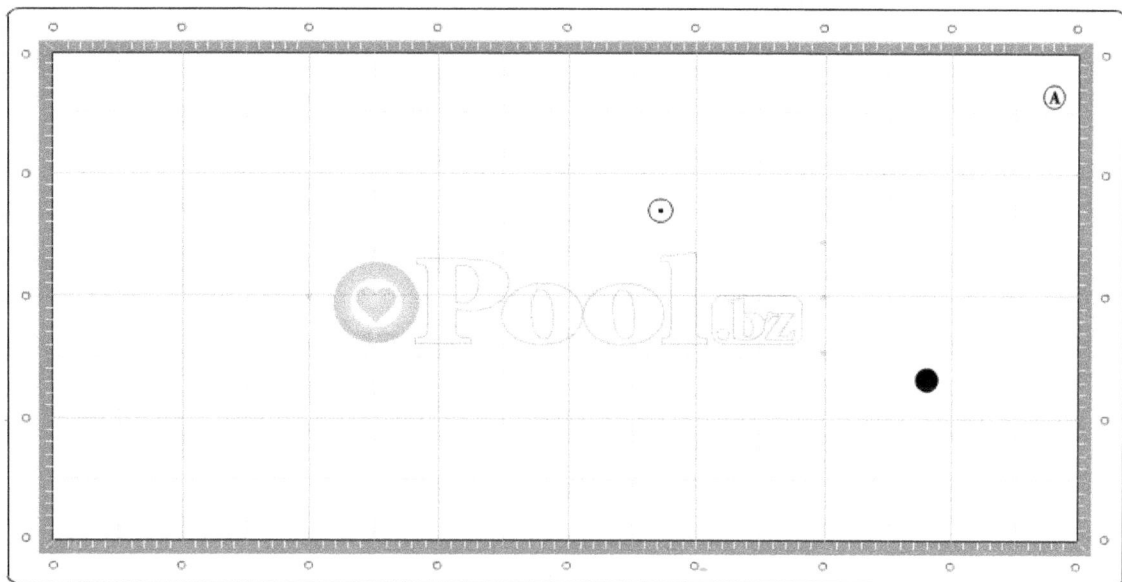

Shot Pattern

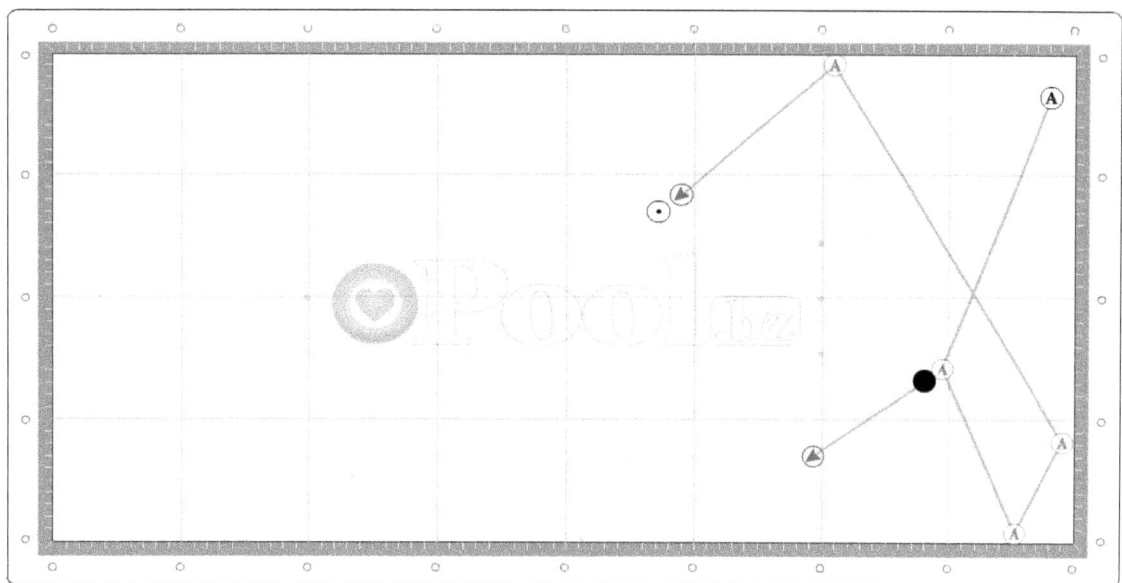

D:4c – Setup

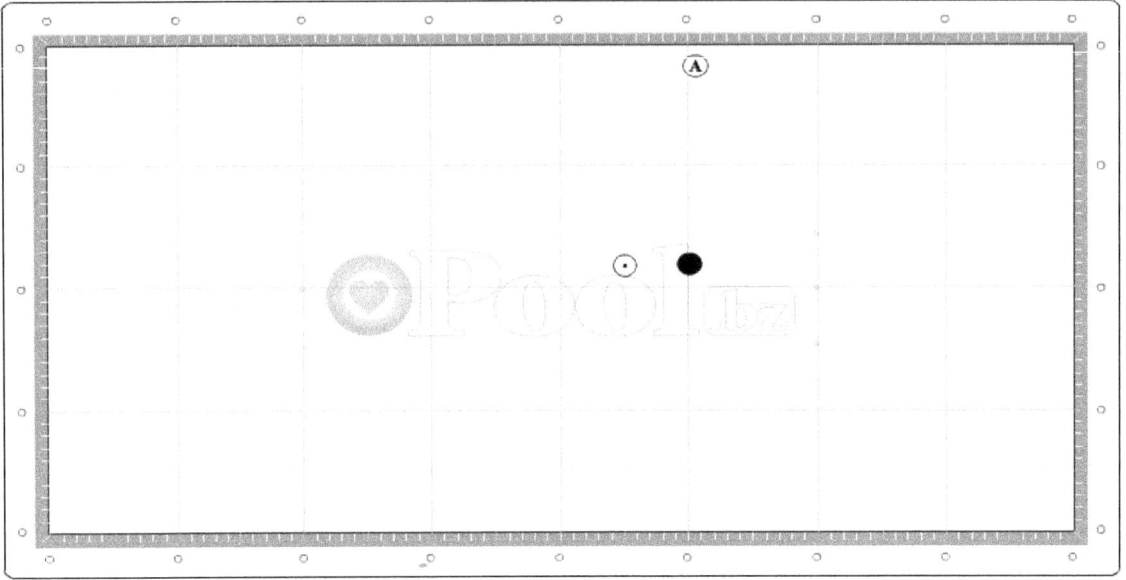

Shot Pattern

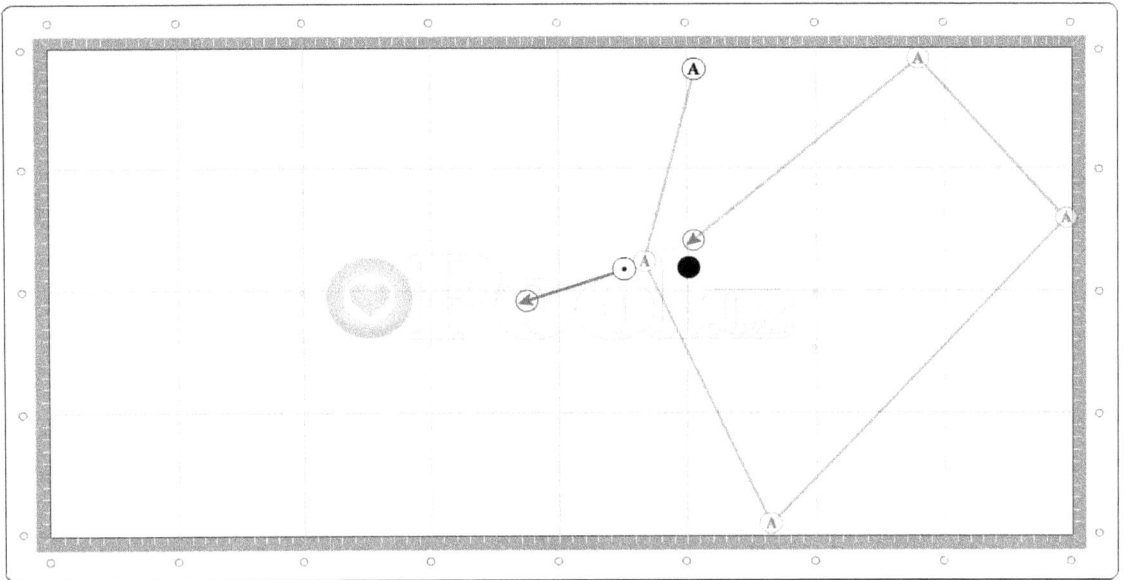

D:4d – Setup

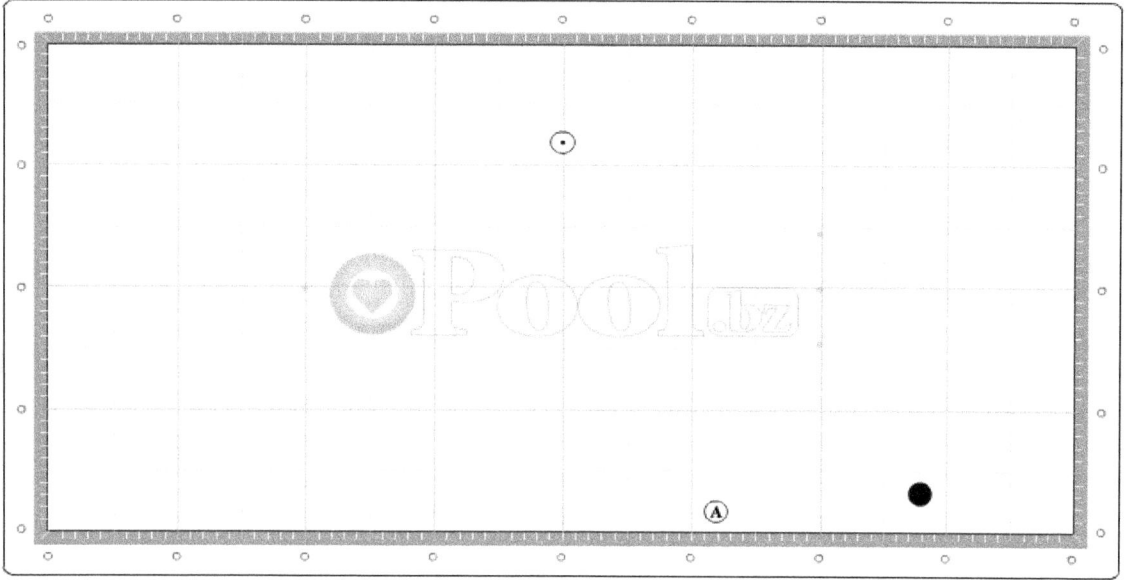

Shot Pattern

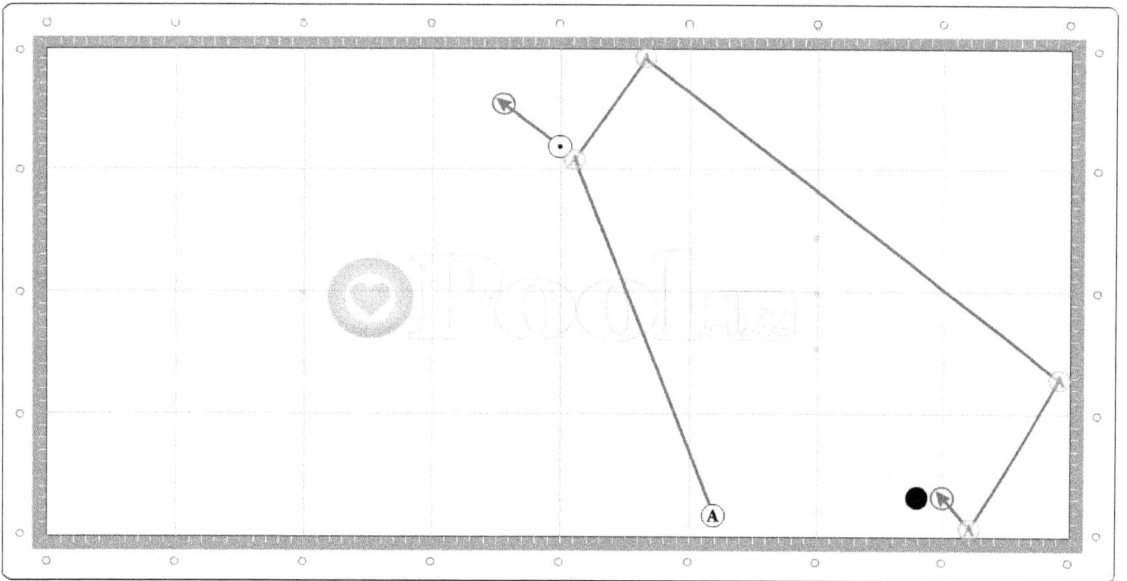

D: Group 5

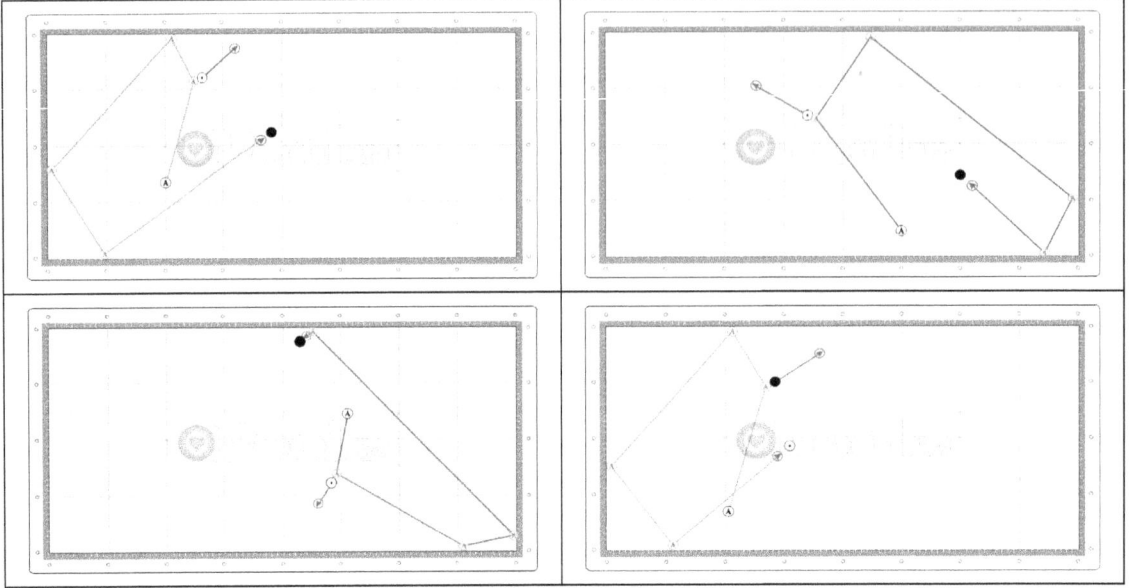

Analysis:

D:5a. _____

D:5b. _____

D:5c. _____

D:5d. _____

D:5a – Setup

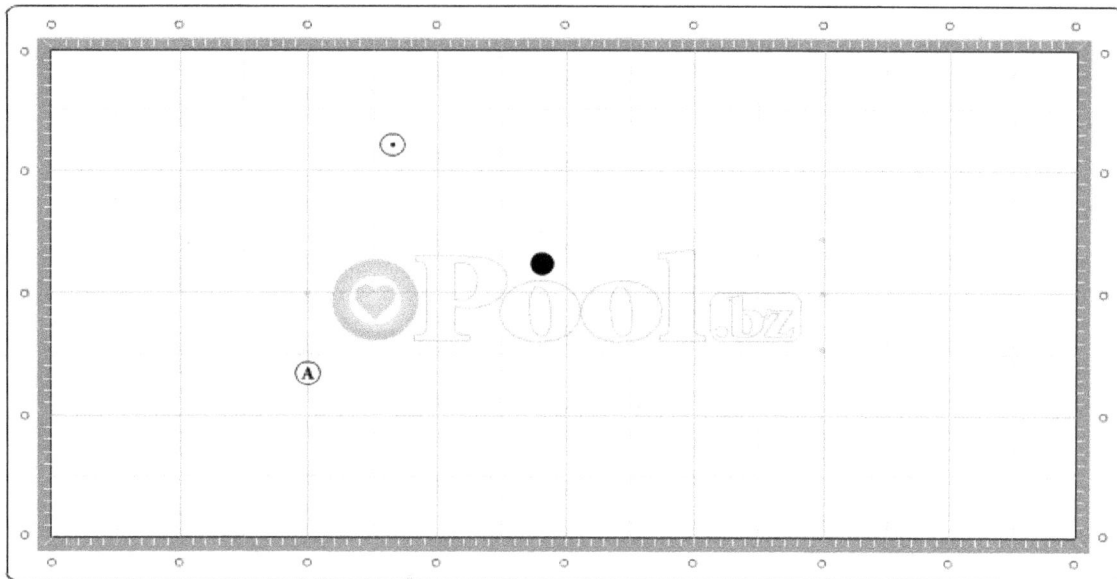

Shot Pattern

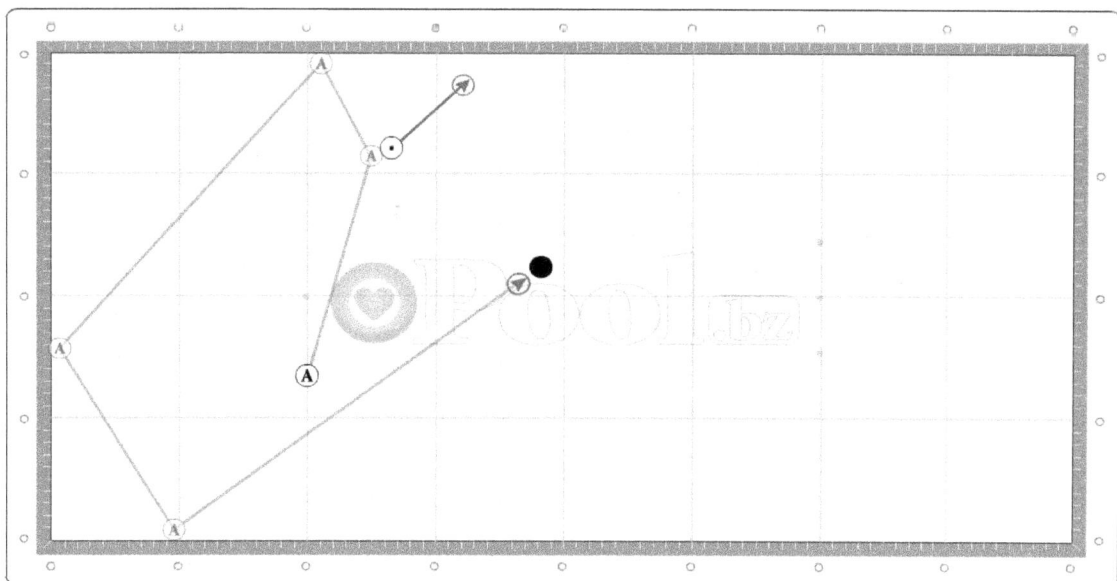

D:5b – Setup

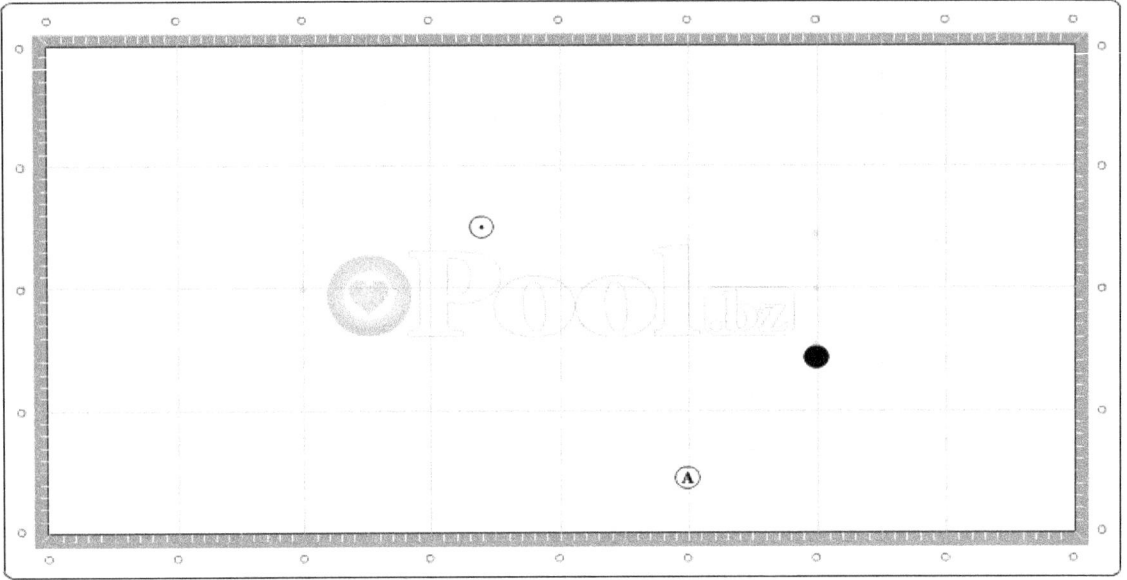

Shot Pattern

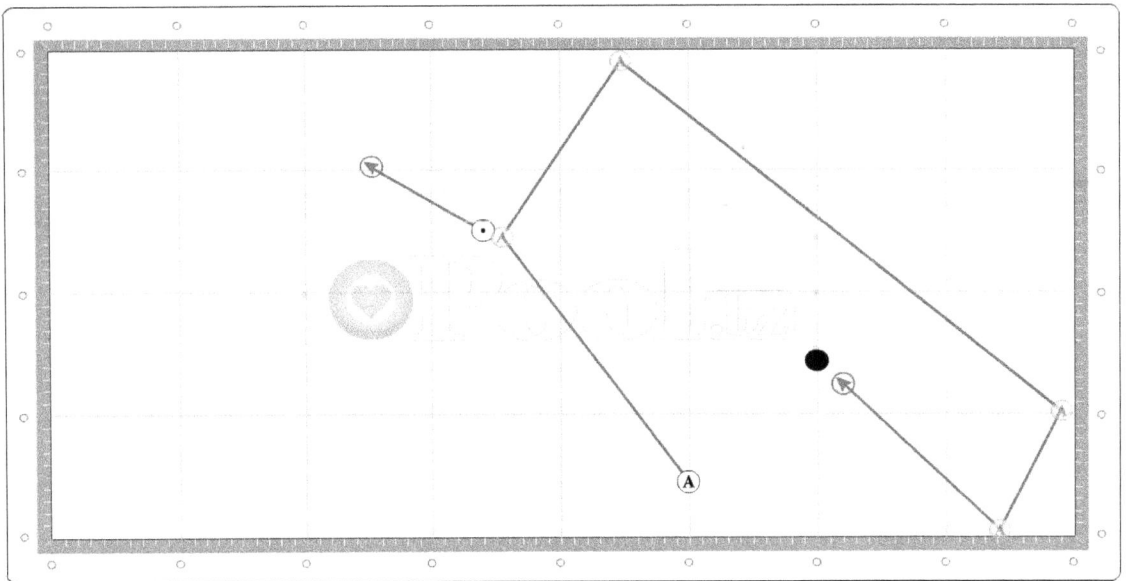

D:5c – Setup

Shot Pattern

D:5d – Setup

Shot Pattern

D: Group 6

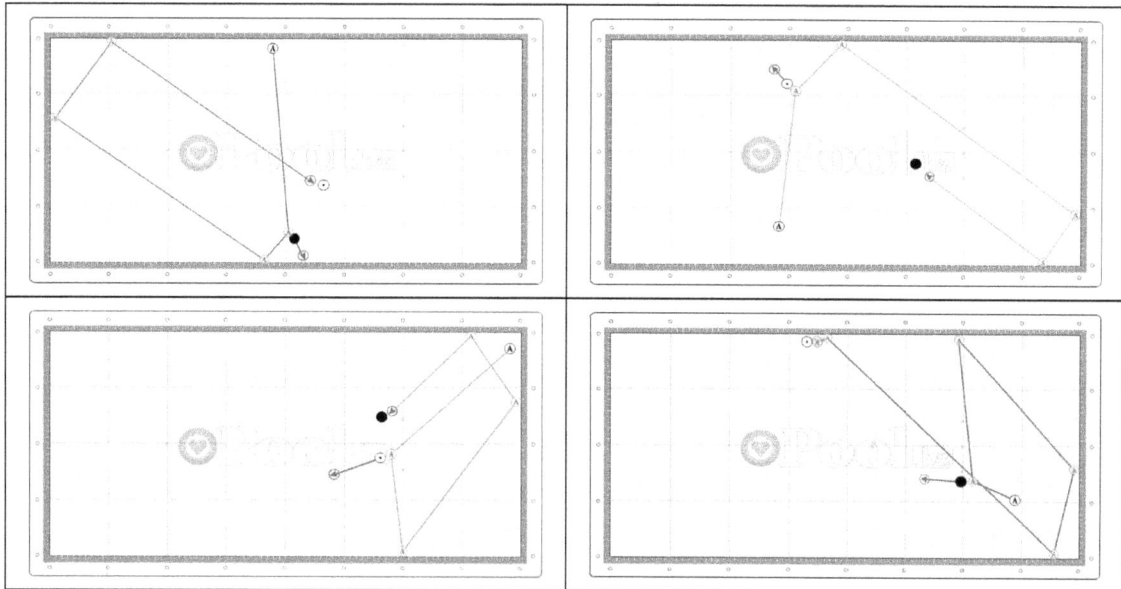

Analysis:

D:6a. _____

D:6b. _____

D:6c. _____

D:6d. _____

D:6a – Setup

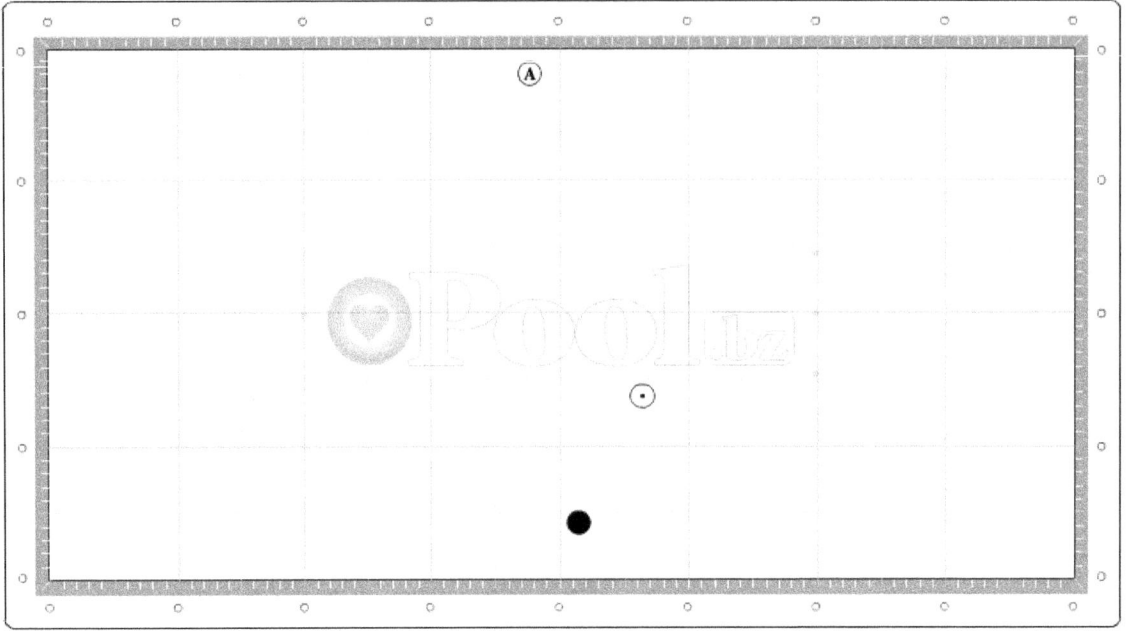

Shot Pattern

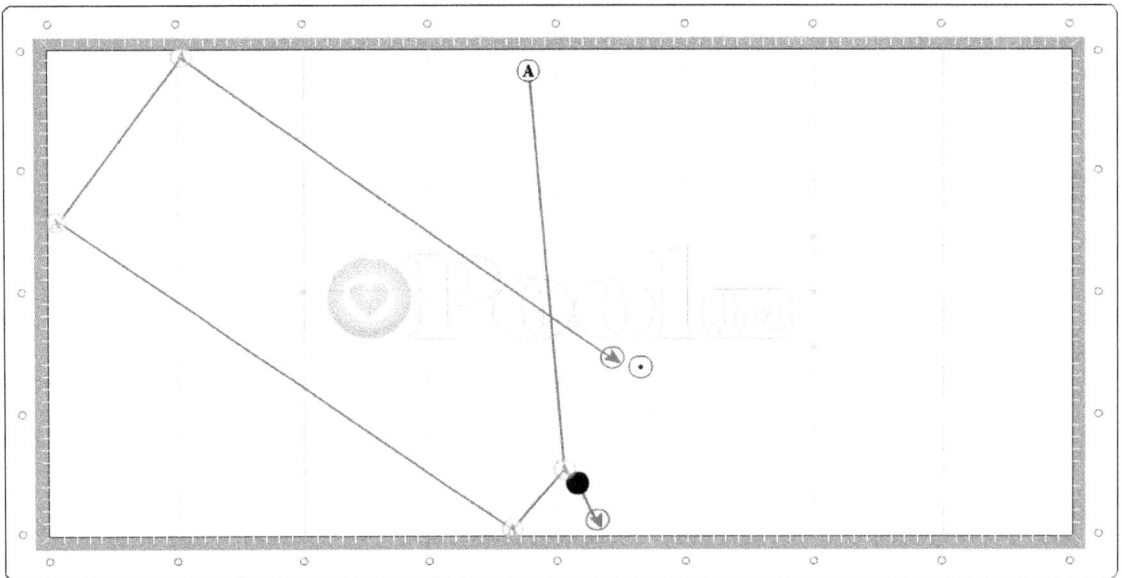

D:6b – Setup

Shot Pattern

D:6c – Setup

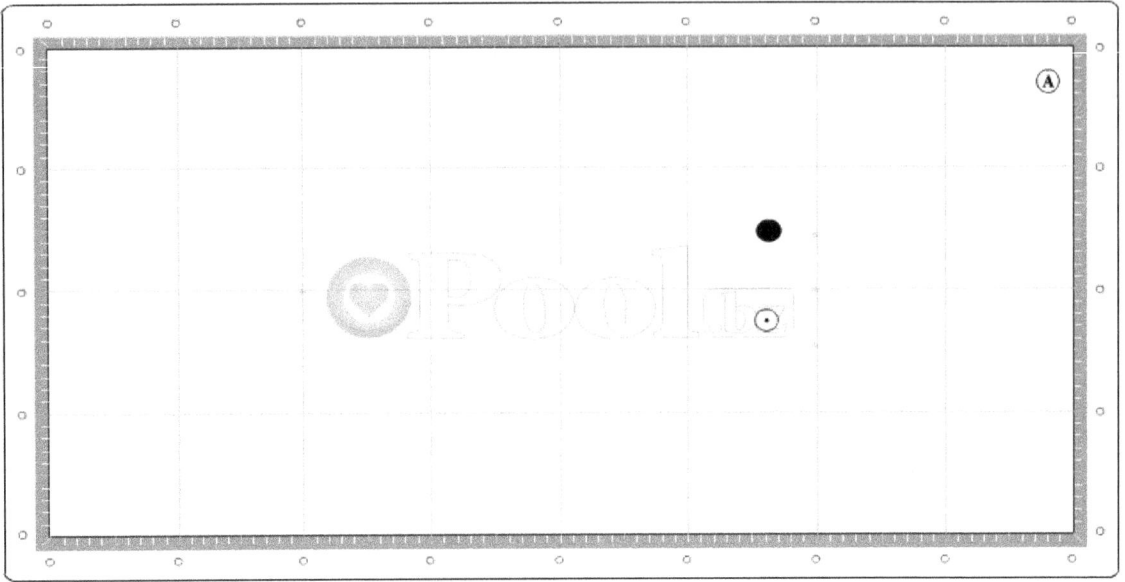

Shot Pattern

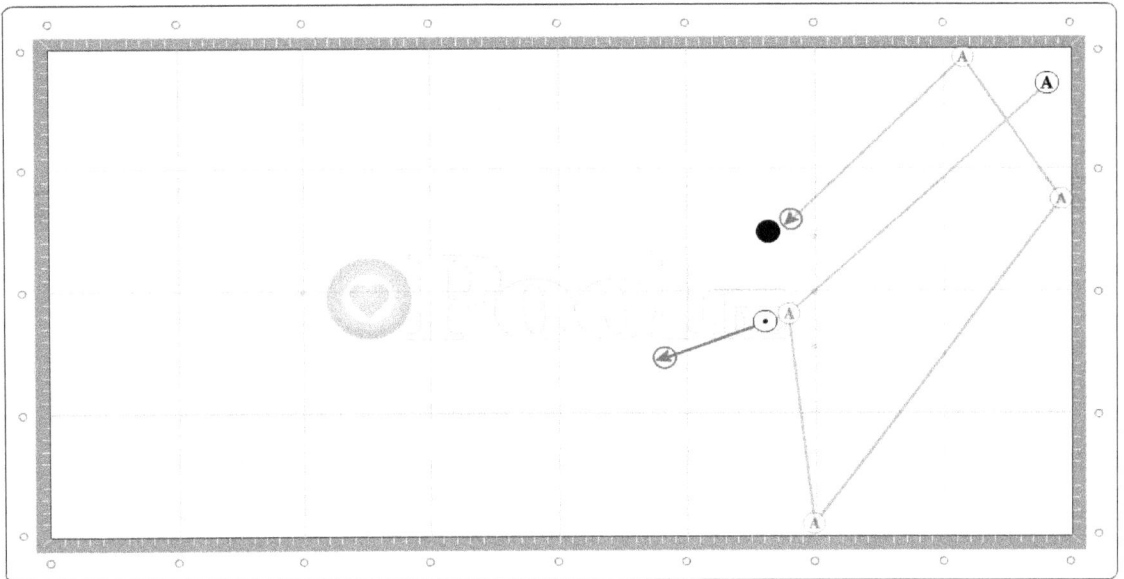

D:6d – Setup

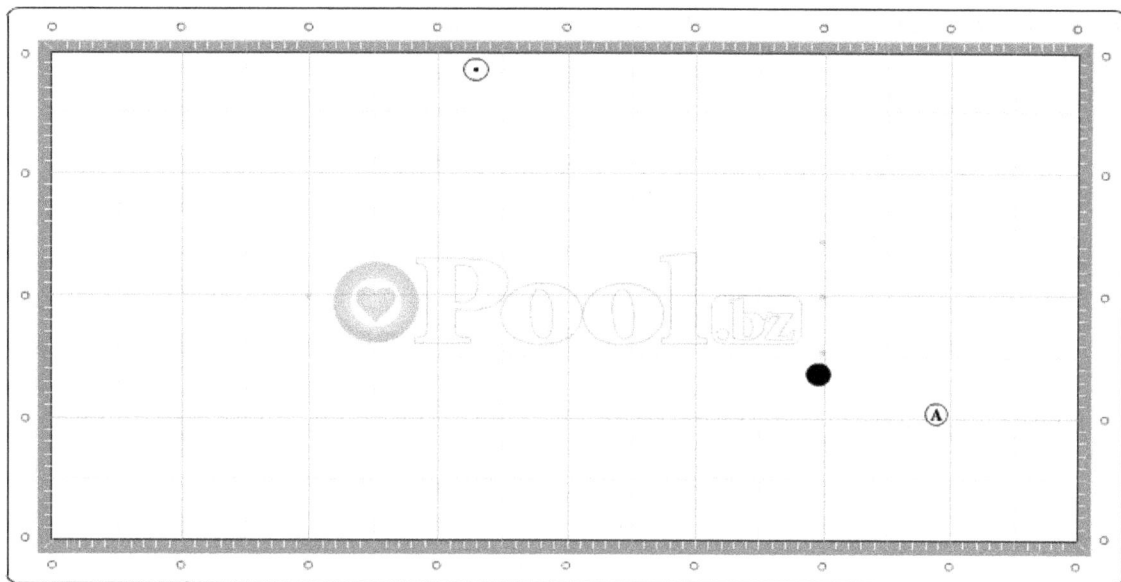

Shot Pattern

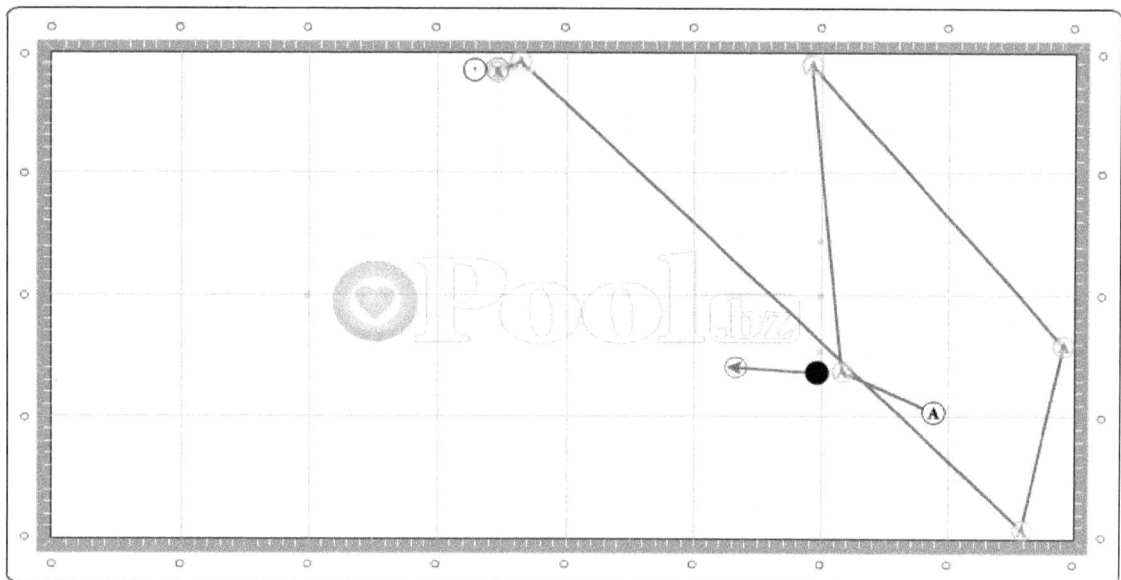

E: Extended Leg

On these shots, the CB comes off the first OB and follows the half-table circle pattern. The third leg of the pattern goes outside the half-table area – to contact the second OB and make the score.

E: Group 1

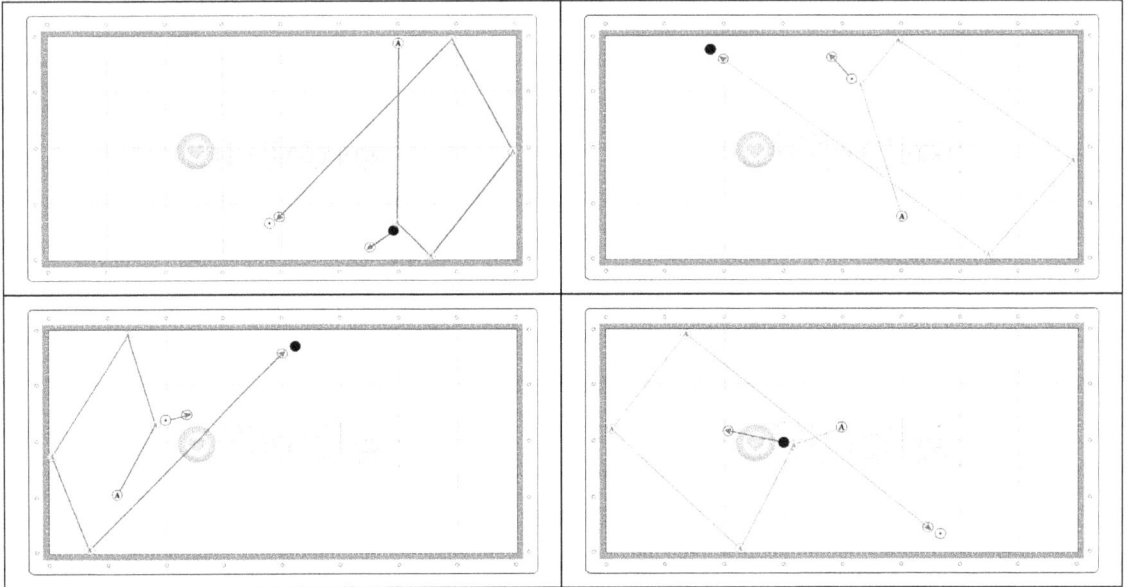

Analysis:

E:1a. _____

E:1b. _____

E:1c. _____

E:1d. _____

E:1a – Setup

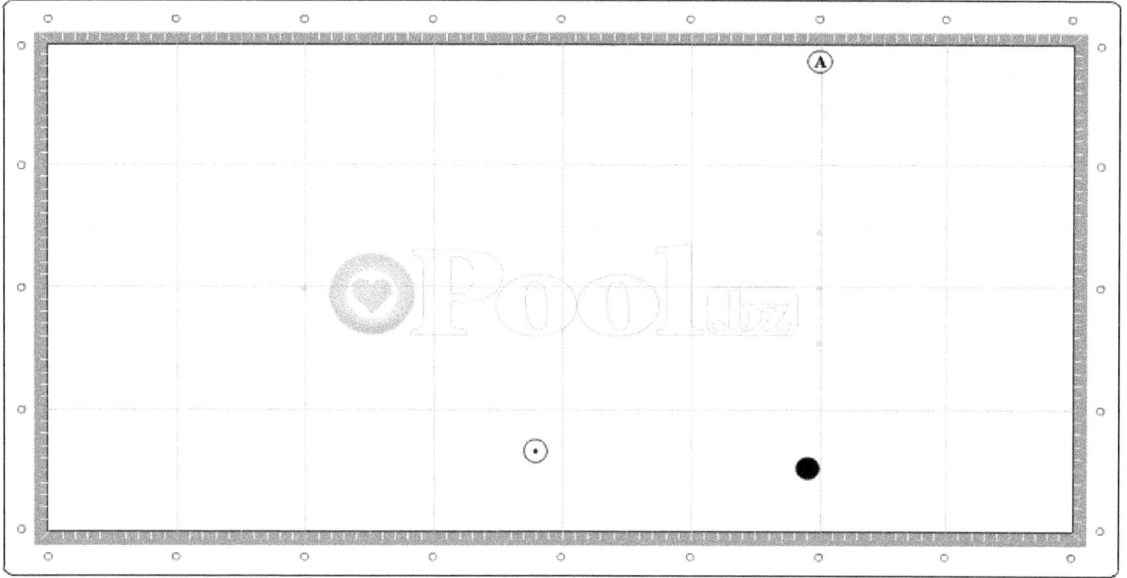

Shot Pattern

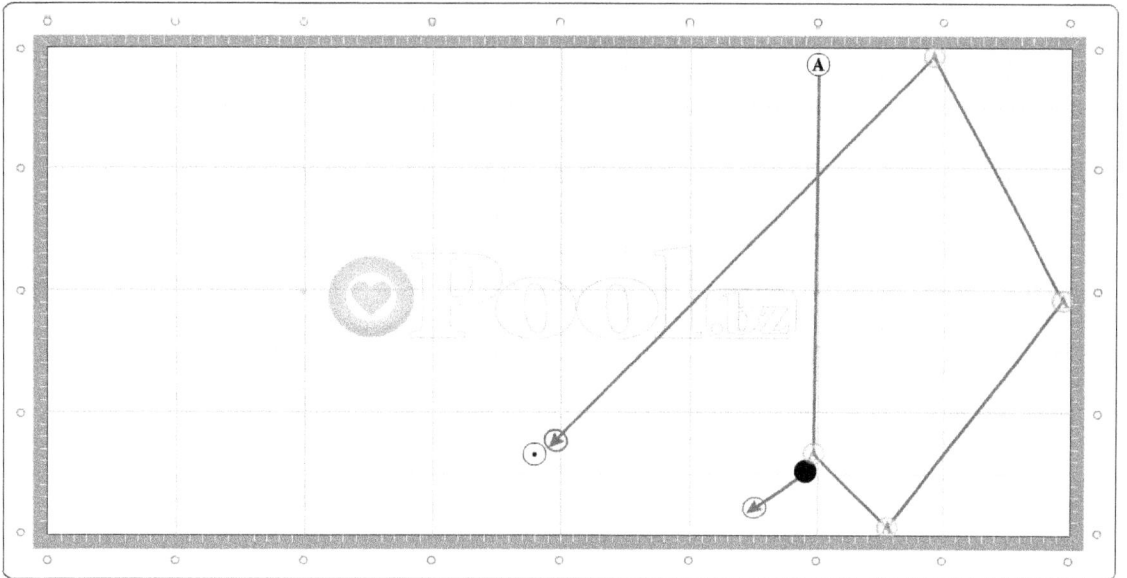

E:1b – Setup

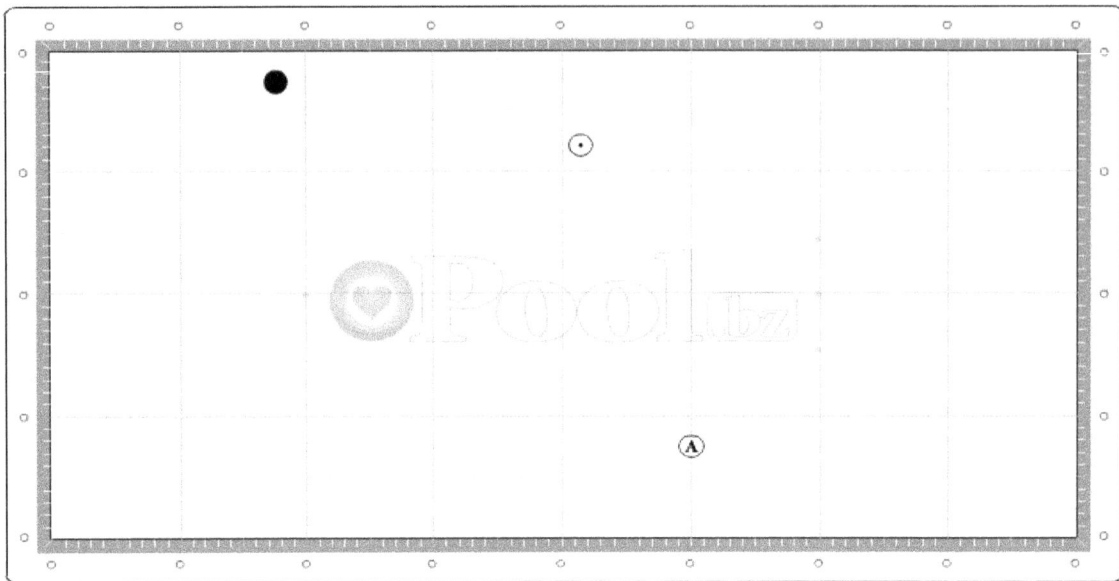

Shot Pattern

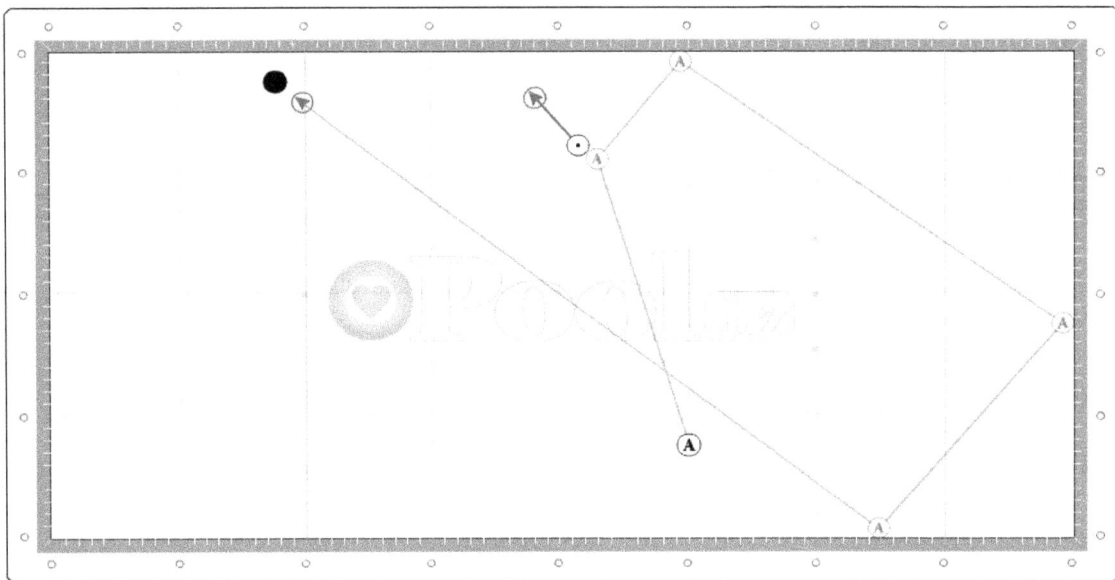

E:1c – Setup

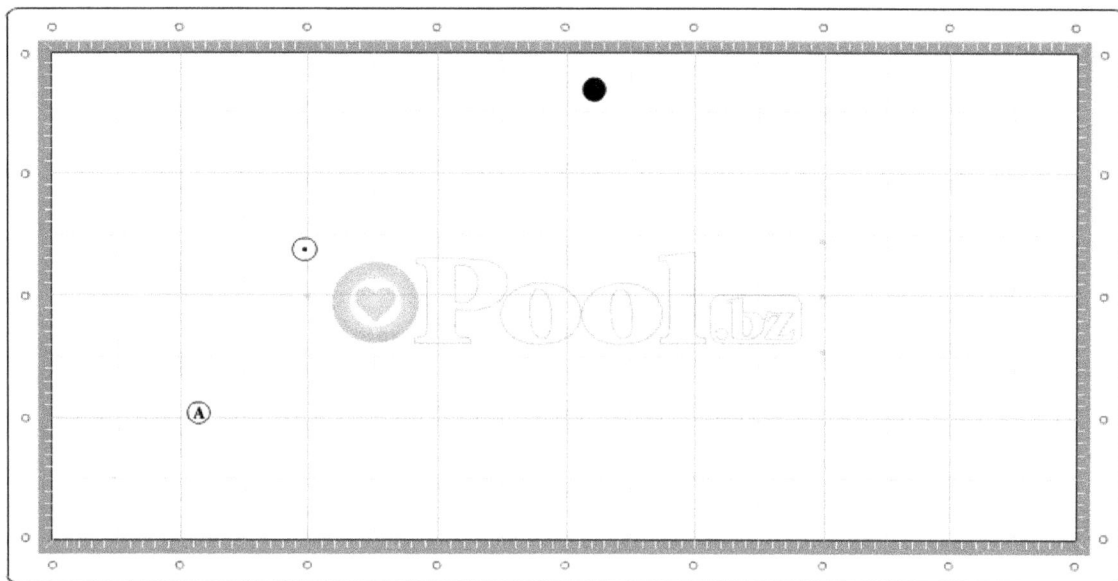

Shot Pattern

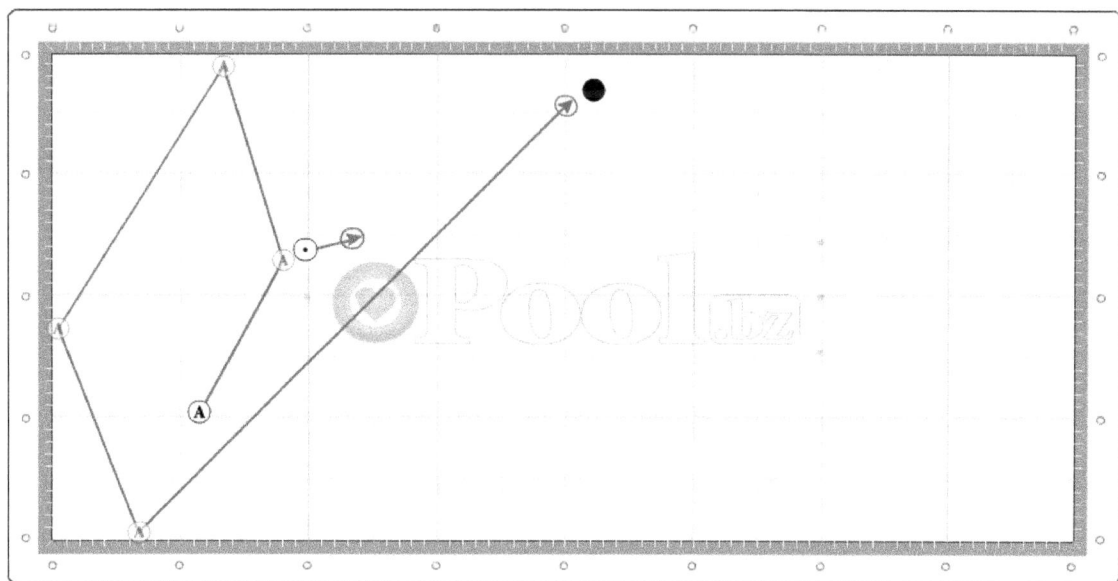

E:1d – Setup

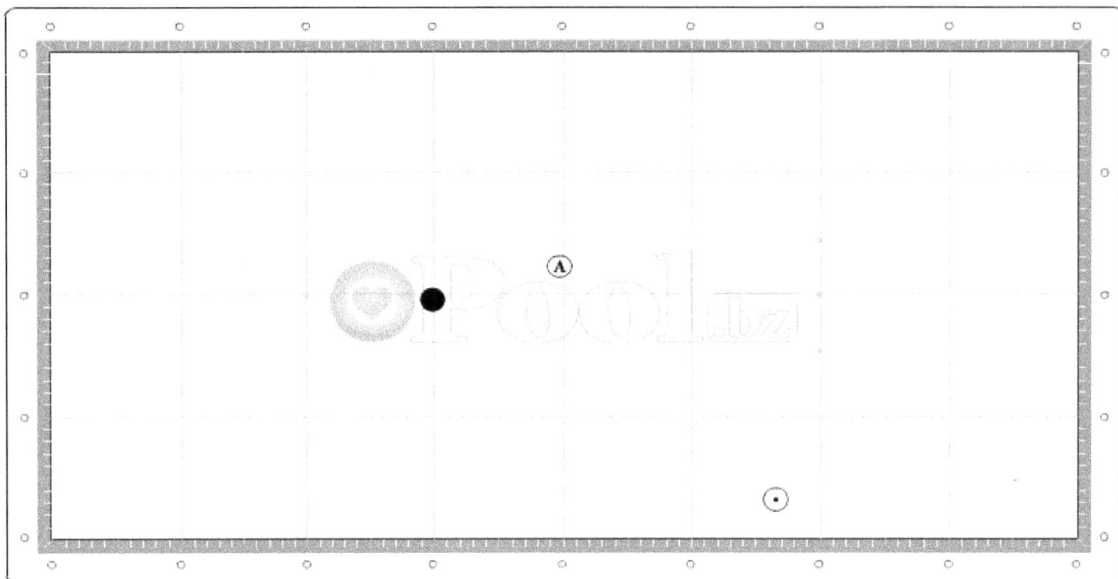

Shot Pattern

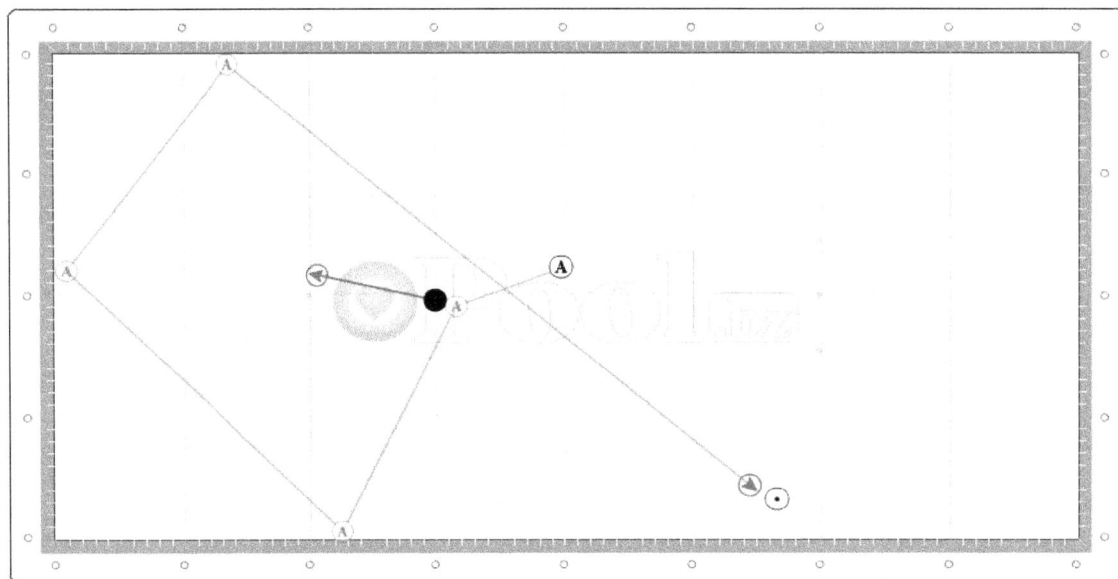

E: Group 2

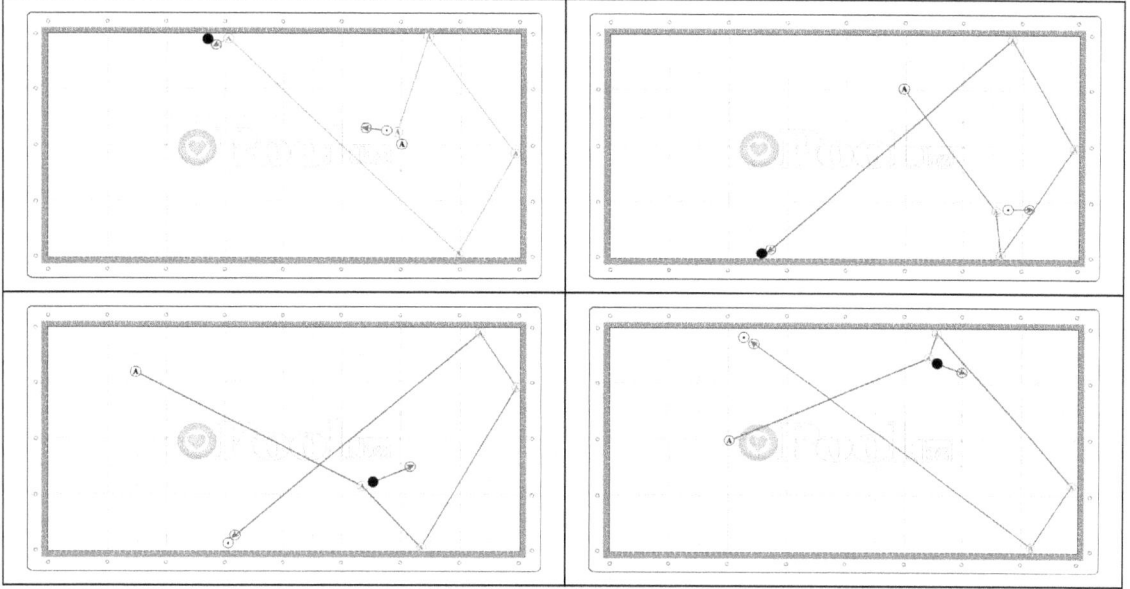

Analysis:

E:2a. _____

E:2b. _____

E:2c. _____

E:2d. _____

E:2a – Setup

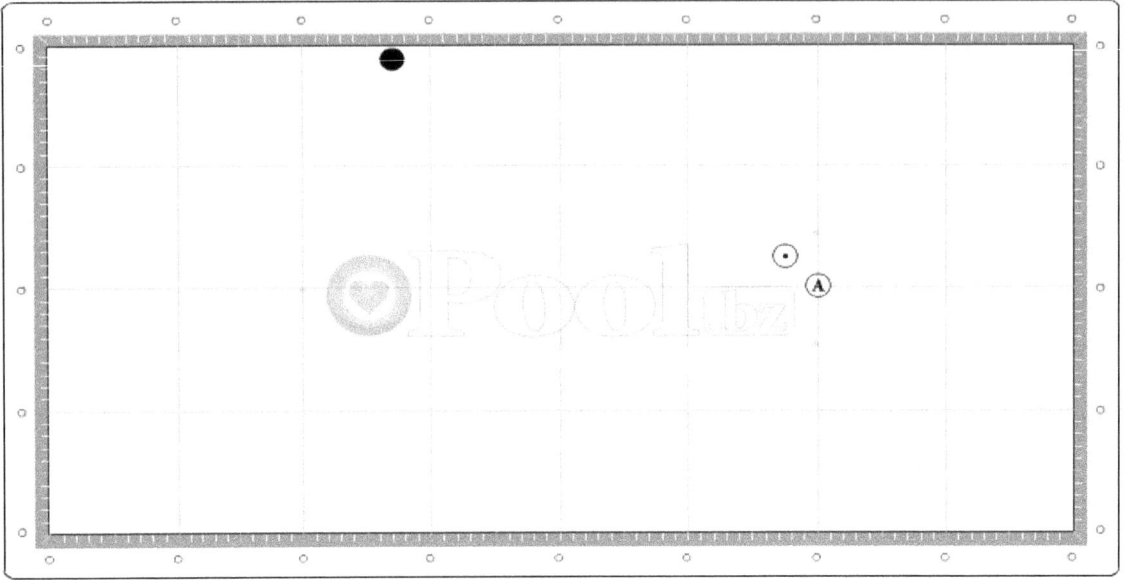

Shot Pattern

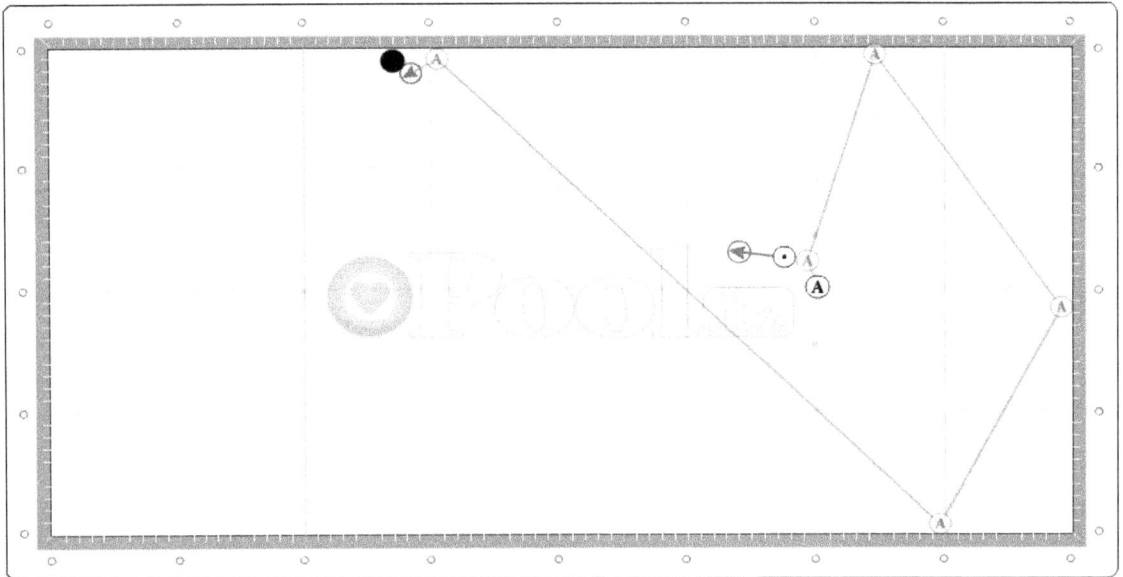

E:2b – Setup

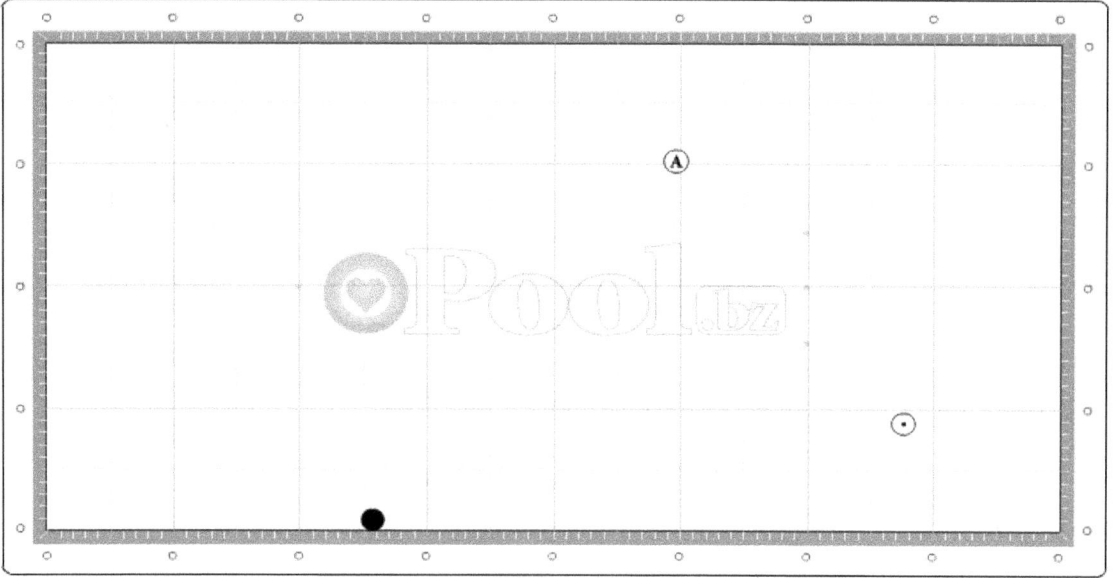

Shot Pattern

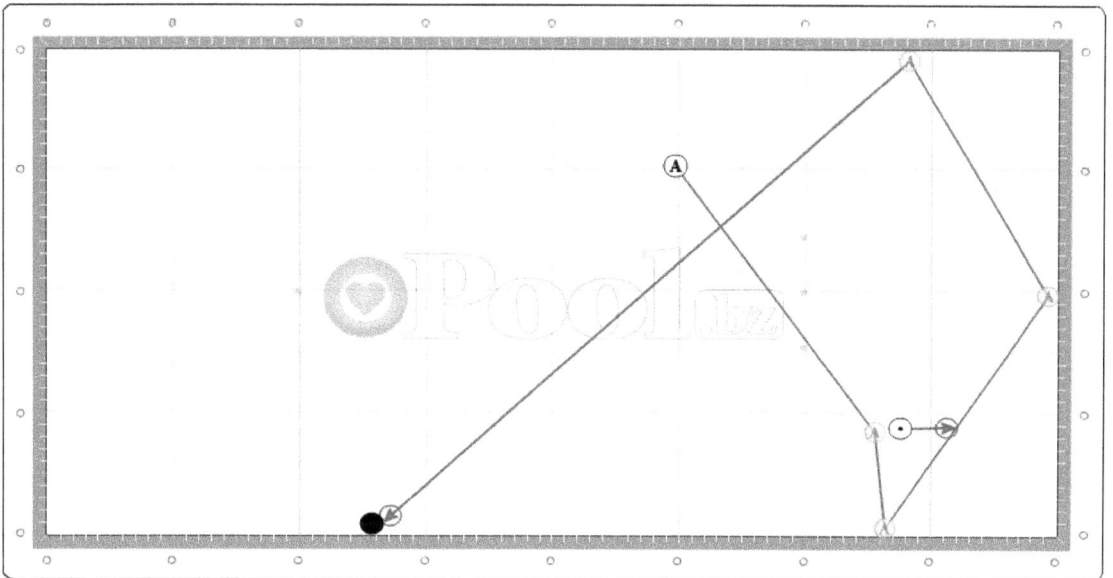

E:2c – Setup

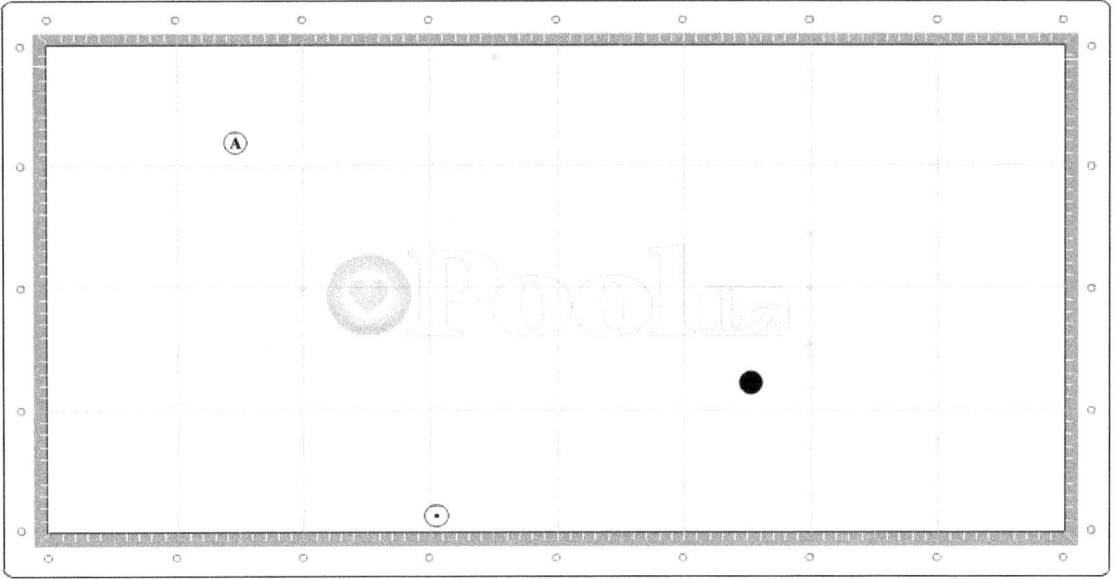

Shot Pattern

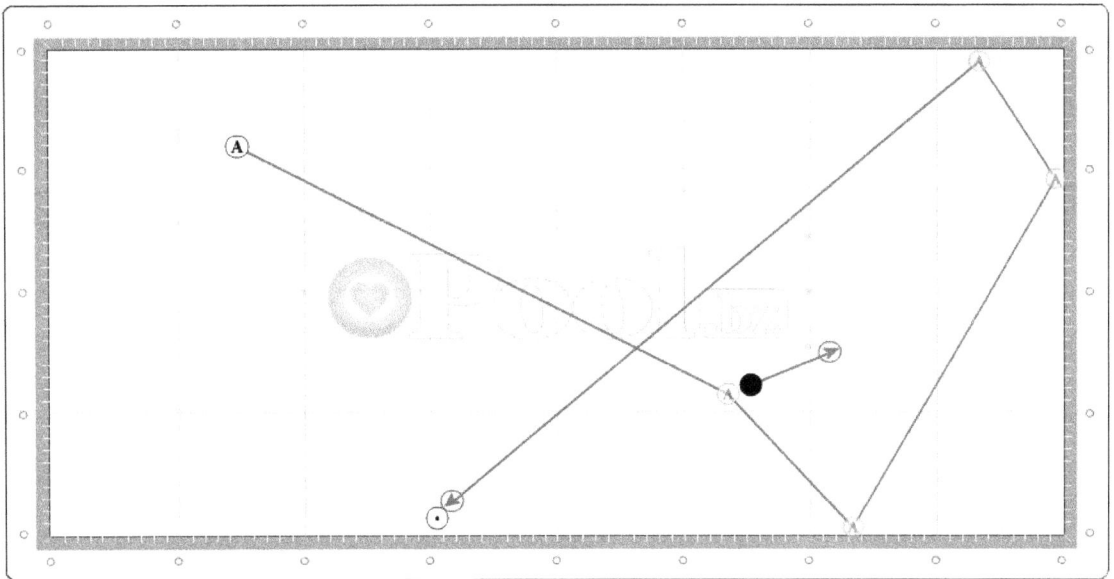

E:2d – Setup

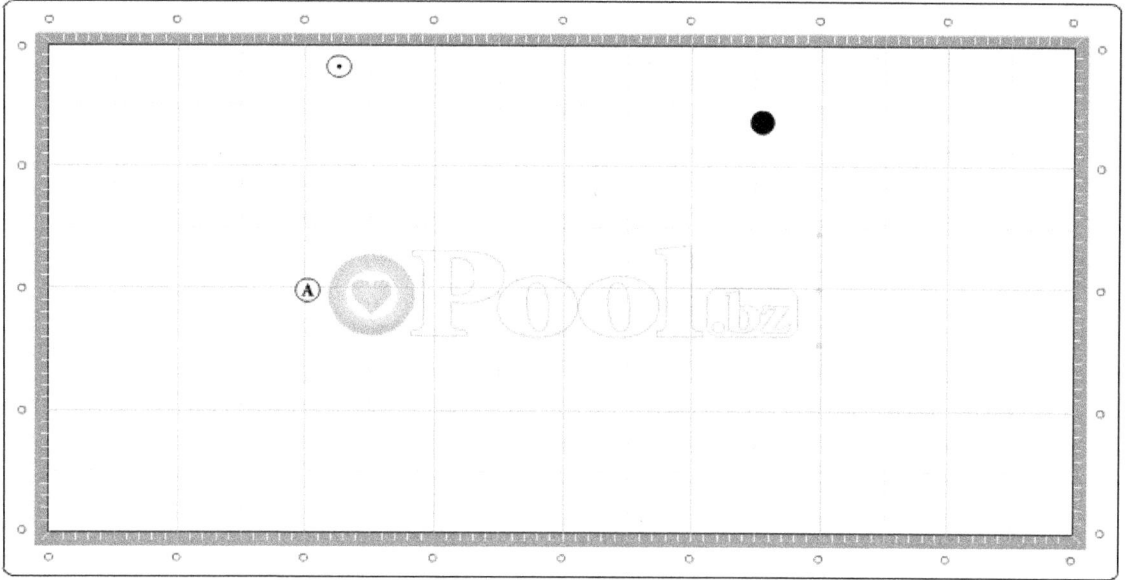

Shot Pattern

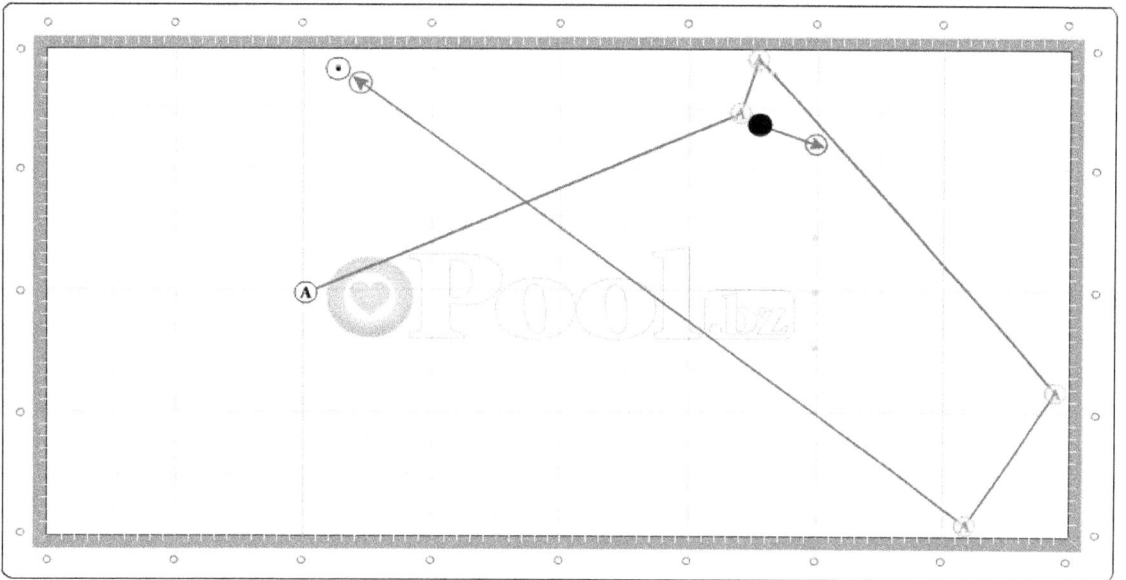

F: Extended Extra Rail

On these shots, the CB comes off the first OB and follows the regular half-table circle pattern. The CB extends into the other half of the table. This set of shots shows the CB coming off the long rail and then to the other end of the table. This is where the CB connects with the second OB.

F: Group 1

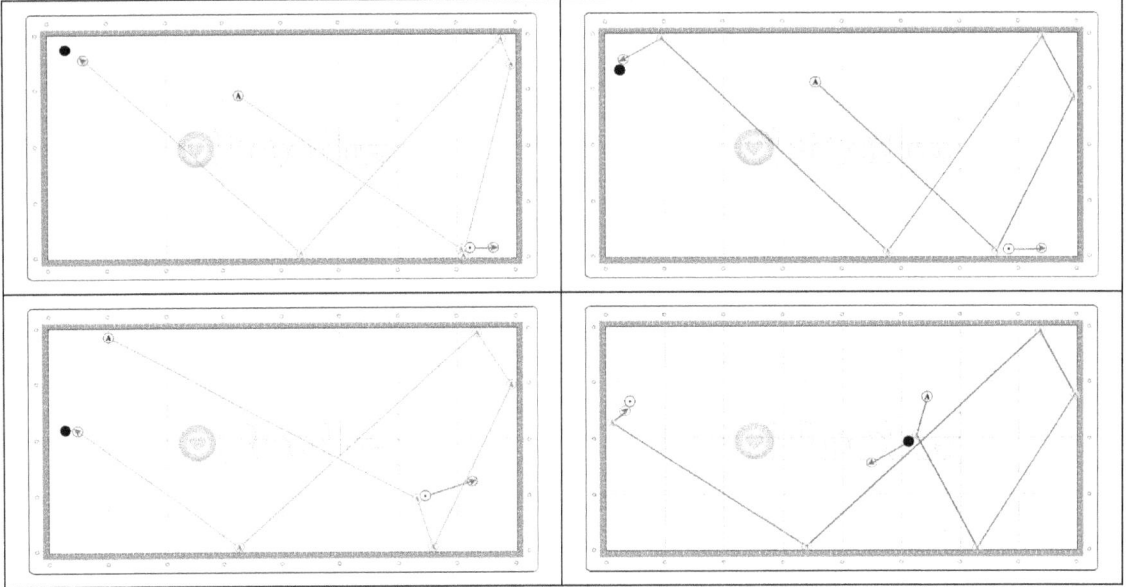

Analysis:

F:1a. _____

F:1b. _____

F:1c. _____

F:1d. _____

F:1a – Setup

Shot Pattern

F:1b – Setup

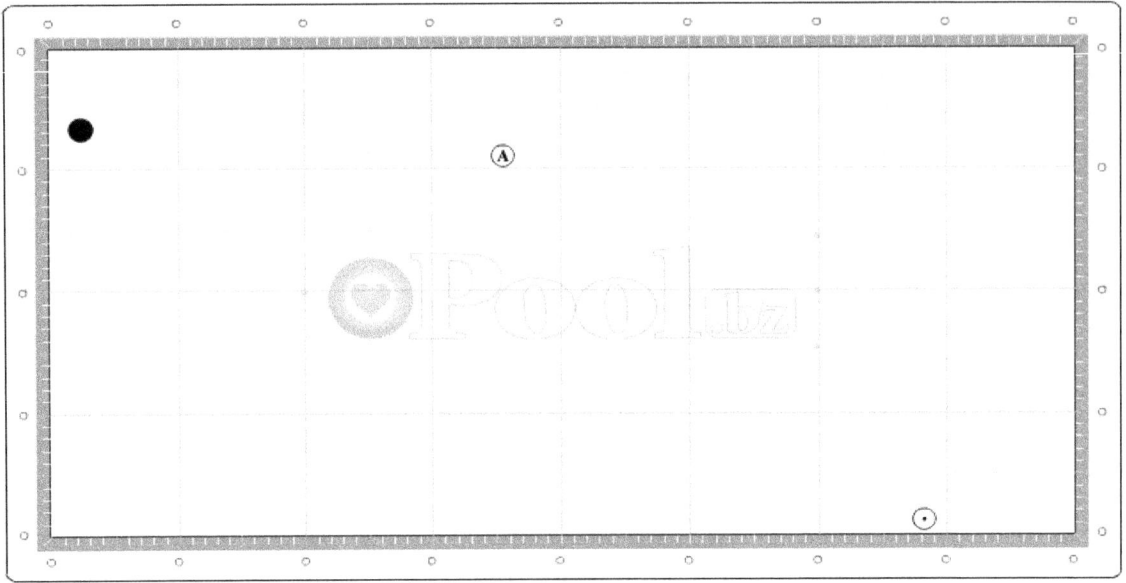

Shot Pattern

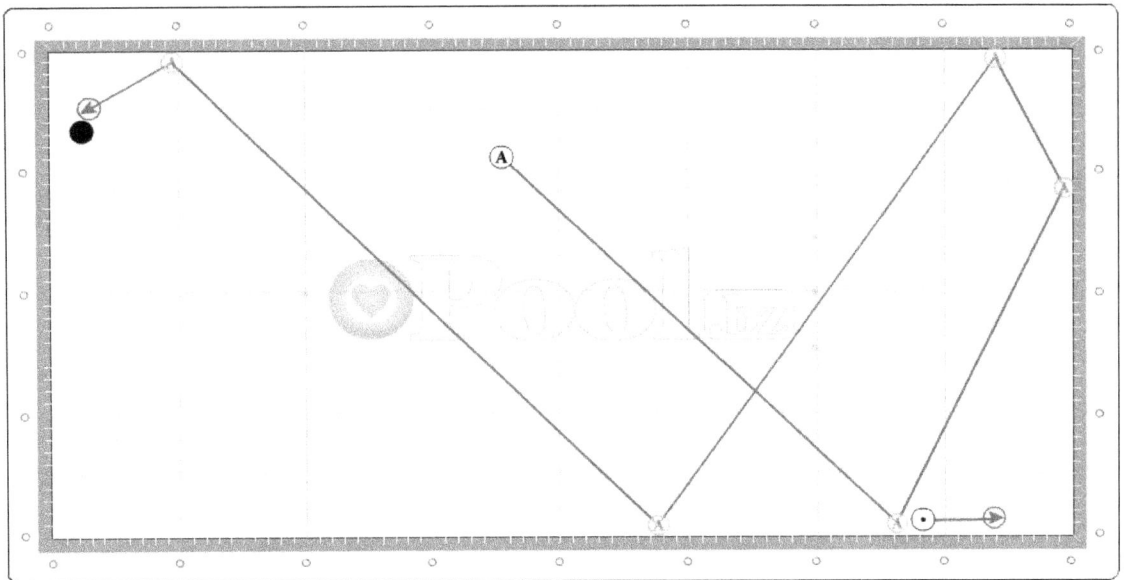

F:1c – Setup

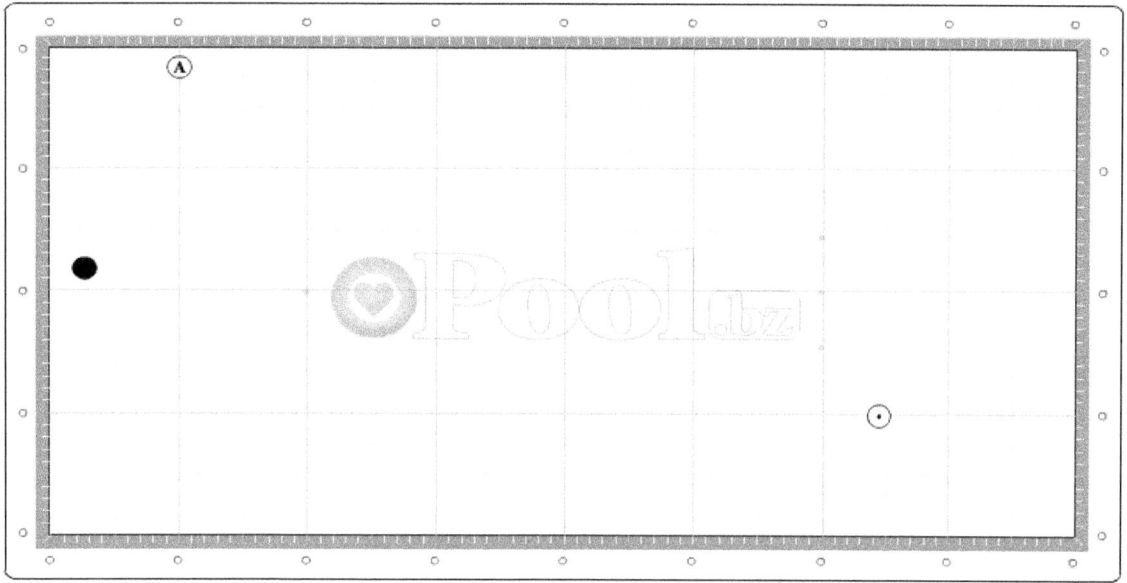

Shot Pattern

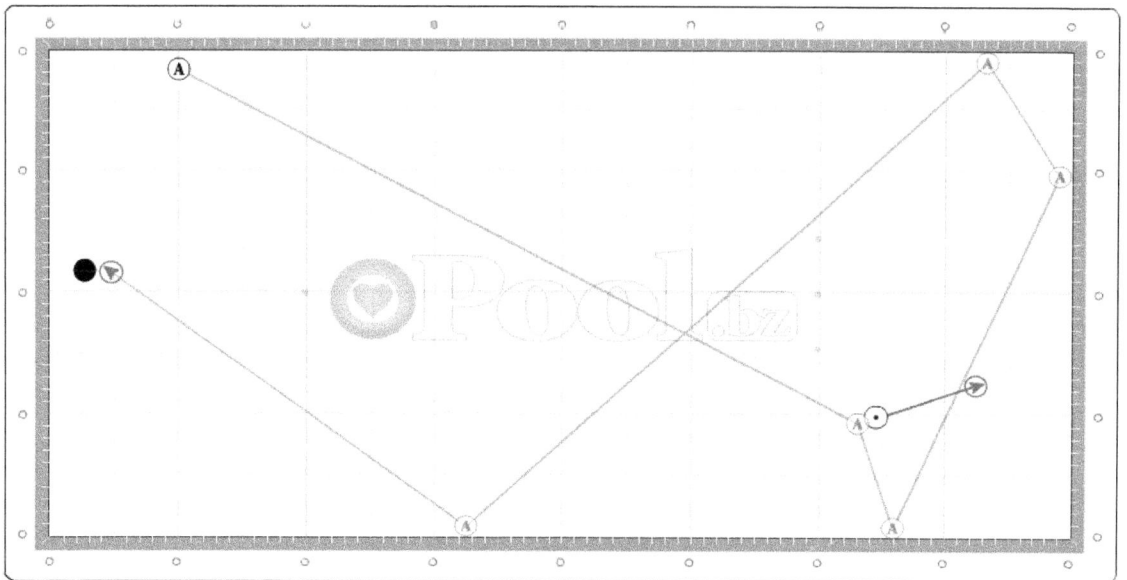

F:1d – Setup

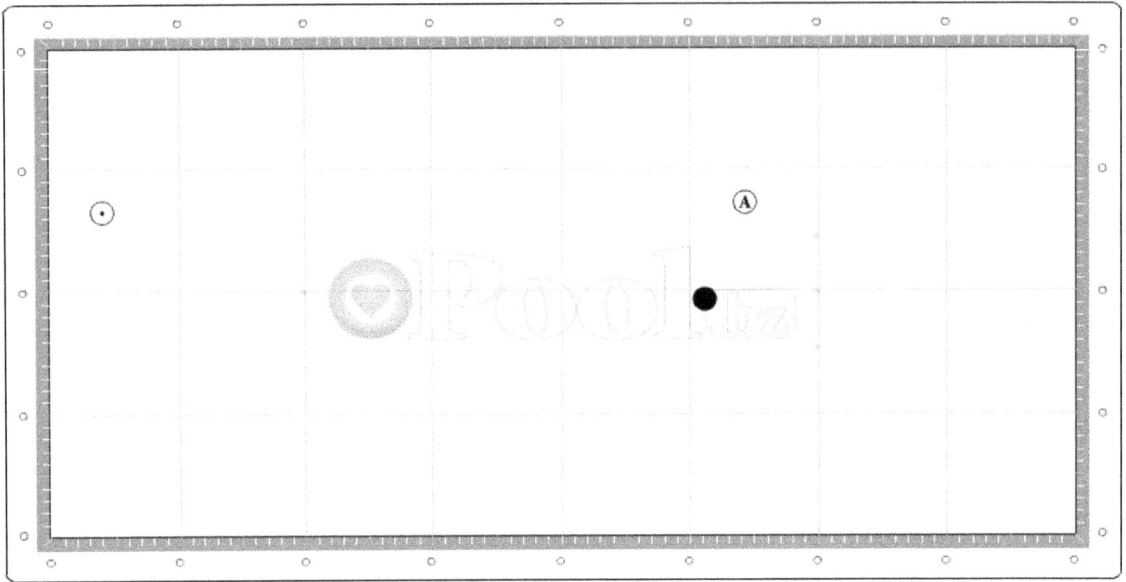

Shot Pattern

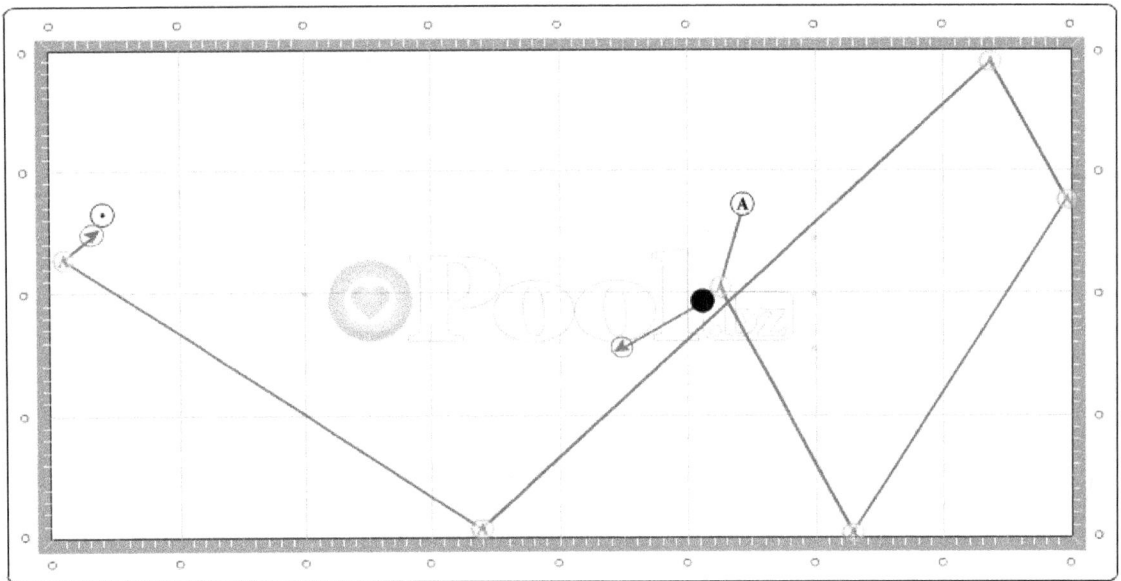

F: Group 2

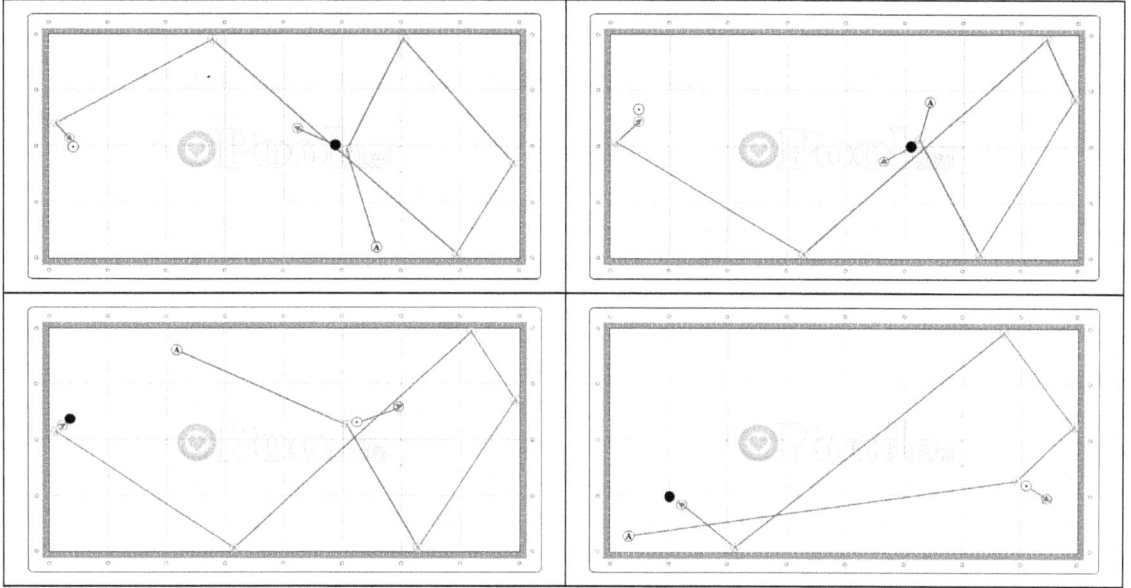

Analysis:

F:2a. _____

F:2b. _____

F:2c. _____

F:2d. _____

F:2a – Setup

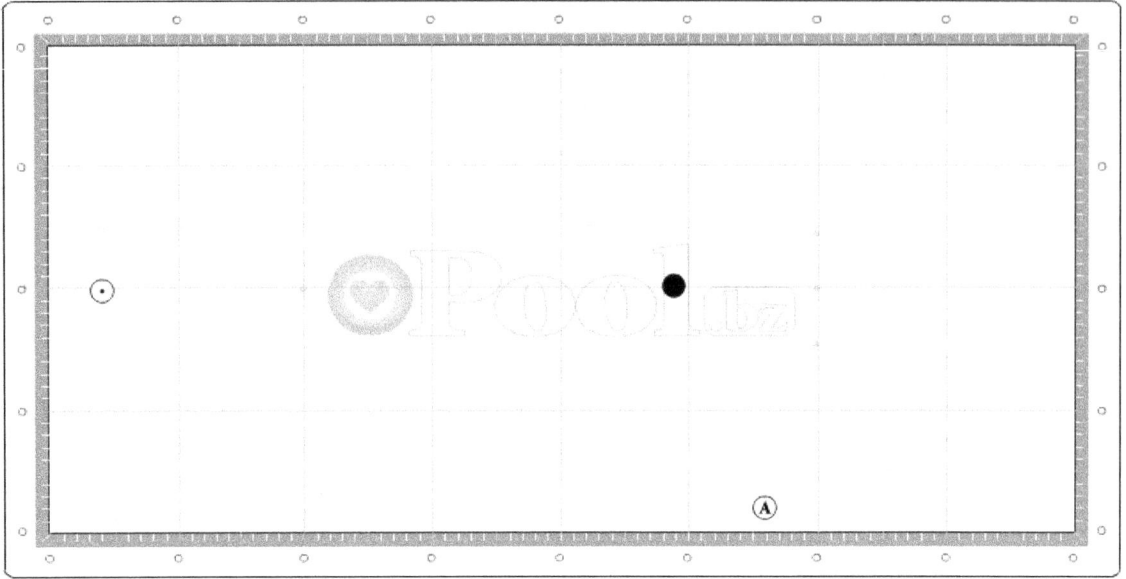

Shot Pattern

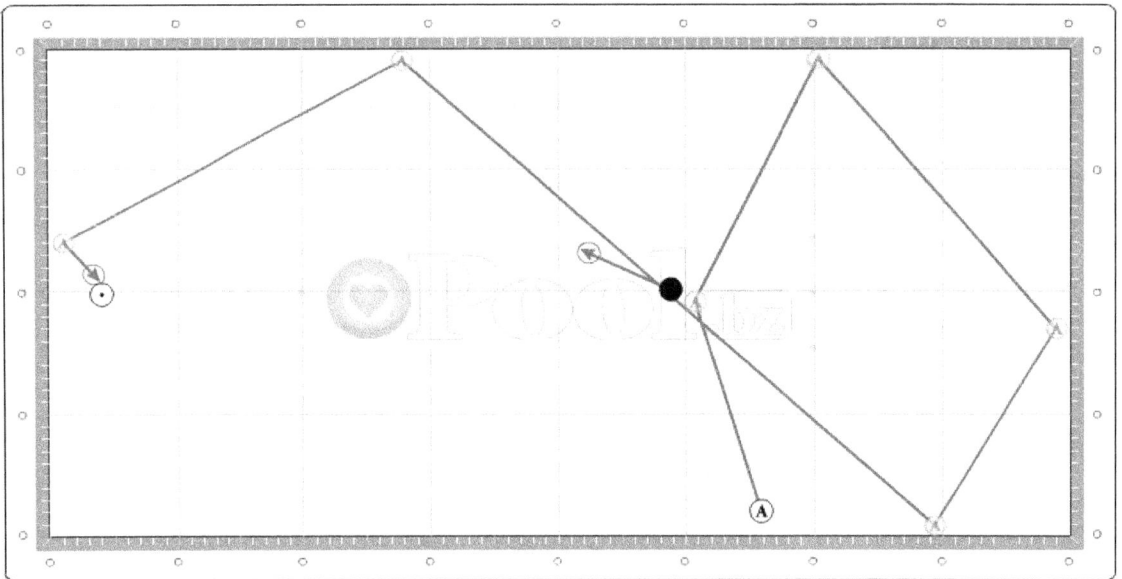

F:2b – Setup

Shot Pattern

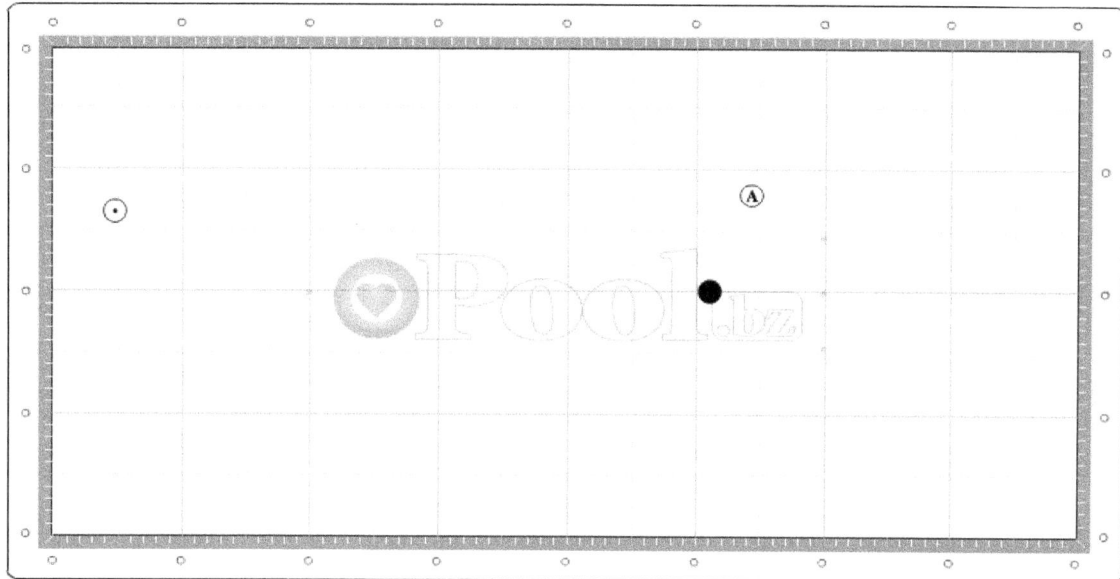

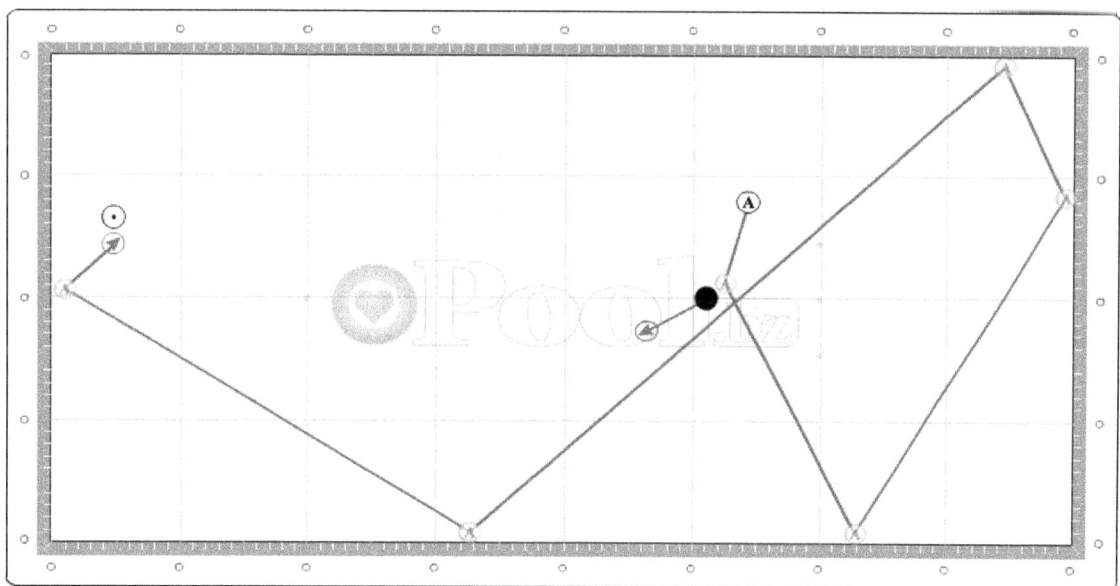

F:2c – Setup

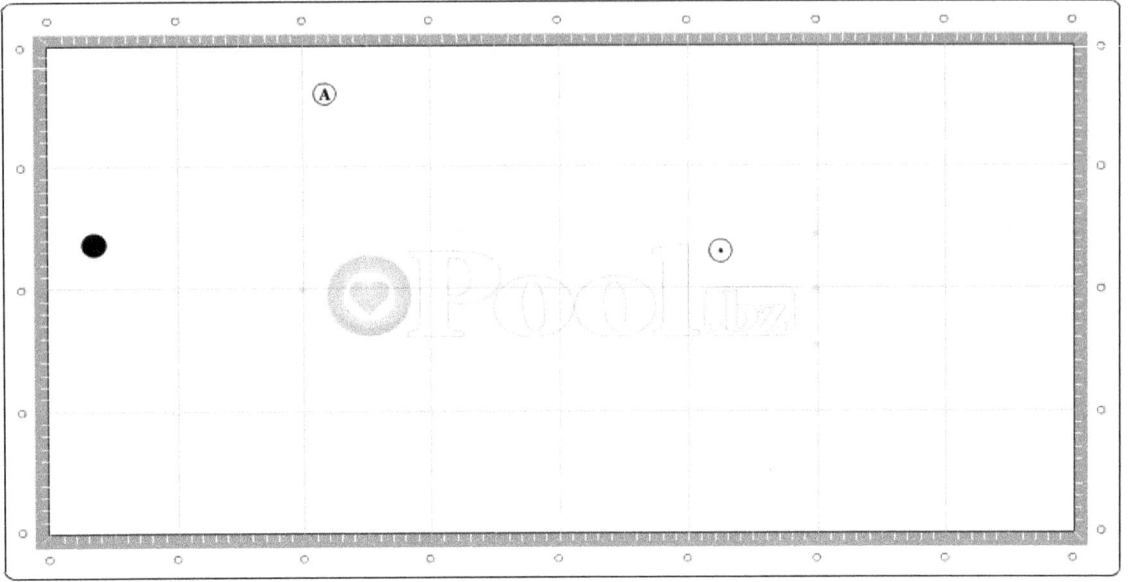

Shot Pattern

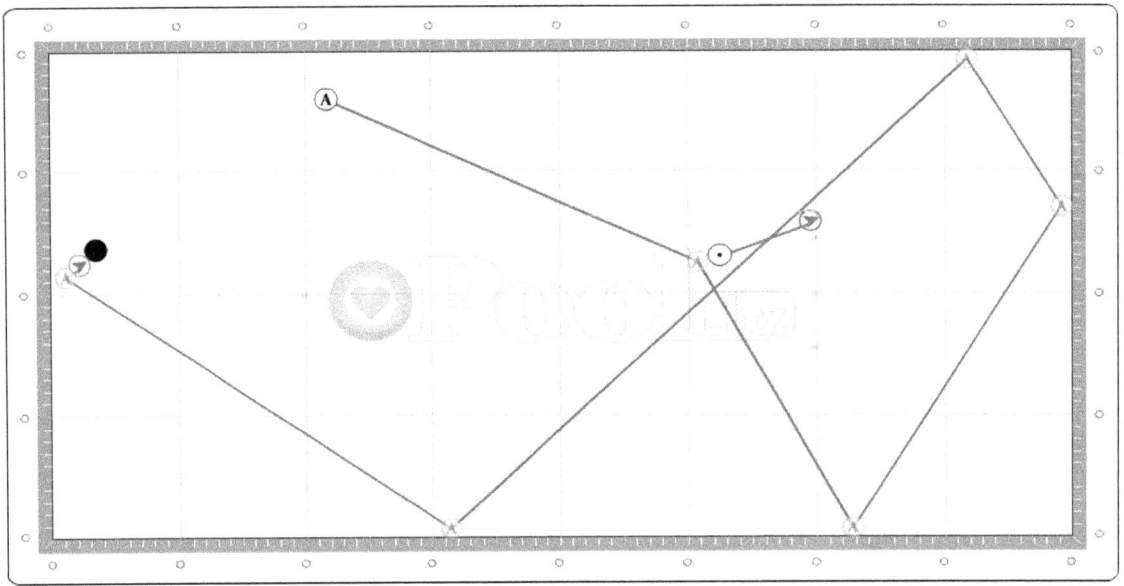

F:2d – Setup

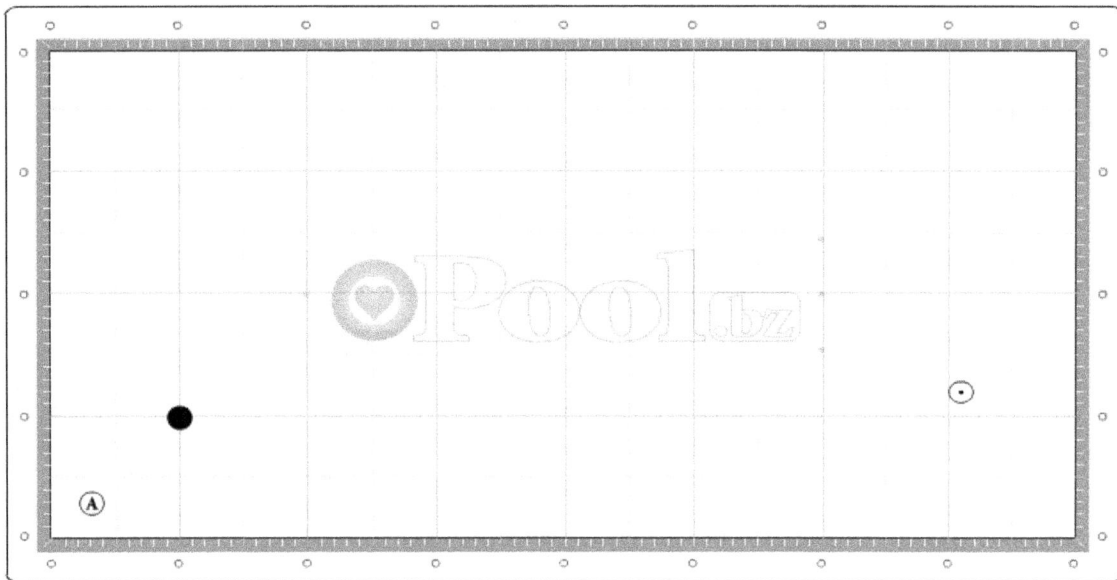

Shot Pattern

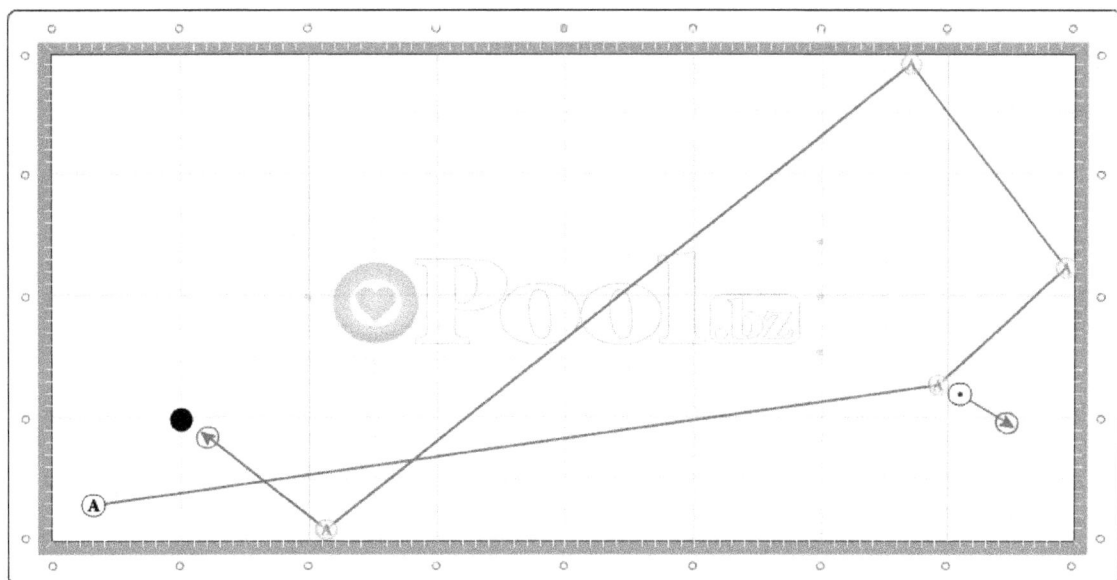

F: Group 3

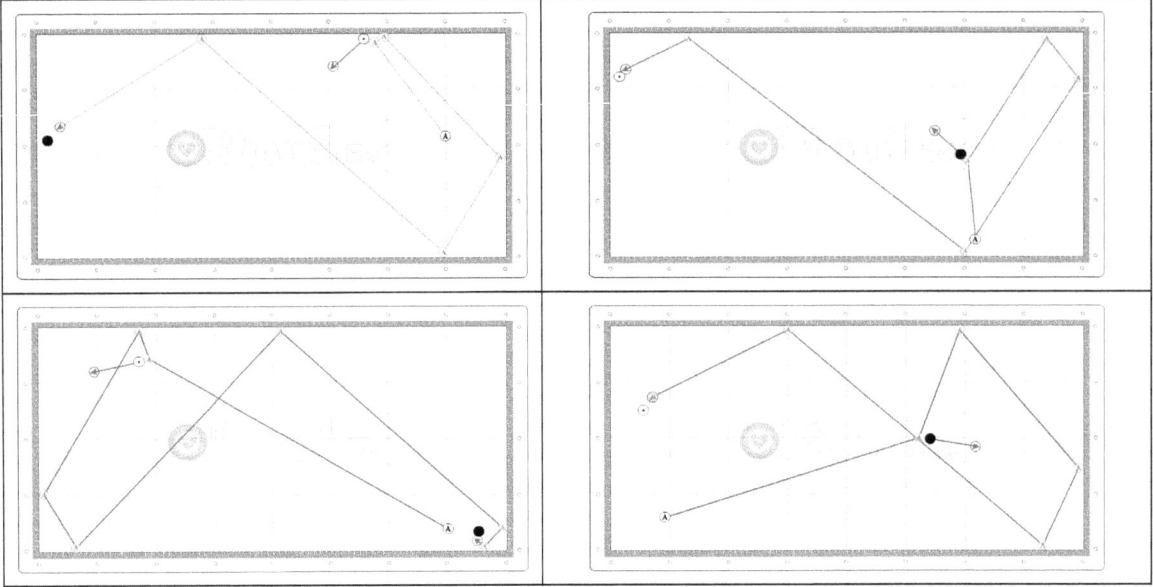

Analysis:

F:3a. _____

F:3b. _____

F:3c. _____

F:3d. _____

F:3a – Setup

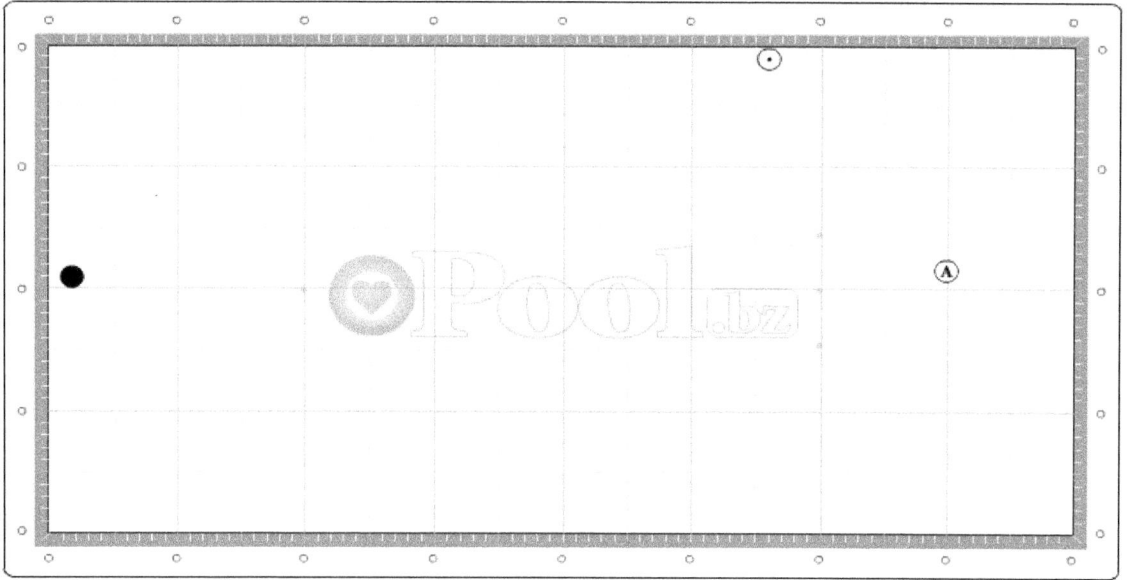

Shot Patter

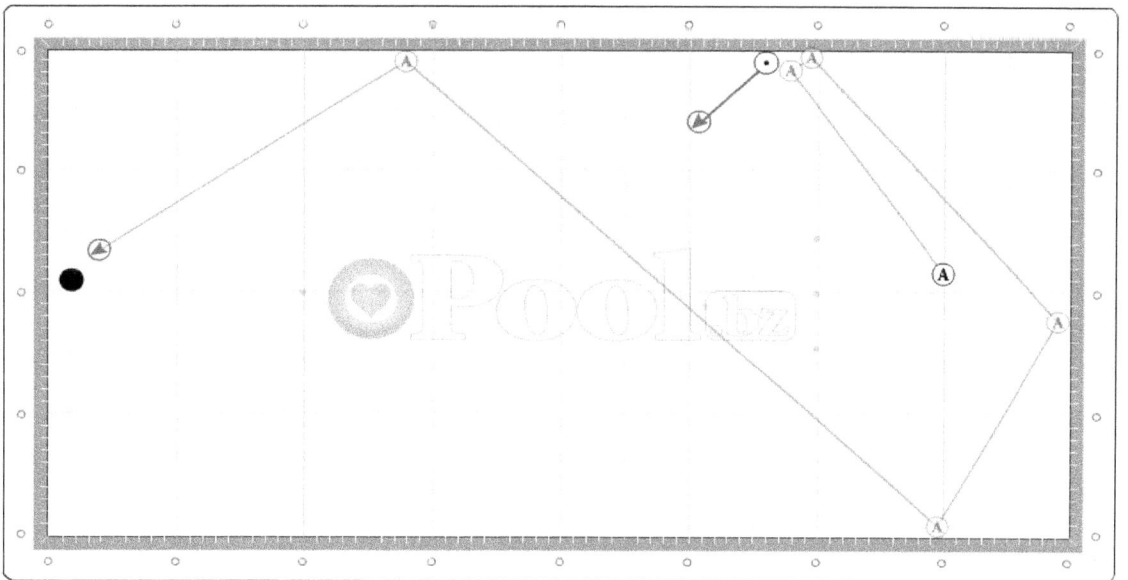

F:3b – Setup

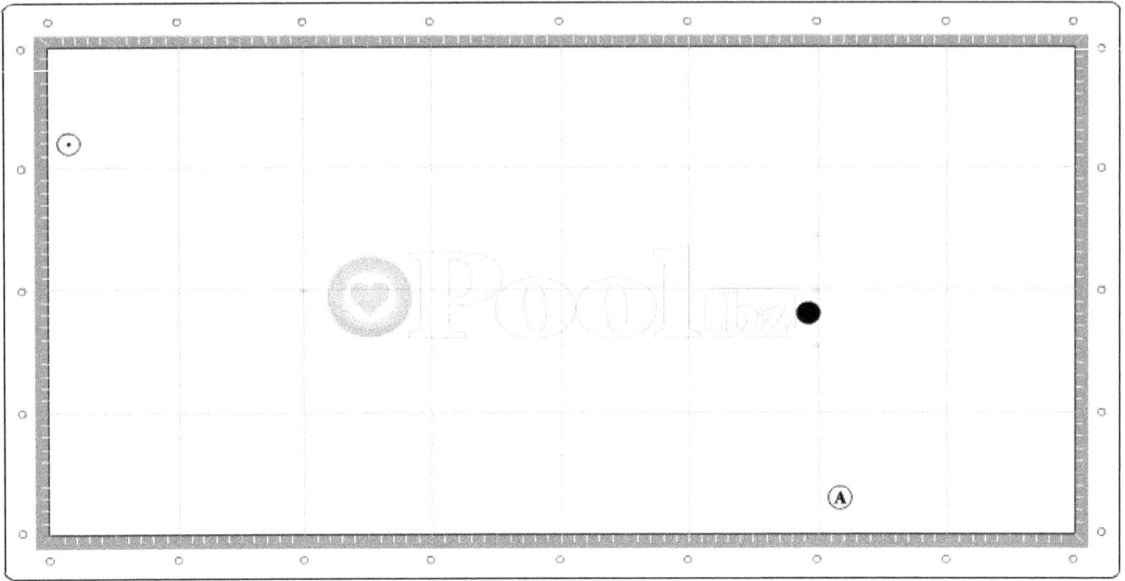

Shot Pattern

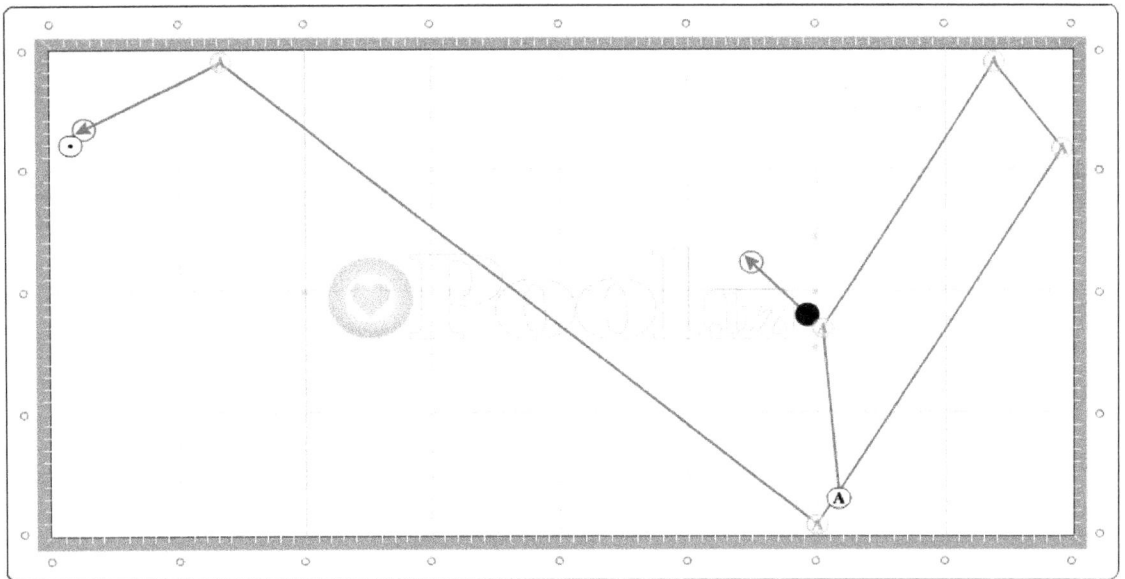

F:3c – Setup

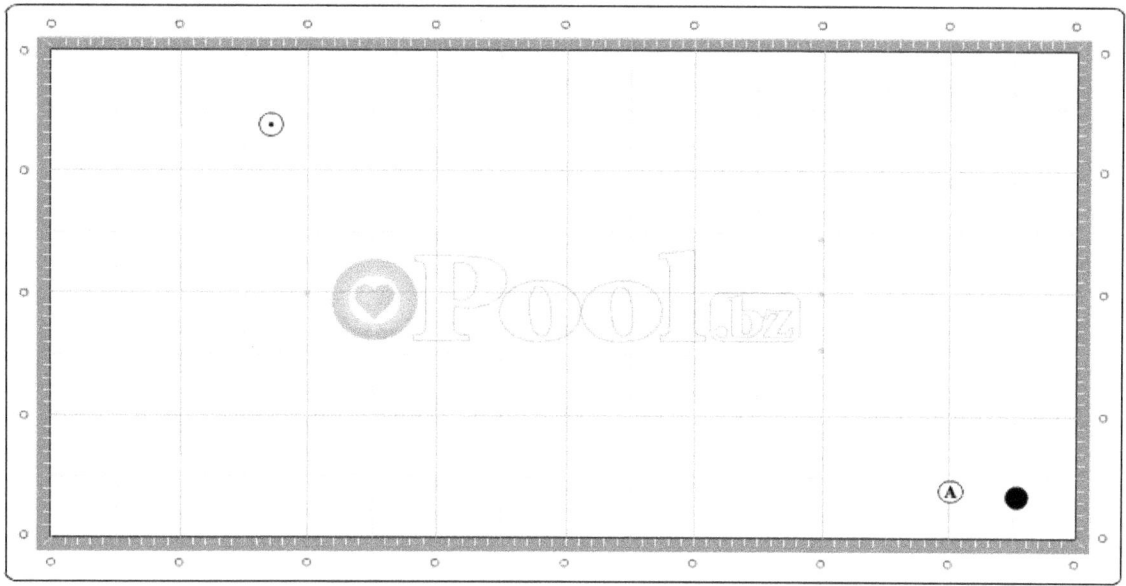

Shot Pattern

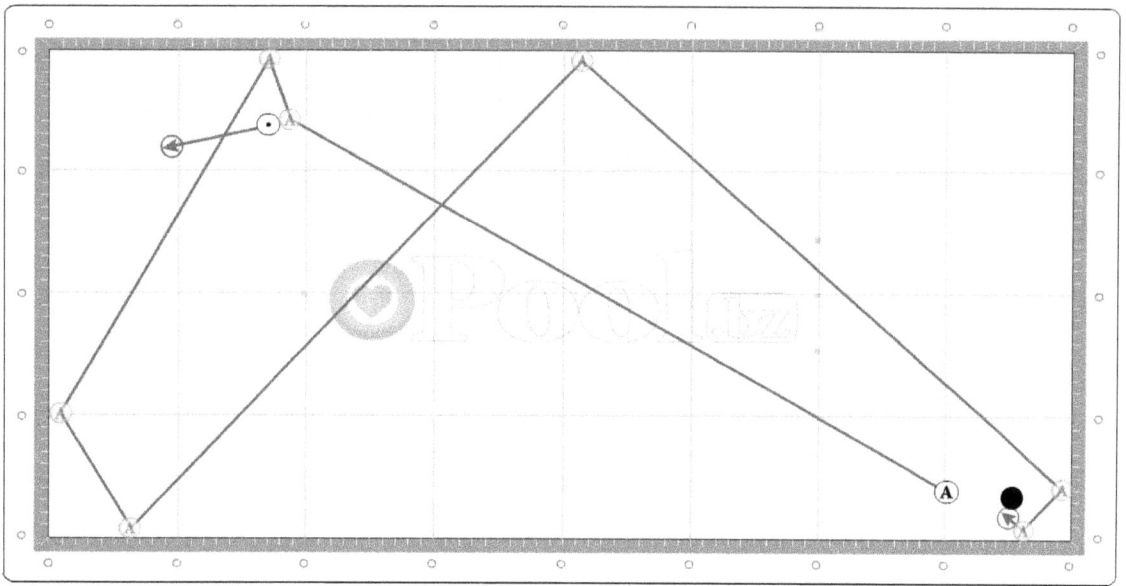

F:3d – Setup

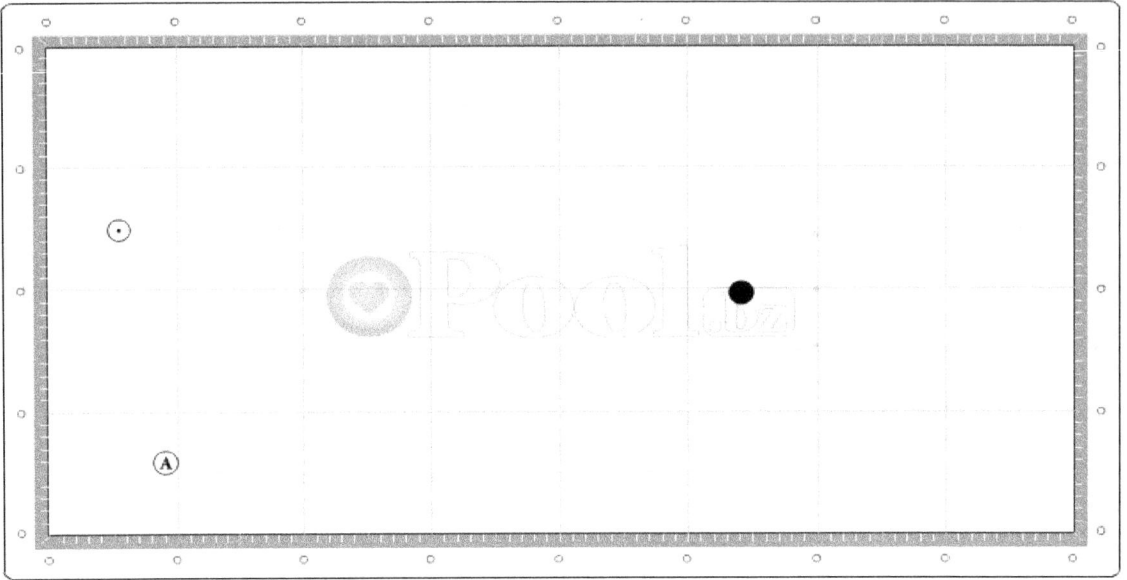

Shot Pattern

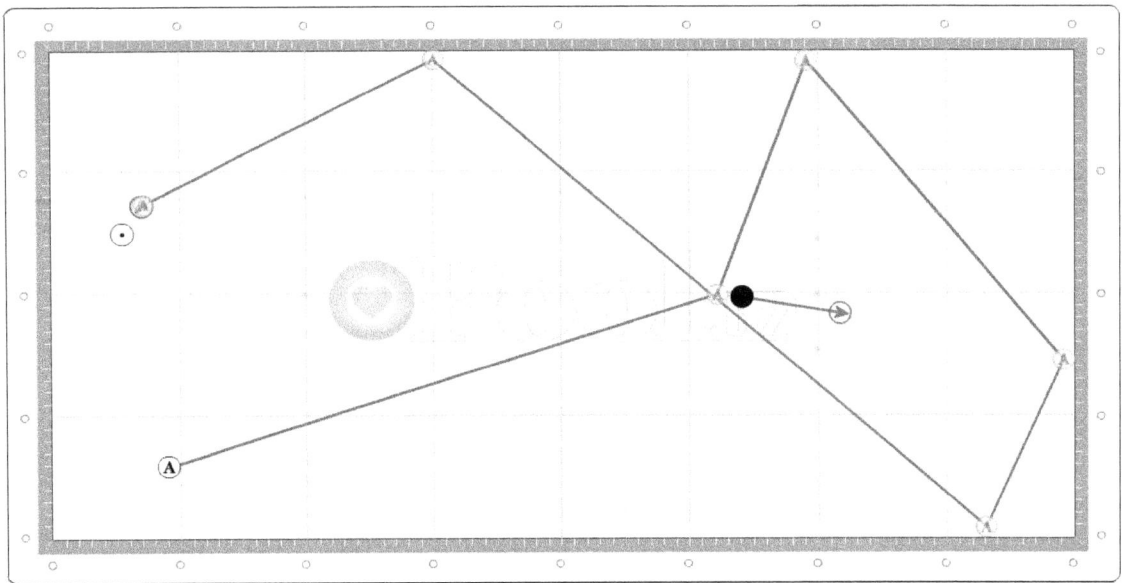